Warrior's Odyssey
SPIRIT OF CRAZY HORSE

ED MCGAA / EAGLE MAN

PROLOGUE

I trace myself back to Holy Dog Face Woman (Oglala), mother-in-law to my great-grandfather, William McGaa, a Scots gun trader. She interpreted for him among the Sioux, notably Chief Red Cloud of the Oglala Lakota and Chief Spotted Tail (Sichangu Lakota (Sioux)). On my mother's side was Maggie Hard Ground, daughter of Cheyenne Looking Glass and Oglala Big Horn veteran, Charging Shield. Maggie's daughter, Ella Kills Buffalo, married Jack Russell in Germany. She was a dancer and Jack was an interpreter in Wild Bill Cody's Exhibition to Europe. My mother was conceived in Germany.

My tribe once ranged from the Dakotas all the way to the eastern slopes of the Rockies north to the Big Horns. In 1775 the Lakota Oglala and Sichangu crossed the Missouri with 2,000 Arikara horses—their former owners defenseless against diseases borne by travelers on steamboats. The Sioux wisely avoided trading with the vessel and waited a moon, predicting the Arikara would be doomed. Overnight, they became the most powerful tribe on the Great Plains. Prior to the Civil War, the Sioux interest in William McGaa, along with his partner John Adams, was guns. The Winchester was invented in mid 1850s and found its way West to keep the repeater manufacturer from going bankrupt. The corrupt War Department foolishly turned down the more efficient weapon due to collusion with Springfield Arms. Buying off the War Department officials and congressional members eventually cost an eight-to-one Cavalry loss ratio at the hands of the Sioux warriors who fired their repeaters accurately while Mongolian-style riding—both hands free—against a US Army largely equipped with a single-shot Springfield 45.70s and reined horses.

McGaa and Adams, from Wigtowne Bay, Scotland, set up a trading post on Cherry Creek to supply Oregon Trail pioneers. Some pioneers stayed; they founded the town of Denver. Main Street was named McGaa Street, later changed to Holiday Street (Doc Holiday) and lastly Market Street. The county was named Adams County. McGaa's wife was a pretty breed, Jennie Adams. After Custer's defeat in 1876, McGaa's family retreated from vigilante Chivington terrorism to the Oglala Sioux Reservation. Holy Dog Face rode at the helm of a two-horse buggy team, her teenaged grandson William Denver McGaa—the first child born in Denver—rode horseback while his sister Jesse rode in the buggy. William Senior was dead and his wife drowned in the Poudre River. Both grandchildren became large landowners on the northern edge of the Oglala Reservation. Jesse McGaa married Gus Craven and began the Open Buckle Ranch south of Kadoka. My father was William Denver McGaa II, and my brother was William Denver McGaa III (he had no progeny).

CONTENTS

ACKNOWLEDGEMENTS

Bill Eagle Feather

Frank Fools Crow

Ben Black Elk

Beautiful Connie Bowen

Dr. John Bryde

Col. Bill Redel, USMC

Col. Pat Casey, USMC

Col. Guy M. Cloud, USMC

Col. Guy (Moose) Campo, USMC

William Denver McGaa, my Dad

Most all are deceased

FORWARD

So fortunate was I to have more adventure than most men, at least according to my own comprehension. I was born in a time and locale of open space which swept outward to one's questing vision. Like the picture of the Sioux woman on horseback; in my Creator's Code book, moving was not much of a problem back when. In my early youth, what ownership there was, it was a generous ownership.

"You kids. Be careful out there," Old Pete growled as he waved us on through an open gate across a cattle guard. "Mah Gaw, you keep an eye on 'em, no shootin' near the cattle, you hear?"
Old Pete had a bounteous spread down where Rapid Creek meets the Cheyenne. The Cheyenne is mostly born out of Southwestern Black Hills runoff. It crawls slowly, meandering silently across vast Dakota spaces to empty into the broad Missouri. Mule deer (the big deer variety), white tail and antelope were more numerous than the two-legged (human). Eagles were abundant—the big Goldens—at least enough that if you wanted to go see them you could.
Old Pete held up his hand. Despite my being only fourteen—but legally driving—he liked to talk to me. We were about the last state to require a driver's license. It cost something like a dollar at the courthouse. They gave you a ticket with your name printed on it and you drove.
I stopped the forty-two dollar Ford (1934 vintage). Rolled down the window as he walked up close and pointed. "See that section over there." He had told me the same story I was expecting but I wasn't about to say so. "Your Dad put up hay all the way to the Cheyenne." He threw his head back and laughed. "Your Grandma beaded up a pair of moccasins for my wife and me, too." This part of his recollection was new. "Your Dad had to break some horses, mean ones runnin' wild outta the Badlands. One helluva rider." His voice lowered to a whisper. "Now there was a cowboy." He pushed his grizzled head halfway through the open window. "Some breed gal broke his heart. He took off toward Montana country; bustin' horses, ranch to ranch, all way through Powder River Basin. Ranchers back then wouldn't hire Indians, but he'd show up with a letter from the last one who had hired him. Was tied to a saddle early as he could walk. Drank cow's milk from a whiskey bottle, a rag stuffed down its neck when his Ma went dry." Pete winked deviously, drawing up close to almost whisper. "Your Dad told me, the secret to bustin' broncs..." he withdrew and laughed loud up to the chill fall sky, "...was to never get hurt." Pete Lemley slapped his thigh and pulled out a snub nosed .38 Special from his right trouser leg. "Never get hurt!" He laughed raucously and let off a round to the sky. "God-damn! Indians don't

say much, but when they do," he clamored with high pitched laughter, "they're mostly right." He calmed down soberly, pointing the .38 toward the Cheyenne with a solemn warning. "This ain't summer time, kid. They'll be out sunnin' today, gettin' ready to den up. They get ornery then." He jabbed a finger but bent down with a fatherly, protective whisper. "You be damned careful." With that instruction, he re-pocketed the pistol and waved the four of us, one white kid and three Breeds, all Sioux, on through with our loaded .22 rifles. "Ain't had a cottontail for a while. Get some extra. Drop one off," he yelled as we headed for the fallen cottonwoods, chokecherry and wild plum and thorny buffalo berry thickets.

They were loaded with tasty cottontails (rabbits half the size of a jackrabbit) and no doubt rattlesnakes. "No one shoots bullsnakes, understand?" I ordered, stopping the Ford. Most all of them pre-war vehicles were black or grey. Mine must have been wrecked a bit. It was Marine Corps green. "Look at the Goddamn tail before you shoot." We had a couple rookies in back, maybe too anxious to take home anything to eat. I have always been a bit nervous when newbie's are carrying a firearm. I had stopped the Ford by a wild plum. A pair of deer burst out as we placed a round into our chambers. "Pete gets pissed if he finds a dead bull snake shot by some dumb son of a bitch."

Later in my life, I would see that same .38 pulled out in front of a startled group of Rotarians or maybe it was Lions, I can't remember. I was a guest speaker at one of their morning business men's meetings and not long returned from combat flying the F-4. I'll have to tell you about that one if I don't forget. Doc Lemley was Pete's son and he was with me that morning as my guest. Mom said he was always cutting up birds, gophers, prairie dogs and cottontails; studying their insides and drying out their skeletons. He was a healthy influence in my life. He took me up for my first plane ride. A Stinson Station Wagon—left one helluva mark into my young brain. Certainly was a highlight.

Pete was right about the snakes. Like the fourteen-year-old kid that I was, maybe fifteen, but just as stupid, I leaped over a fallen cottonwood toward the sunny side. *A leap into the unknown!* Lot of us do take a leap like that. It can bring all kinds of consequences. A deep cavity on the aging tree's sun side was hollowed back enough for a big rattler to sun itself. "Whirr," it spoke with its tail when I landed. Looking down at that coiled monster, I jammed my gun butt between us and leaped again, crashing into a thorny buffalo berry, cutting myself in various places, but not enough to stop hunting. Thanks to the crisp, autumn air, it didn't strike. Instead it crawled to safety, back up into the hollow log not all that inhibited due to the temperature of its lair heated by the sun. It must have just taken up its warmer station, waiting to heat up enough and strike a cottontail (rabbit) to ease it on into the approaching snows. It was big enough to swallow one. I could have been a goner if it hit me more than once. We were all mesmerized by its size. One of the newbies pulled up his gun, but I pushed the barrel away as the snake crawled to safety. Maybe it could have sat in the sun long enough to strike me. We watched it crawl away. Possibly, that event was the first danger scene in my adventure-filled life.

Later on in life, my hunting dog would be hit by a rattlesnake that size. He lived but suffered through the night. A big rattlesnake has a magic aura, at least for kids. Much later, I would bring my son's hockey player friends out to the remote Dakota Reservation Badlands to shoot prairie dogs on my land. Earlier son's friends the same. Evening time we would harvest a few rattlesnakes coming out to hunt. The 'Rites of Passage' would be held. Young, suburban future men, some a bit overprotected, now bearing their new .22 rifles and a brick of ammunition (500 rounds) would receive their first and most possibly only Nature-based ceremony. The roasted rattlesnake along with baked potatoes, cottontail or out-of-season pheasant would be devoured. Back then prairie dogs were almost an epidemic. Big golden eagles sitting like men upon buttes were visible in the distance, watching, waiting to devour their meal. The bricks would eventually be totally expended the next day. Now in my later life, those are all grown men. A few left still remain single but almost yearly almost I am invited to their weddings. The night before, a raucous howl issued up as I walked into the bar. I was King of those once-youth at that moment and sat and drank to recall those 'Nights of the first passage.' It is truly rewarding indeed.

INTRODUCTION

"He made everything so why should he choose one thing over another?"
—Jerry McGowan, Author - The Place

I never considered a Bio but... in light of recent happenings in my latter life I feel compelled to tell of normal sagas, the warrior picking up lance and shield and going forth against what I consider the evil-makers of doom while I also will tell about what some have encouraged, that I have had, indeed, quite an interesting life. A few damsels in distress even, which I may omit. These adventures were not climbing mountains, sailing around the world or scoring goals, some were battles against what I considered foes at the moment. One battle, with repeated combat scenes demanding extreme training were for the wrong sponsor—which took me years to realize. That was my biggest battle if considering repeated life threatening experiences. Over and over I was shot at, but my belief system was instilled forever more by a powerful, predictive ceremony conducted by Fools Crow, revered Sioux Holy Man who stated, "You will see the enemy 100 times and the bullets will bounce from your airplane."[1]

The other foes who needed to be engaged, combated and spelled out, gave me spiritual relief as well as new knowledge from my actions. The Nation needs to know: Racism, Eurocentric-ism, Redneck-ism, Greed, controlled politicians, cover-ups, manipulating bureaucrats, colluding churches, disrespect, dishonor, Untruth and, since childhood, that terrible word, *Prejudice*—all is very much alive in states far from the Mason/Dixon line. This is a non-fictional odyssey of some happy times as well along with some powerful mentors, mixed in with some solid confrontations and needed exposure. And of course, the dangerous era we now all face, Planetary Heating and Climate Change.

---

[1] Yuwipi Spirit Calling ceremony held at Chief Fools Crow's cabin prior to Vietnam combat tour.

Black Elk of the powerful, forecasting spiritual book, *Black Elk Speaks*, no less of a critical modern day spiritual forecast than the vision of Moses on Mt. Sinai wherein Creator's forbidding of Idol Worship—the Ten Commandments—stated to the interviewing author, John Neihardt, before he began his revelation regarding our planetary dilemma be it cyclical or man induced, "I must tell you of my people before I tell you of my life (primarily his vision) so that you may trust me."

I feel as obligated as Black Elk to tell you of my people in this writing. Two chapters will reflect on Indian Boarding School, of which I was spared. My adventures and/or relevant successes within the other chapters would never have happened had the missionaries had their way and taken me away from my parents which they did to most Indian families every fall for nine long months, and often for some, the entire year. I need not expound further on the tragic results and non-preparation of our Indian youth as a result. Jesus, Jesus, but very little academic preparation for Nature's occupational requirements, demanded from all of us. Therefore I feel justified to inform you of what happened to those of my era and before. Thankfully, Martin L. King's Civil Rights Movement finally awakened America and now the inefficient, destructive boarding schools have been discontinued if not severely reduced. Missionaries, as well, have been curtailed from their high-handed, controlling proselytizing. Our own Spirituality, once banned for nearly a century has been restored for the many who have chosen to return. As long as I am a Teton Lakota, this information cannot be omitted from my life's adventures which began with this constant fear every fall when the missionaries would come to take me away. Unfortunately, the majority of Native American writers have cowardly omitted to tell you what you do not want to hear. Simply look at their writings. Nothing is there.

I have to quote John Fire, narrator of the book, *Lame Deer, Seeker of Visions*. I knew John, he was a close friend of Bill Eagle Feather. Both were pillars beneath our revered leader, Chief Fools Crow, who kept the embers of our Banned-by-Congress, Lakota Spirituality glowing.

John Fire (Sichangu, Lakota Sioux) pierced me in the AIM rescue Sun Dance since Fools Crow was pretty busy with all the new, young Sun Dancers. He used his jack knife. It left the biggest scar.

> *"Before our white brothers arrived to make us 'civilized men', we didn't have any kind of prison. Because of this, we had no delinquents. Without a prison, there can be no delinquents. We had no locks nor keys and therefore among us there were no thieves.*

> *"When someone was so poor that he could not afford a horse, a tent or a blanket, he would, in that case, receive it all as a gift. We were too uncivilized to give great importance to private property. We didn't know*

any kind of money and consequently, the value of a human being was not determined by his wealth. We had no written laws laid down, no lawyers, and no politicians, therefore we were not able to cheat and swindle one another.

We were really in bad shape before the white men arrived and I don't know how to explain how we were able to manage without these fundamental things that (so they tell us) are so necessary for a civilized society."

—*John Fire Lame Deer-Seeker of Visions, Author Richard Erdoes, Sioux Lakota (1903-1976)*

A man can have many highlights in his life. As the world population magnifies, however, fewer men have more adventures: especially the thrilling, spellbinding, exciting ones—such exhilaration, even placing you into a state of numbing shock, it being more than the mind can handle. Some faint and not from pain. As a child, I fainted a few times but I don't recall such as an adult. When you are in an uncontrolled inverted spin following an engine suffocating Surface to Air Missile blast and realize you may crash, to survive you simply must concentrate with all your wits. "Concentrate, concentrate," is what your mind tells you. It is the same when two nose tires have been blown to rumbling smoking rims and you are doing 200 to 220 knots bouncing in both after burners half way down a runway deciding whether to lift aloft or take the wire at the end. The 'Death's Door' adventures are the most memorable, naturally. Coming up right to the slanting edge of a roaring sucking stream and a loose rock slides underfoot; a pair of Great Whites stalking you; landing a huge jet with a hung bomb on a black rainy night, low on fuel such that an engine quits on the taxiway; reaching for that ejection release but your hands frozen from centrifugal force. Aviation guarantees you many a 'deaths door' and not all necessarily combat; several coiled, concealed rattlesnakes, a blast of 12-gauge wind rippling your pant leg from your alert son behind you; even a burly, ugly grey-black Panama Bushmaster, coiled boldly on your path as deadly as the Great Whites. Yes, looking, feeling that other world, oh, so now, so close, is quite an event. I have faced it many times, more so than a dozen men put together. Some of those, however, especially when you see those that went through that fated door, can be so tragic that a once wholesome mind can be severely affected.

For some, most now, there is but nothing. Life is but an adventureless task. The real reason why made-up movies thrive. Vicarious becomes the consuming modus. To feed one's self and their family, the *Task* spawns nothing to focus upon with rapturous memory and worse, on into age, a blank scenario. Worry becomes the focus. Worry to survive and worry about how one's progeny will survive while being chained to the *Task*. We all know rightfully, truthfully worry since our misguided, greed afflicted, trafficked government has managed to mortgage our generations unborn (our offspring and their offspring and so on) while we haughtily complain about China's lack of Human Rights and Church Denial. Odd isn't it? China's progeny are not mortgaged! It is the absence of land, mainly, my humble opinion: less game, less room, crowded horizons; so much absence of what we call the Wild. Two-legged, more and more now, have little adventure. The catalytic Wild is exponentially disappearing.

The Indian had tremendous adventures, especially the Northeastern; Iroquois, Mohawk, Cherokee and Sioux. The Sioux went west and had more adventures yet, a wise move, surviving intact for at least another two centuries, or three or close to it. No 'Trail of Tears' for the Sioux. Instead they were killing their oppressors—eight to one toward the end of their journey in the 1800s. Better than walking toward your cultural death as the Cherokees had to do. The Sioux would retain their culture and their religion, too, despite the unconstitutional Christian missionary lobbying of Congress to ban for a century our own Spirituality. Fanaticism about who IS God will do those things. The Cherokee lost theirs and went on to call themselves civilized. Now they follow Jesus and not their ancestors' old successful beliefs. Some, like we Sioux, are starting to go back, however. We never mortgaged our Generations Unborn.

Spirituality

Spirituality is more explanatory when comparing it to the White Man's beliefs. How they believe in a Higher Power: Our pre-assimilation beliefs are quite contrary to what the White Man, the *Wahshichu*, holds. That bothers him, but how he believes does not bother us. It really doesn't, as long as he does not meddle with us and keeps his ways to himself around us—which he finds it impossible to do. We do not attempt to convert him. Why does he constantly try to convert and 'save' us? Planetary Heating/Climate Change? I guess we have to 'save' him but it will be fruitless. Why should a White Man listen to an Indian?

Creator?

We have basically four major ceremonies which we commonly practice: (Yes, we do believe in an Ultimate Power.) Four of our major beseeching ceremonies to Great Mystery are:

Sun Dance—Tribal Ceremony

Sweat Lodge—Group Ceremony

Spirit Calling—Specific Calling

Vision Quest—Individual Ceremony

Several other supporting ceremonies inter-twine within these major ceremonies. For example, Pipe Ceremony opens each one. The first three ceremonies I shall elaborate on with my related experiences. Vision Quest is rather simple, although very deep for the participant. You simply go to an isolated area wherein one will find the least distraction and beseech to your Creator or Higher Power concept for a day or two or up to four days. Some Christian friends told me their Jesus did the same. Odd, how they have not carried this into their present customs. Hard to imagine Joel Osteen, Pat Robertson, or fat Jerry Falwell beseeching alone to Creator for four days without sustenance on a hot Badland butte. Isolation obviously provides focus. Focus hopefully brings sought after spiritual insight. Most participants fast and drink no water unless one is a diabetic or has another form of related ill-health. This is not intended to be an explanatory book of Indian ceremony, culture and history, however.

I guess you could liken us to the Jews. No matter how much you try and persecute us, even starve us in your concentration camps, like Auschwitz, Belsen, Buchenwald or Pine Ridge Reservation, Rosebud, Eagle Butte or Navajo Rock, we will not go your way, especially with your religion. We just are not going to give up ours and I don't expect Israel to do so either. You can still keep yours—we won't try and take it away from you. To us, Creator, *Wankan Tanka* (Great Mystery) is simply that. Why fight over what neither of us knows for sure?

Maybe we need the Jews to explain this to you. They are more *Wahshichu* (White Man) than we are. Maybe that will make it easier. They don't want to have you take away their Spiritual/Religious beliefs. They won't let you.

For some, especially those of color, even though they may be so fortunate to have been able to progress onward into the adventuresome realm, their experiences with racism will indeed come up—the pall of frustration, in one form or another. Rarely does the man of color escape such frustrating injustice. For the young man, he most often must ignore or even bend or bow, probably the latter, otherwise he will become branded with various adjectives: recalcitrant, un-coachable, unworkable, troublesome and, worse, militant. Hence he will become unemployable or, worse, lose his occupation. There are many men of color however who will do injustice's bidding, too many, Clarence Thomas the former Monsanto lawyer, comes to mind—he is no Thurgood Marshal. A career ahead of the young Indian man demands so often that he must concede. If he stands too taut, he is overwhelmed.

For the old man, however, what does he have to lose? If he believes in a Spirit World that lies Beyond; that is his personal choice. My dutiful, loyal to his family, father was stubbornly traditional despite a far more trying time than mine. Is there one? Who knows? If a two-legged happens to think so, such thought will spur him on and simply adhere to what appears on the back cover of my latest book, *Spirituality for America*.

There are two kinds of people in this world.

The first seeks knowledge, while the second seeks gratification.

The first trembles with anger when injustice is done to others; the second is numb and unconcerned.

The first recognizes their duty to speak out; the second dismisses injustice as being out of their hands or simply "the way it is."

The first is loyal and loving to their human and non-human brothers and sisters; the second is loyal to their nation.

The first rejects dogma and thinks independently; the second blindly respects authority and bitterly ridicules free thinkers.

The first is humble, always knowing that they could be wrong; the second rigidly adheres to beliefs which ossify with time.

The first removes themselves from contributing to the system of oppression in any and all ways; the second does nothing because they are comfortable.

Which one are you?

This will not be a book complaining about life, however. A bit of exposure, yes. For injustice always needs to be exposed. Overall, for all of the adventure I experienced, why should I complain? I have had a wondrous life so full of beautiful adventure and of course many gorgeous, knowledge-seeking, observant dear friends. Probably every wonderful woman that I have had the great fortune to be romantically affiliated with have been an absolute plus in my life. None I ever met in a bar, saloon, night club either. Luckily; I just never came across in those places and am far from being a 'Teetotaler' or overly religious. So many believe the old Nature based Way, this provides such deep-thinking people who are very earth based but yet, not fanatical as so many religions spawn. What a happy, confident group to know in life and, our belief, in the afterlife, as well, where all Truth reigns. At least we hope so. Yes, hopefully Creator is All Truth. Wouldn't it then have an All-Truthful Beyond World for us? We are fairly practical with our suppositions.

Even at older age, one should move onward. For those who have been exposed, however, they must learn: *Do not threaten a Sioux warrior who may well or may not be in his latter stages. You won't get away with it. He can come after you. Look out!* A later chapter will bring out some serious mistreatment from several people that should not have happened if we respect and believe in God's Truth, but it did. Yes, these disparaging human beings are named, too. Why not? Truth is Truth. One cannot totally rectify injustice but it needs to be exposed to protect the innocent, their future. Whether or not the perpetrators receive needed correction here in this life's journey, at least, we may never know but their history, their track record needs to be exposed at least, somewhere. Next to Truth, Knowledge is close to being as important for Human's Ethics and Morality. The Age of Communication is upon us. Someday it may be the hopeful tool to elevate us away from the extreme flaws that human manages to devise and perpetuate.

Actually, this work holds a high degree of pleasantness and harmony, a bit of humor, and yes, Spirituality. My childhood was indeed pleasant and loaded with child pleasing adventure. Some mothers might shudder at how loose the reins were upon us. It possibly could be a wonder how we all made it—my peers at least— to adulthood. No plastic toys, no TV tubes, no electronic games keeping us sedentary. What kind of legs will today's youth have when they are my age, I have to ask.

I mentioned Vision Quest. One of my earliest 'Spiritual Adventures' which sent me to Bear Butte Mountain in the Black Hills of Dakota. "Go up there and beseech to *Wakan Tanka* (Great Spirit) before you come back to do the Sun Dance with us." Such were my instructions from the Sioux holy men, Fools Crow and Chief Eagle Feather. I will not go into detail of that experience. For the curious, it is in several of my books. Instead, I will recount a subsequent adventure at Bear Butte (vision quest) Mountain in keeping with the intended tone and play of fate of many adventures in my life. There exists a statement among combat pilots: Long periods of extreme solace, serene contentment and then…moments of sheer, unexpected life threatening drama.

The British Broadcasting Company contacted me to participate in a documentary they were making regarding the return of our Sioux/Lakota Spirituality. My role was to project/portray the modern Indian who had gone out into the so-called 'White Man's World,' met his relative successes and yet returned to the 'Old Way', at least back to the 'Spiritual Old Way.' I was dating the beautiful Western Flight attendant at the time who appears on the first page of my last writing. She went with me to the Black Hills to meet the Brits and their camera crew. They had interviewed several medicine men regarding the return of our Spiritual freedom in the advent of Martin Luther King's successful Human Rights campaign. One holy man had even conducted an appreciating sweat lodge which had been partially recorded. My task was to take the Brits up in a twin engine airplane because of its allowance of needed extra filming room from the cockpit. I flew above Bear Butte Mountain where many vision quests take place. I had to hold a tight circle, requiring a steeply lowered wing to allow the cameraman a view of the mountain below through the cockpit window and including me as I described Vision Quest. I started at several thousand feet above the mountain at high power and picked up extra needed airspeed to hold the tight descending turn. Unexpectedly, as I finished my descriptive script, I had lowered to within the wind shear envelope of the mountain and caught a sudden downdraft and approached a bit too close for comfort—stall condition. The airplane shook in anticipation while the stall warning horn blared. I flattened my wing level, holding my dive down the mountainside for extra airspeed, narrowly missing tall pine trees. We safely sailed low over the prairie. Only I and the stewardess knew what had happened; the Englishmen were beaming with satisfaction regarding the interview.

1 NAMING

Some folks know me through my books; my Spirituality side (*Mother Earth Spirituality*—close to fiftieth reprinting) and the most recent writing, *Spirituality for America*. The latter is fairly heavy on modern issues— Climate Change, Planetary Heating and my blaming those dilemmas on overpopulation—and pointing the accusative finger at Organized Religion, the major culprit behind membership spawning, dangerous, deadly, destructive Overpopulation which is leading us to planetary devastation now fast upon us.

Observed evidence worldwide cannot be truthfully denied. If a writer declares that Creator is believed to be 'All Truth' which he declares through his direct observation of Creator's Nature (no existing superstitions evident), then it would be hypocritical would it not for him to omit such obvious evidentiary evidence? Just to be politically obsequious or avoid offending a narrower-minded readership (while the planet plunges into obvious glacier melting Climate Change—I may add)? Observed evidence worldwide cannot be truthfully denied. No less than a United Nations declaration, a National Federal Assessment and even the Retired Generals and Admirals association including two Department of Defense heads have declared Planetary Heating as an extreme issue regarding world civilization.

Regardless, even the most overzealous religious fanatic has to look down from a ship's rail cruising the now open Arctic sea lanes at a floating, starved to death polar bear with a vanishing Greenland glacier for a background and must have to wonder: *'This planet. Is it, really, truly heating?'* A huge ice shelf, not just some mere iceberg has floated by Nov Scotia. It is hard to convince those folks that Planetary Heating is just some Al Gorian invention.

Cornwell, Carroll and Zucotti

The RCC (Roman Catholic Church) took extreme issue with John Cornwell, unleashing an all-out war effort to vilify him for his *Hitler's Pope.* They are not pleased either with James Carroll, a former priest and author of *Constantine's Sword.* Both men set out to write positively about the wartime pope when the usually secretive Vatican, surprisingly, opened up its files due to a newly elected open minded pope who did not last long. As I write this, we have what appears is the greatest pope of them all. I only hope Pope Francis does not depart us early. These two authors, Cornwell and Carroll, were so shocked at what they discovered that they could not and would not lie about the clear evidence within the wartime records. Susan Zucotti, a Jewish author of *Underneath His Very Windows*—Pius XII's cowardly denial to save, at least make a humanitarian attempt, 4,200 Jews, corralled and bound for Auschwitz to be gassed. Sporadic gunfire raged to round up recalcitrant Vatican neighborhood Jews and yet the Vicar of Christ never intervened, not even a phone call to the German commandant in Rome and now, beatified by the resigned Pope Ratzinger for canonization. I must yet seem to them (the RCC) as too small a fish to fry. Be nice for me if they remain so consoled.

Well, despite Spirituality and Planetary Issues, what is there to know about, Eagle Man? How did I come to receive that name?

Ben Black Elk

I was just a kid playing cowboy and Indian around the 4th of July. Another neighborhood kid and I were banging away with our cap guns at each other and both of us yelling that we had shot the other dead. Cap guns held small rolls of miniature blasting powder caps that would make a loud pop and some smoke when the pistol's hammer struck the cap of powder. Don't know what happened to them. They all disappeared, like my $42 dollar Ford and quarter-dollar gas! The roll allowed numerous 'shots' at your opponent. They were also an exceptionally inexpensive training method for training hunting dogs to get used to gunfire. Real shells are a bit costly for training. (Hope I remember to explain how to train a dog from being gun shy, and how to pick out your hunting pup, too. Don't just look for size, color or how pretty.)

We were innocently blasting away at each other, hiding behind several sheds, one an abandoned chicken coop, when Ben Black Elk drove up. Ben was just an ordinary Indian then and liked to talk Sioux with my parents. We had a whole city block almost, well maybe at least half a block, a big lawn and even an orchard of plums mostly, an apple and a cherry tree, too. Raising chickens were still legal in city limits: so that meant a mini-wheat field to feed them. Ben Black Elk came quite often as his wife would want to visit her sister and probably wanted to hear Spanish no different than how Ben enjoyed the old Sioux language with my parents. He talked often about, "My Father's book," but no one paid much attention. *Black Elk Speaks* had been printed in the early thirties, authored by Nebraska's Poet Laureate, John Neihardt. It sat, however for years, unknown and sold as remainders for forty cents a copy. Many of you readers are quite familiar with the story, but for the benefit of the unknowing, this book would finally rise and literally be read by millions throughout the world and in numerous languages.

Ben's father was Nicholas Black Elk and he spoke no English. As a young boy, around early 1870s, he received a powerful vision that revealed the Mystery of Spiritual Imagery not in accord to man designed Biblical or Koranic imagery but one based on Creator's observed Nature. This is an important statement in regards to understanding Religion versus Spirituality. Religion is based on what Man tells us. Spirituality is based on what we can glean from Nature. Oh yes, Nature has much to tell us and is doing so every day.

He was carried up to the Spirit World onto a vast plain teeming with herds of wild and free animals as well as unbridled horses of many colors. Within a tall lodge, he was given audience to the Six Powers of the Universe. Each direction, West, North, East and South, spoke as a wizened old man. You have to admit that there are Four Directions and a bit more visible than what Organized Religion attempts to proselytize to us. I can feel the North and South Powers—cold and heat. I can observe the red dawn of the East and darkening dusk of the West Power. The West Power spoke, but first gave him a bow: "You will be allowed to destroy and allowed to make live." All spoke to him revealing Knowledge. The Sky Spirit and the Earth Spirit spoke last. The Earth Spirit, whom I regard as Mother Earth herself, did not address Black Elk directly but rather beckoned all the powers including Black Elk to come look down at Earth and view what the future would bring. There among the confluence of three foul, polluted rivers with bloated fish floating was a Blue Man of corruption and doom. On shore animals were dying, birds were falling from the sky, and the air was putrid. Planetary Heating of our planet due to the corruptive greed of modern man's ways? Is that the one percent we are suffering under now? Did Creator forecast that the Earth would be in serious catastrophe in but a short century or two? Was Creator warning us of Planetary Heating mainly due to a runaway over-population which Organized Religion and Dominant Society Commerce champions despite the peril it portends? Likewise, did Creator respond to Moses way back when several millennia ago?

It is not difficult for a Traditional leaning Indian to believe that Moses had his vision on Mt. Sinai. Creator was quite concerned and did address the tribe of Moses to communicate its laws. Did Creator decide that the world now needed to know the direction it was heading through allowing Its Six Powers to communicate?

This message is too intricate for a young boy to make up—he would grow to become gifted in Spirit, and a powerful healer. His revelation is based on Creator's most powerful creations. The North Power exists! Get lost in it during its fury and try to escape from its death-dealing grasp. If you succeed you will have definitely acquired new respecting knowledge. "Does the North Power exist?" You will be sitting shaking from chills in your vehicle hoping to be rescued. "Yes! Definitely. No question. The North Power is a definite Entity." We do not worship these entities, only Creator, but certainly realize they exist.

My Spirituality teaches me that Creator is All Truth and All Knowledge which we should seek and hold dear. Black Elk received powerful new knowledge from his engagement with the Six Powers. Earth Spirit led the five Powers down to attack the Blue Man but failed to destroy it. Earth Spirit called up to Black Elk to come down and help destroy the Blue Man. Now that he had powerful new knowledge his bow changed to a spear and he charged down and killed the Blue Man. His new knowledge from the Six Powers gave him the ability to do what the Six Powers could not. Joseph

Campbell, when queried by the well-known interviewer, Bill Moyers, about his travels throughout the world studying Indigenous belief: "What is the best example of this Spiritual Imagery you speak of?" Without pause Campbell answered, "Black Elk's Vision."

If I am going to base my life upon prophesy, I want to base it upon Creation-reflective accuracy, not babbling parables that say absolutely nothing about what is beginning to appear as the most dangerous civilization destroying force in human history. Planetary Heating! For those who are 'Biblically Faithful,' take solace, however. Evidently if your Black Book is so faultless, then the masses have nothing to worry about, do they? Planetary Heating and Climate Change nor the false flag of causative overpopulation does not exist if your black book never mentions it, does it? Furthermore, your Jesus says nothing. Can we take that omission as "Worry Not?" I do hope you are right with such faithful supposition. If, however, Climate Change does move on exponentially, then would you admit that the human race is in dire trouble?

Ben Black Elk was sent to Carlisle Indian Boarding School in faraway Pennsylvania where he learned to speak English. In the thirties he interpreted every word of *Black Elk Speaks* from his Father to John Neihardt.

Ben looked at me and muttered to my mother. She called me over and introduced me to Ben. She said he was going to give me an Indian name— Eagle Boy, '*Wanblee Hokeshilah*' she pronounced it. I was more interested in resuming my game and was happy that she dismissed me. I do still remember Ben looking down at me with a broad grin.

Twenty some years later, he parleyed with Chief Fools Crow and Bill Eagle Feather within the Sun Dance Intercessor's tipi (Intercessor is the Sun Dance leader/Organizer, the main Medicine/Holy Man) and they changed my name to *Wanblee Wichasha*—Eagle Man. It was the summer after my combat flying in 'Nam. I had just come in from a morning sweat lodge ceremony and was toweling down, stepping out of my wet swimming trunks into dry ones and then putting on my Sun Dance skirt. Ben also brought his father's peace pipe and had me carry it in my first Sun Dance. That was in late '60s. A hot August at Pine Ridge. Only a few supporters attended those early Sun Dances (such was the power/influence of the Reservation missionaries). Within a few short years, however, our Spirituality (The Indian

22

Way) spread like wildfire. That is how I got my name.

The vision within Fools Crow's ceremony was the catalyst of my life. You would not be reading this book if I never came to know it. I would no doubt be a skeleton well cleaned by jungle ants, encapsulated within the broken wreckage of a McDonnell F-4 Phantom fighter-attack bomber brought down by a Vietnamese Russian made surface-to-air-missile. No one gets hit by a SAM missile, loses an engine from the blast and lives to tell about it…let alone turning around and going in to kill the launching site. No…not unless they had powerful, intervening Spiritual help—My Belief! I will tell you about that close call in detail later.

To know me, to know the warrior within, the writer, you have to know the Vision.

There is a big difference between Spirituality and Religion. Religion is obviously Man-made, Man-created, Man-organized even though most claim that God, Higher Power, Holy Sahib, Bwana Big Jim or Mumbo Jumbo, Bwana Big Lulu or whom or whatever one desires to call it is from God's special interest in them and them only. For many, *IT* came down special from the skies and anointed their particular religious movement…and nobody else's beliefs or religious/spiritual interpretations.

On the other hand, Spirituality is a people's belief system generally based on observation of Nature, assuming that this Higher Power is a Maker, Designer, Creator. Man statements are never regarded as higher as or more reliable than what we can learn from Nature—God's, Benevolent Creator's—creation. Nature does not lie nor does she exaggerate, does she? Man does. I have discovered which one of the two I choose to trust. Most folks, however, choose to trust Man over Nature despite the Planet racing headlong toward Man's doom, or at least, horrendous misery for the few survivors. We traditional believing Indians call those gullible, naive ones, Sheeples! They are blinded by Celebrity Watch, the daring, diving-cleavage Kardashians, whomever the hell they are, and ahhh…luxury seeking or at least materialistic fantasy even if you live in a trailer house. At least the homeless know no fantasy, they are at the bottom where there is no fantasy. Pure survival can erase the hell outta fantasy. At this stage in life, Human is oblivious to Planetary Heating and Climate Change despite its obvious warnings. Oh! How they are about to drastically change! Yes—made to change by Mother Nature!

It is going to become quite interesting in just a few years. Too bad, for me, that I probably will not get to witness from here but I sure as heck will from Beyond. Nature has no superstitions. Man does. Man claims that God forgives, especially the Christians' state so. Maybe it is the reason that they exhibit such a lack of true moral, ethical discipline, especially among themselves. Nature's tornado or hurricane comes through and causes tremendous havoc. She never returns and puts it all back together again, does she? Is Creator telling us what we do here is harmful to others, the animal world and the Earth Mother? Those negative actions are untruthful and contrary to what Creator shows us in Its Nature—my belief. There is no forgiveness and we will answer for the harm we do to others in the after world. Nature controls! Puny, ego-filled Man does not! The harmed ones will chastise us in the Spirit World for our greed-based ignorance. They do not enter into the Spirit World without a memory—would you not deduce? Maybe Creator gave us that memory so we can chastise the guilty ones who personally screwed us over and not *IT*. *IT* probably has bigger, more important issues concerning Its vast Universe. Conversely, the good that we do, respect and generosity, we will be honored in that Beyond World because we remember the good that people do for us, do we not? It is All Truth vs un-Truth. It is all written down in each person's memory. That is a Spiritual Belief of most Indigenous.

The Who, Where, When, What

I was born on an Indian reservation way out in western South Dakota a few years before World War II. My parents had a small ranch next to my grandfather's huge, fenceless spread on the Pine Ridge Sioux Reservation. 'Rez' is what we 'Skins' (Indians, Sioux) call a reservation. I had good parents. They stayed together through thick and thin—mostly thin at first, damn thin.

Sioux never had big families until the preaching missionaries came along, especially the Catholics. The Jesuit Order were the main culprits for changing that part of our Oglala Sioux culture. My mom, a devout Catholic, had thirteen children. I was the tail gunner. We were all about two years apart so that meant I had several brothers and sisters that could easily have been my parents. One older brother became like a dad to me and provided most of my kid-needs—baseball glove, fishing rod, BB gun. As I grew, I also got his

.22 pump rifle, .22 shells lying loose on his dresser, trout fish hooks, tapered leaders and an occasional reel replacement. Reels don't work well after several falls stir up sand or mud. But, I am getting ahead of my story.

My sisters and brothers attended the Indian boarding schools at the Indian Agency called Pine Ridge, thirty to forty miles further south. The main buildings at Pine Ridge were the Indian Agency, which by then had changed its name to Bureau of Indian Affairs. A smaller building was the Oglala Sioux Tribal Council headquarters, which then, was where the mostly powerless tribal leader once termed Chief held office but now is called the Tribal President. The power balance has shifted somewhat especially after Martin Luther King's Civil Rights Movement. West of the Agency, the Public Health Hospital was a fairly modern structure for its time with several floors staffed with doctors and nurses.

South was the sprawling federal government boarding school that had its own brand of discipline for the students ranging from grade one through twelve. Balls and chains were attached to runaway youth and empty rooms served as jail cells for those who failed to obey the rules. Further west was the equally sized Catholic Boarding School, called Holy Rosary Mission, staffed by black-cloth Fathers (Jesuit priests), Jesuit brothers and hooded nuns making up the main body of teachers. Holy Rosary was akin to one big farm with dormitories attached. A prominent, steepled church, considered rather large for its time, was centrally located on the school grounds with outlying cattle, dairy, crop and hay lands. Student labor was put to adequate use manning chicken and hog yards as well. Discipline and methods for maintaining strict conformity were no less stringent from the government school termed Oglala Community Grade and High School. Beatings, even for the girls, were common. Worse than beatings or inhumane confinement was the unpreparedness, the distortion of educational focus which the Eurocentric false superiority held over a vanquished race. This was their greatest crime, in my opinion, an utter lack of academic preparedness.

I do not want to expose the Catholics alone. Other reservations were allotted dominance by the federal government to Protestant missionaries and their cruelty, pedophilia and inhumanity were just as infamous. Canada, they say, at least by the Indians there, was even worse. Huge lawsuits, mainly about pedophilia, have been recently filed in Canada.

Every fall, my siblings would go away for nine months. Those who could, would catch a ride home at Christmas time and most came back for summer. Some stayed over at the mission boarding school the full nine months. My parents were so poor that some were farmed out to aunts and uncles during the summers. Cousins liked to play with their own age group so in some ways it worked out, maybe for the better. Hard to say.

U.S. Marshal

World War Two came. Our lives changed abruptly. The Marshal attempted to come into our small ranch, but blowing alkali sand across one part of the road my grandfather had made trapped him for most of the day. When he did show up he had some papers. "You got to get outta here in thirty days." The star badge and six-shooter he wore denoted authority. "Bombing Range. U.S. government orders," he said and flashed the papers.

My Dad had to adapt and fairly quick. The northern end of the hundred mile long by nearly as wide reservation, at least a fourth of it, was to be converted into a bombing and .50 caliber machine gun practice range. Too dangerous for human habitat, cows and horses too.

For a while my parents stayed with the Red Cloud family in Pine Ridge. Word got around that jobs were available in Rapid City, a three-hour car ride away in those days. The Army Air Corps was building an air base for mostly B-24 bomber crews to train and head for England where a high casualty ratio was waiting. The young men were steadily enlisting and leaving. Workers at the air base, any kind, skilled or unskilled were needed. Even Indians were hired.

My dad went from a cowboy to a construction worker, and for me it was the best break of my still young life. I would not be attending Indian Boarding School. A later chapter will cover what boarding school was like. Adolf Hitler and Hideki Tojo should never be given any accolades whatsoever for all the death and destruction they brought on by false inspiration of their naive masses, but I have to admit that what they catalyzed changed my life for the better. Moving off the reservation was the best thing yet to happen to me. No boarding school! I would get a decent education. The same as the white kids got.

My dad was a good man, but he was so much older than most other neighborhood dads and came from such a changing past that he could not identify with and did not want to adjust completely to the dominant society world he wound up in. I played sports, but never had a parent to watch me. My dad was a quiet, providing person. He just did not want to sit within a cheering, yelling group of white people. My oldest brother was a star baseball pitcher, a South Dakota Hall of Famer, and I guess years back my parents went to watch him play, but time went on.

My dad never drove a car but he was such a reliable worker that the construction boss would come early to pick him up and get out to the job site early. My dad was a 'mud mixer,' meaning he mixed cement for the brick layers who can get pretty fussy about how their cement is mixed and made available. They preferred my dad hence he was always employed. A long way from roping steers and cutting calves. He and I hunted cottontail rabbits, at times, along with my brother who had a car. Other than that I was fairly much on my own for recreation which I had no trouble finding.

I have absolutely no remorse. I understand why, that is all that matters. When I was quite small, like most everyone, I just do not recall a helluva lot about that part of childhood. It had to be quite comfortable even though I cannot remember. When I was real small, I surely must have had adequate parental love, and my sister, two years older received it, too. We played a lot together and both look back with pleasant memories.

Probably the most disastrous institution for me to avoid was the Indian Boarding School. Yes, I know I am being repetitive, but maybe I am like the Jew who will tell about his concentration camp experience. Not many of the few still living, I understand, will talk about it. They just cannot and will not do it. I have a chapter coming up that I won't find pleasant and I would like to omit, but I know I have to do it. Boarding school played such havoc in the lives of Indians that it has to be told. We do have a bevy of Indian writers, however, who never mention it, nor the Canton Indian Insane Asylum—all Indian and federally built and staffed wherein most of our innocent Medicine Men and Women were institutionalized. One hundred and twenty graves there are proof.

Yes, so many of them died there. They want me to tell that this was wrong, and at least expose the cowards who sent them there to die. Mainly, I think that they want me to warn my audience that too much zealotry can cause extreme suffering and that a hopeful future society can forbid such atrocity. *Avatar* touched on this concept, my opinion. Unlike most, if not all, of the 'Sweet Good Indian' writers, the South Dakota Humanities Council parades in front of the public. This writer however, yes, *me*, I will tell you about both and even offer a few pictures. Cowardice, cover-up, happy talk and sugar coating are not my forte.

Of the early breed families that sided with the missionaries, how many knew and maybe even helped plan Canton Insane Asylum? Did these Indians voice any objection to the illegal incarceration and often the deaths of their very own tribal people, all over the issue of religious belief? Ella Deloria is on record as a harsh condemner of what her own ancestors believed (and incidentally provided a far higher lifestyle of ethics and morals down through centuries). Vine Deloria, the celebrated Indian writer, her nephew, is from the most well-known Indian missionary family among the Sioux. His last book is dedicated to those missionaries. His great-grandfather was told by God to go out and kill four Indians, which he did. His last book is dedicated to that person. Deloria's Aunt Ella was an adamant denouncer of all things Spiritual among the traditional Indians. I met her several times when I was a law student. She condemned both Russell Means and me for taking part in the resurging Sun Dance. Vine's father, Vine Senior, Ella's brother, I will give credit for stating in the last page of his memoir: 'And when I die, I want Captain Ed McGaa to fly my ashes over the Badlands.' (Or words to this effect.) I believe he was commemorating my stance for the return of the Sun Dance and our Spirituality back then. It was a bit late in his life for switching, but probably he was making an attempt or felt that the old Way held a lot of good for Indian People. By then, our Spiritual Way was a growing flame from a once almost dying ember. Of course, I was never contacted by his family to spread his ashes from an airplane.

2 MISSIONARY BOARDING SCHOOL

There are many stories and many story tellers. Most will tell you what you want to hear, but only a few will tell you what the Blue Man forces don't want you to know.
—Thunder Owl—Mdewakanton Sioux

Yah, Joe (Thunder Owl). And here it is the next century and the goddamn academic stooges (Indian writers, authors) still ain't got the guts to tell about what Boarding School really was—all the damage it did and still does-and the Canton Insane Asylum either!

I mentioned that most of my brothers and sisters attended Holy Rosary Mission and that discipline and methods for maintaining strict conformance were no different than the government boarding school. Worse, no doubt, due in part to the highly unnatural vows the clergy took for a lifetime—'devout celibacy.' (To somehow please God!) Pedophilia was more rampant than at the government boarding school. Anger also was vented considerably, brought on, my belief, by such an unnatural vow that presented itself ever so strongly by each approaching day as the avowed one got older. Later lawsuits would bear this supposition out.

I described Missionary Boarding School in one of my early writings. The main characters in this portrayal are real. Some are the composite of several characters. I did have an older brother who was quite strong for his age (more than one actually). He tangled with an overbearing priest and the priest lost. He was expelled in absentia after he ran away and joined the military. The brothers within are a combination of several brothers. Cross Dog, whom you shall soon meet, what happened to him is all factual. While the following is fictionalized, the story is true.

High aloft, a pair of eagles scanned a prairie dog town. It was an unusual winter day. Warm wind and sunshine had enticed the stubby tailed creatures and now evening was drawing jackrabbits from their dens. To the south, the eagles could view the missionary boarding school. Northward, the desolate Badlands stretched for almost a hundred miles. In that vastness of silence, high walls crested with cedar and isolated wind carved buttes touched down to alkali flats, gullies, creeks and a lone river knowing no street or village. Only a post office/store and a few cattle ranches upon fenceless range bore witness to two-legged (human). The rest belonged to the eagles, owls, rattlesnakes, bull snakes, kangaroo rats, prairie dogs, rabbits, deer, antelope, badgers, bobcats and coyotes. In those days, maybe a few mountain sheep and possibly a pair of prairie wolves still lingered—such was its remoteness and solitude.

The Indian boarding school was a sprawling establishment. The Church had acquired hundreds of acres; choice bottom land, once covered with buffalo grass, now sprouted hay pasture, grain fields and garden plots. So far, it was a mild winter, the first Sunday of December and pond ice had formed only once. A statue, proclaimed by the Jesuits as the 'Mother of God', beamed down on open water melted by a warm Chinook which had been blowing on and off for about a week. Upstream from the pond, red brick buildings, classrooms and dormitories clustered around a spired church. Several battered cars, mostly '30s vintage, were parked in a graveled lot. A sporty team of matched dappled grays pulled a buggy up to the church. Another team, plow horses hooked to a wagon, stood in sharp contrast next to a shiny black sedan. The fenders and grill of the new 1941 Ford gleamed from a fresh wash and polishing by boarding school students. The West River Bishop's Mass was about to conclude a weekend retreat. Most of the brothers, priests and sisters had been sequestered in silence and subsequently, all mission school activities had been curtailed. Even radios had been banned for the weekend; such was the devotion to solitude, isolation and contemplation. Barns, hog houses, chicken coops and machinery sheds spread out downstream. Range cattle stood inside a fenced enclosure, isolated from a herd of milk cows waiting to be stanchioned for the evening's milking. Hogs grunted in the hog yard while a pair of roosters tried to outdo each other for the last crow.

Oglala Sioux youth scurried around the milk cows like trained sheep dogs, obedient to the barking commands of well-muscled Jesuit brothers. A bell tolled from the church, and the brothers fell silent for a few moments. At the opening of a cattle gate behind a hesitant milk cow, one youth looked perplexed. He didn't know whether to follow the last command of the Jesuit or the dictate of the bell. He wisely dropped one knee to the ground in an act of prayer while the milk cow ambled back to a tuft of hay she had pulled from a feeding stall. On a hillside rising beyond the church steeple, a cemetery waited beneath leafless cottonwood and elm trees. Tombstones and wooden crosses arranged in rows poked out of brown winter grass and clusters of tumbleweeds. In the center of the fenced graveyard, a European-featured human God was nailed grotesquely to a cross and another life-sized statue of the grieving Mother of God also bore distinct European features.

Three boys hidden by stacks of prairie hay behind the hog house ignored the bell while it tolled. Two half-breeds listened closely to a full-blood boy pronouncing Sioux words. "*Pilamiya*," Cross Dog spoke, then went on to enunciate each syllable. "*Pee lahm eey yah. Pee lahm eey yah.*" He paused to explain in English. "*Pilamiya*. That means, thank you." He repeated, "*Pilamiya*," then added a new word, speaking yet in syllables. "*Pee lahm eey yah wee choh nee.*" In heavily accented, guttural English he said, "Now say it."

"*Pilamiya wichoni.*" Lawrence, the older of the two half-breeds, answered comfortably with almost as much Siouan accent as the full-blood, Cross Dog. Lawrence was the oldest of the trio, almost too old looking for high school. He was strong in build like Cross Dog but lighter complexioned. The youngest of the three, Kyle, was still in his early years of grade school. He was thinner than Lawrence and close to his brother in degree of complexion. All had the pronounced hawkish Siouan nose and rangy bearing. The two older boys, still growing, were close to six feet.

"Real good, brother," Cross Dog responded while he gathered up loose hay to make a comfortable mound. The full-blood could have displayed a fiercer look but the hunger and loneliness in his eyes erased it. "*Pilamiya wichoni.* That means, I am thankful for my life. That is a powerful prayer or something good to say to the Big Spirit *Wakan Tanka*." Cross Dog was not a blood relative but used the customary term of relationship reserved for a close friend.

"*Wakan Tanka*," Lawrence replied. "I know that is the Great Spirit, Great Mystery, but what else does your father and your grandfather say about that word? They were all holy men, weren't they?" The half-breed spoke with a calm self-confidence.

Cross Dog looked around cautiously and nodded affirmatively. "They must have been. I get beaten at this school more than anyone else…and I don't look for trouble."

"Why don't you just throw in with these Catholics? That's what I told my little brother. Lay low and keep your mouth shut. What they say ain't any mystery. Hell, he's even made his first communion."

"*Wakan Tanka*, means Big Holy…Big Everything," Cross Dog responded in halting English, ignoring the advice. The *wahshichus* (white men) have a word. You just said it." A glimmer of deep pride still flared within the full-blood.

"You mean Great Mystery or Great Holy," Lawrence offered.

"Yes that's the word. This 'Great Mystery', it is too powerful to be killed and hung up to die like the *wahshichu* claims. I am too old now to believe that. For your little brother, I can understand but I would be lying if I say that I believe the way the *wahshichu* wants me to."

Lawrence chewed on a stem of hay. "That's why the Brothers of the Cross are beating the shit out of you and not giving you as much to eat. But as long as I'm around, you'll eat." With that statement the husky youth pulled a half loaf of bakery bread out from a gunny sack. He broke off two small pieces, handing one to his brother and then passed the major portion to the full-blood. He reached down into the grain sack and served up four boiled potatoes. He offered two to Cross Dog, one to Kyle and took the smallest for himself. Kyle handed his larger potato back to Lawrence, then swiped the smallest potato out of his brother's hand despite a bite already taken. Lawrence laughed in admiration. "Heyyyy, heyyy, look at this little guy. Already he's learning to be an Indian." He pointed his potato at Kyle. "Cross Dog, my brother, you look after this little guy next year. Keep the bullies away from him." He noted a sparrow looking down from the roof of the hog house. He broke a pebble-sized crumb and threw it up to the bird. "That little bird is our witness. Beat the shit out of them the first week of school. That's the way I've always done it. I taught you enough about boxing. You can do it."

Cross Dog ate his potato and smiled confidently. "You still plan on joining the Army?" he asked after he swallowed the first potato and reached for the bread.

"A Sioux should never join the Army. Goddamn cavalry," Lawrence spat the words. "Going to try the Marines. Don't know if they will take an Indian. They don't allow Negroes in the Marines. Navy doesn't either. That's what I heard. Don't know what they'll say to an Indian."

"I think I heard about the Marines but never saw any. Are they the ones with that real pretty uniform, all red, white and blue?"

"That's them. But guess they don't wear it much. Just for show and parades. I guess they are some real tough sons-a-bitches."

Cross Dog admired the way Lawrence could swear and sound like a white man. He wanted to swear like Lawrence and promised himself he would practice swearing once he could get away and be by himself. Lawrence had learned to swear from working summers in the West River lumber mills next to white men. He was a baseball player, too, for the lumber mill team; even though he was Indian, he was that good. He liked Lawrence. Not many full-bloods had the opportunity to hang around with half-breeds. The school seemed to reward the half-breeds more and was harder on the full-bloods. But Lawrence, he was different. He didn't care whether you were full-blood, half-breed or even quarter-breed. He could outbox anyone in the school, even the brothers, and they knew it. Took three to hold him down for a beating. Cross Dog's chest rose. Took three of them, last time he was beat and he had gotten a couple of good licks on that one smart aleck brother, the one that really hated Indians, especially the full-bloods. He looked at Lawrence. "My father saw real live soldiers, right here on the reservation."

Lawrence threw his hay straw to the wind and offered another piece of bread to the sparrow. "So did mine. That's the reason none of us should join the Army. They worked hand in hand with these goddamned missionaries. I heard they left not too long ago. They still got a fort north of West River.

Don't know whether they use it or not."

Cross Dog liked the way Lawrence was so unafraid of the missionaries. So many of the breeds and even the full-bloods thought that the priests and nuns had some sort of hidden power through their Jesus, but not Lawrence. The way Lawrence could fight, he didn't have to take anything from anybody. No priest or brother could take him alone. At the age of six, Lawrence had been severely weaned when he entered boarding school. Those were the lonely years. The isolation from his parents and grandmother left a growing hardness that developed into a bold disdain for the missionaries. Cross Dog looked at the lengthening shadows and knew it was time to resume his language teaching. "Your parents speak good Indian, Kyle. You had better learn from them when you go back home this summer."

"Our mom, the priests have got a hold on her. She won't let us learn. Dad, he sneaks, like you have to. He teaches me sometimes," Lawrence spoke as he looked at Kyle. "Dad's afraid of the priests. He believes the same way as you do but he says the priests are powerful with the way they can be boss, and you best stay out of their way." He paused and studied his younger brother. "It can all cause this little guy a hard time. Me, I'm getting the hell out of here. Wish to hell I could take Kyle with me." With a perplexed, worried look he found a cocklebur in a tuft of hay and threw it at the hog house.

"What about your brother Hobart?"

Lawrence scowled. He reached into the sack and pulled out an empty pint jar. "Kyle, go down to the creek and get us a drink of water," he commanded. Kyle responded with a quick hop to his feet, eager to please. "And get the water upstream from where the cows drink," Lawrence called after him.

Once the boy was out of earshot, Lawrence growled with sarcasm, "My dear brother Hobart. That son...of...a...bitch. That son...of...a...bitch." Lawrence noted the quizzical look on Cross Dog's face. He stammered, adding hurriedly, "I don't mean my mother is a bitch. I like my mom and she would probably kill me if she ever heard me call one of my brothers or sisters that. But, it is about the only way I can say how I feel about Hobart." The breed's voice carried a warning note. "Stay away from that guy and my sister

Leona. Both of them are out for themselves."

"They don't even bother to look in my direction or any of the rest of the full-bloods," Cross Dog replied. "Your sister Mildred, she talks to me and has even snuck me some bread, once or twice. Gave me some apples last Christmas."

"She's okay," Lawrence added. "Long as she stays away from those other two."

As Kyle ambled down to the streambed, a bearded Jesuit brother pitched wads of manure out of the cattle barn into a manure spreader. Milking chores exempted some brothers from the final retreat hours. Raised on a harsh Kansas wheat farm, Brother Herman had known nothing but work. He was solid muscle and could outlast anyone at the Mission when it came to cutting wood, fencing, milking and a host of unending tasks to care for the fields, animals and gardens. Recreation, sports, social festivities and girls were never an experience to the Jesuit. Most German farm families steeped in Catholic tradition selected at least one or even two of their own to serve the church; and he had been chosen—no questions asked. Raised in sheer discipline and religious fervor, he had never expressed remorse or questioned authority regarding personal ambition or worldly desires. Out of curiosity, he watched the boy with the jar shuffling along. He returned to the milking area and gathered up more manure with his shovel. After the manure loader was nearly full he noted the boy returning with his water jar back toward the hog house. He tossed his shovel into the manure load and proceeded to sneak in a low, clumsy crouch toward the front of the hog house.

By the time they had finished their bread, both boys were thirsty and appreciated the cold spring water brought by their companion. Cross Dog took a long drink before handing the pint jar to Lawrence. He smacked his broad lips as he spoke, "Well, let's find out how your little brother is doing at learning Indian. Now say my name in Lakota, Kyle."

Kyle was proud that the older boy included him in his lessons. "*Hinya za, hin yan za shaunnka.*" he pronounced his answer, trying to copy his brother's Siouan accent.

Cross Dog rolled back from his perch of gathered hay in laughter. He poked his head up again with tears in his eyes. "Again," he commanded.

"Hinya ẓa, hin yan ẓa shaunnka."

Cross Dog disappeared behind the hay mound again, moaning in laughter. He poked his head up. "Remember how I told you to say horse? Now say that."

"Tah Shaunnk ah Wah kahn."

Cross Dog fell back from behind the hay mound, this time landing with a thud on a bare patch of ground. Lawrence caught on to the joke and rolled away from his brother in laughter. He held his sides and stared up at the sky. "What does that mean, Kyle?"

"It means Big Dog Holy. That's what Cross Dog told me," he answered with a proud smile. "Is that what you guys are laughing at? When Indians first saw a horse, they said it was a big dog and since a man was riding it, they said it had to be holy." Kyle beamed. "*Tah* means big, *shaunnka* is dog and *wakan* is holy. Big Dog Holy."

Cross Dog leaned closer, his mouth agape with a huge grin. "Little guy, I don't mean to make fun of you but it is really funny how you say 'dog.' 'Dog' is supposed to be said like this, *Shuuuunn-kah. Shuuuunn-kah.*" He overly pronounced the syllables. "*Oooohhn-kah, oooohhn-kah* not *shahhnn-kah*," he tried to sound the way *wahshichus* pronounced Sioux words. "You are saying *Shaunnnnnk-ah.* There is a big difference between *Shuuuunn-kah,* and *Shahunnnnnk-ah.*" He couldn't finish his explanation and started laughing so hard he had to quit looking at the younger Sioux. Every time he looked at Kyle his laughter would get the best of him. Lawrence remained on the ground laughing up at the clouds turning red from the sunset.

So used to being raised in an environment where children were seldom ridiculed, Kyle couldn't help but to laugh along with the two older boys, happy to be responsible for such a degree of amusement at the restrictive, rule-bound school. Finally, Lawrence joined in on the mirthful explanation. "What he wants to say, little brother, is that when you are saying "*shaunhka*" the way you say it, you mean a 'woman's thing,' you know, that thing she pees through between her legs. You are calling Cross Dog an angry woman's thing.

Shuunka is the way you are supposed to say 'dog.' A 'horse' you are calling 'a great big woman's thing that is holy.' In Indian, that really sounds funny. *Tah* means 'big'. *Tah shaunka* means 'a great big woman's thing.' You know, *shaunka* is the same thing that babies come out of." He dropped down quickly and howled at the sky. "White people, *wahshichus*, they call it a pussy. We call it *shaunka.*"

All three sprawled in helpless laughter. Kyle Charging Shield howled along with the two bigger boys, knowing that he would never forget this lesson.

At the corner of the hog house, Brother Herman wanted to rush in and end such hooliganism but he knew he couldn't handle Lawrence. The Sioux was a shade taller and too quick with his fists. He would tell Father Prefect. The Father would punish them. Punish them all. They'd get the belts for this, even that young one. They'd get it harder than those two girls got it last time. He had been thinking about the last beating as the boys were talking and laughing. As he relished the thought of holding down the girl for Father Prefect, it began to happen again and it wouldn't go away. It wouldn't go away from his dreams either.

Brother Herman began to look worried. Beads of sweat rolled down his brow. He would have to go to confession. How could this be happening? He had a rock-hard erection and it wouldn't go away. While Lawrence was explaining what was down between a woman's legs he even had a slight ejaculation when he heard the word *pussy*. And then thinking about that Sioux girl moaning when she had caught each blow of the belt; her pain, and those damned unforgettable moans, even her smell was haunting. And then when her dress got pulled up and he saw her legs…the damn sight and the sounds wouldn't go away. And just now he had even delighted in such a foul evil word. How could he tell this in confession? He would agonize but he would never be able to tell. This was evil. Yes, it had to be some form of evil. These boys and their laughter, it had to be evil. They had caused him to sin. Yes, he was guilty. Guilty of some sin but God only knew. Maybe it was a merciful God or maybe the fires of everlasting hell awaited him, but he would never tell it in confession because no one would understand and the confession wouldn't make it go away anyhow. He did not understand. He was perplexed. He wished he never had snuck up on the evil boys behind the hog house.

Mulling over the report in his sparse, solitary office, Father Prefect sat tensely rigid. Upon the rolls of the Jesuit Order, Reverend Paul Buchwald, S.J., was his name. Since he had been assigned as Mission Disciplinarian he preferred to be addressed as Father Prefect. The waning moon made a silhouette out of the church spire through his window. His thoughts focused on discipline and order. Many a lash had fallen upon recalcitrant Indian youth for the breaking of rules. Rules were designed by learned men to keep order, perfection and obedience to a holy, controlled society. Even some of the girls had to be lashed. Mostly full-bloods. The breeds could be punished with less severe punishment, it seemed. But the full-bloods! God knows they were but a generation or two away from arch paganism. None of their ancestors knew the risen Christ. It was God's redemption, God's resurrection, and God's perfection that often had to be beaten into them lest they lose their wretched souls!

Paul Buchwald heard approaching footsteps in the hallway. He imagined he could smell manure from Brother Herman even though he had given him strict orders not to bring the boys until he had fully bathed. He could smell manure! It wasn't imagination! It had to be Brother Herman. God help him if he had not bathed! He would make him stay up all night saying rosaries for his disobedience.

"Is that you, Brother Herman?" he barked, convinced the smell was not mere imagination. "Bring in the boys," he commanded not waiting for an answer.

Brother Herman stumbled in with a rim of hog manure covering the seam stitched to bind the sole and toe of his boots. Buchwald's top lip drew back and upwards as if to hold back the smell. Long in the manure shed and hog yard, Brother Herman was oblivious to odors even after he had showered and soaped and lathered and put on clean clothes. His erection had risen again as he lathered but he wouldn't tell that in confession. The boys...the laughing, evil boys, they were responsible for this reoccurrence of sin. They should be beaten. Beaten for their laughter and the sin that was descending upon him.

Buchwald looked at his watch. He had an important meeting scheduled with Father Superior. New donations from wealthy eastern patrons; more letters to write by the students and the retreat had kept him from his business duties. Money was more important than beating these ignorant pagans. A new form letter would be drafted for them to copy. The breed kids, especially the quarter-breeds, were best at writing the soliciting letters. They made the least mistakes. He would be late if he did not act promptly. There would be no time for a lengthy speech and it wouldn't work on the older two anyway…and ugh, that damned smell of Brother Herman. He planned to expel Lawrence in the spring as soon as horse breaking was over. Lawrence was as good as his father at breaking horses. Finally, they would be rid of the belligerent breed. The younger one would shape up in due time. And Cross Dog. The Devil would get Cross Dog. The sons of the holy men; they were too brainwashed in the old traditions. They had to be isolated and even starved down to keep from spreading their evil influence. They either ran away for good or committed suicide. There wasn't much hope for them. Besides, they could poison the minds of the rest. It was a worthy sacrifice. All could not be saved. Even the Bible said similarly. He noted the black missal standing upright on his desktop; his book of prayers and devotions sandwiched between a heavy pair of polished agate bookends. Every word was actually written by the hand and voice of God the Savior.

Two priests and two brothers brought in the older boys. Father Buchwald looked nervous. Both seemed to have grown in stature. Lawrence was big enough but yet it seemed he had suddenly become larger and even stronger looking. Twitching nervously Lawrence looked down at the floor. Buchwald looked over at Cross Dog and found him shaking with fear

Damn, he thought, these boys should have been tied. But they're scared and there's six of us, he tried to reassure himself. Brother Herman went back into the hallway and with a firm hold on Kyle's ear, pulled him into the crowded office.

"Lawrence and Cross Dog. You are charged with speaking Indian within this institution. This act is forbidden at U.S. Government Boarding Schools and this rule includes Mission Schools upon Federal Reservations. We of the Jesuit Order pride ourselves in being lenient as God is caring but we must follow government dictates that foster discipline and good order. You are also charged with using foul, obscene words as witnessed by Brother Herman in your sojourn behind the hog house." Buchwald frowned. He wanted to sound formal and military for the sake of the newest priest holding on to Lawrence. He noted that the priest, somewhat effeminate, appeared fearful by the look in his eyes. *Hog house… hog house*, damn that took away from the formality of the charge, his mind wandered uneasily as he looked at the young priest. "Kyle, you are so equally charged," he added with a loss of forcefulness.

Brother Herman thrust the youngest of the accused forward to within an arm's length of the Prefect. Buchwald reached behind the side of his desk to draw out a thick leather strap. He folded it once and held it under Kyle's nose. The priest felt a surge of power as Kyle's eyes widened. The boy had felt the sting of the strap before. Kyle smelled the leather over the hog manure on Brother Herman's shoes and began to be afraid but he was more afraid for Cross Dog and his brother.

"Bring the accused forward," Buchwald commanded with warden-like authority. Cross Dog held back as if afraid while Lawrence stepped forward. Buchwald made a polite gesture. "The first shall get the least of the lashes while the last shall receive the most." He wanted to pit both of the older Indians against each other. Neither of the two older boys indicated an acknowledgment. Lawrence took another small step forward but hung his head low as if to convey a conciliatory gesture. "As an indication of my leniency, I shall not punish the youngest within this room as harshly but nevertheless, he shall receive his due." With that statement he was pleased to see Lawrence nodding in acknowledgment. A stool was pulled out from a closet. Lawrence moved forward and bent over, his backside to the disciplinarian priest. The youngest priest was over anxious to let go of the accused and stood with a girlish pose—his mouth open with a chagrined gape and knees knocking—while a brother, smaller than Lawrence, still clung rather awkwardly and loosely to the Indian's muscled arm. "Brother Herman, switch with your companion holding Lawrence," Buchwald barked. The smaller brother moved to stand beside Kyle.

At the touch of Lawrence, Brother Herman was brought back to the last beating. The pair of full-blood girls that had run away; both of them had got the strap and he, Brother Herman, had to hold them. He had an uncontrolled erection while they were being beaten and had ejaculated when the girl's dress came up. It was a good thing that he had worn his long flowing habit. Now he was beginning to come erect thinking back to the girls, their moans and grunts. They were full-bloods and refused to scream out like most of the breed girls did. It was the closest he had ever been to a girl…Yes…he could revel in it! Those moans…he could still hear her moaning!

Buchwald reared back in the crowded room, letting the strap loose to its full extension and accidentally bumping one of the agate slabs on his desk. His balance shifted slightly and as he brought the strap down hard, his aim was amiss and he partially missed the backside of Lawrence. Brother Herman let out a howl from the end of the strap stinging him solidly upon his erection. The brother began dancing a jig, howling in pain.

It happened. Not according to plan but close to it. Lawrence came up strong with an elbow to Buchwald's temple sending him down and out cold. Cross Dog spun free from his two handlers. A brother went down gasping from a vicious jab to his throat. One of the stone desk slabs smashed down across the ankle of the brother next to Kyle, sending him limping and howling out of the office. Kyle took the remaining bookstand and crashed it on Brother Herman's foot, fracturing his instep. The two remaining priests were no match. One priest sailed out the window, receiving cuts from jagged glass. The effeminate priest cried out in fear and began sobbing as he was stuffed into the closet, brandished by the stool across his backside.

Under the clouded moon, the boys hustled down the gravel road leading away from the reservation, bearing a gunny sack and bound for the railroad tracks connecting to West River. Whenever a car would come from the direction of the Mission, they would hide off to the side of the road until it passed. Few cars passed from either direction as the night drew on. Back at the Mission, the infirmary was too busy tending to the injured to bother looking for runaways. Lawrence had always planned to run away and kept a sack of stores put away for the occasion. They would be long gone before the Mission could track them. They would catch a freight train at the bottom of the first steep grade and by morning they would be in West River. Enough Indians, including an uncle working at the lumber mill, were camped along Rapid Creek. They felt confident they could hide for a while.

When they came to the grade, they hid beneath a tall stand of chokecherry bushes. The Chinook wind blowing out of the Badlands kept them warm. Cross Dog told them that the Chinook was a good omen and the waning moon hiding behind the clouds was a sign that the spirits were with them. Kyle didn't know about spirits but he liked Cross Dog. He figured that spirits must be like guardian angels. His legs ached, making him appreciate the rest. "What exactly is a spirit?" he asked Cross Dog.

"Being Indian, I have to say truthfully I don't know for sure," the full-blood replied. "I suspect it is simply a person that was here before and has gone on."

"You mean a ghost?" Kyle's voice wavered.

Cross Dog laughed. "Ghosts," he spat the word. "That's what those missionaries preach to keep you scared so you won't run away." He held up his hand. "A spirit isn't like a scary ghost. It is a helper. It can watch over you and help you out, especially if you do something important like going off to war. A spirit helper is a good thing to have on your side."

"How do you know this?" Kyle pressed.

"I have seen many *Yuwipi* (*You wee pee*) ceremonies and these spirit helpers came in. I would be lying if I said that I didn't hear them and even see them—in a way." There was no hesitancy or stammering in Cross Dog's response.

"Kyle," Lawrence spoke. "You are too young to hear this and it probably scares you. But I went to a *Yuwipi* once. It was powerful and these spirit helpers came in and made some helluva big predictions. They always make good predictions, I mean they are in line with what the people are asking. I wouldn't call them ghosts. They ain't spooky like it sounds. I want you to believe me." He looked at his brother closely. "Have I ever lied to you?"

The younger boy was starting to droop. "No," he answered quietly before laying his head in his brother's lap. "You mean they ain't nothin' like a devil?" he mumbled.

Cross Dog spat an answer, "Our *Wakan Tanka* is too powerful to have to make what the *wahshichus* believe in. We never had a devil before they brought it here!"

"Fucking missionaries and their goddamned made up devils and Satans." Lawrence growled as he defiantly looked back toward the Mission. "Yeah, the sons a bitches, they brought the devil here. Our people never had a devil before the white man brought it." After a pause he added, "I learned that from my grandmother."

Lawrence broke out some bread and each boy ate a mouthful, washing it down with water from a quart-sized jar. Before long they were rehashing their episode. "You did a good job shaking," Lawrence complimented Cross Dog. "I figured if we didn't get tied up, then we could get the jump on them."

Cross Dog laughed and looked at Kyle who was now fast asleep. "Your little brother, there. He did his job well. I always had a good feeling toward those fancy rocks that Buchwald kept on his desk. All along they had some good medicine inside of them. Kyle really bombed them two brothers with those rocks. Maybe he'll grow up and fly an airplane. He'll be bombing the Germans if we get into a war with them."

"The white man will never let an Indian fly an airplane but we might go to war with more than the Germans. They say the Japanese are making trouble. That one cook that lets me sneak you food, he's always telling me what's going on from a newspaper the mailman brings." A coyote's doleful howl made the breed's head nod. "I'm starting to get sleepy but one of us has to stay awake to hear the train."

Cross Dog looked back down the track and rose. "I'm going to put my head on the rail and listen for the train. They say that you can hear it coming from a long ways off." He turned with a strange smile. "You get some sleep and I'll wake you up when I get tired...if the train hasn't come by."

Lawrence called after him, "Cross Dog, Brother, I have one last question before I sleep. Why do you think the disciplinarian put you on half rations? Was it because you are a full-blood or your father and grandfather were holy men?"

Cross Dog laughed and walked off, speaking back over his shoulder, "It was because I would never take a name."

"A name? What do you mean?"

"You are Lawrence and Kyle is Kyle...Mildred, Leona and Hobart...Paul and Herman." His voice rose. Deep pride could be sensed. All hunger and the loneliness vanished. Even Cross Dog's face took on a fierce warrior's expression. "Me, I am just Cross Dog and only Cross Dog...like Crazy Horse, Chips, and Red Cloud. The priest...Father Prefect told me I could have double rations for a month if I would just set an example, make Holy Communion and take a holy name...even one like his." His voice lowered. "I am a traditional Indian. I couldn't do it." Sternly he spoke, "It would be a lie to myself." An owl hooted loud and clear. "It would be a lie to myself," Cross Dog repeated softly. "Thanks to you Brother, you kept me from starving. I'll make it up to you some day. I'll look out for you and that is a firm promise." There was a resolute echo to Cross Dog's words, as if somehow, he would carry out his promise.

Several tears for Cross Dog flowed from Lawrence as he drifted into sleep. The full-blood's pronouncement ushered in a lonely feeling. Cross Dog was so alone at the Mission. He wished that none of them would ever have to return to the boarding school. He could hear the soft hum of "heyyy, heyyy, heyyy" as the full-blood walked away. He looked up to see Cross Dog hunkering down on the railroad bed, placing his ear on the track. A muffled "heyyy, heyyy, heyyy" could still be heard. The coyotes howled while a pair of owls echoed their chorus. Both breeds slept and for the moment, Cross Dog was free.

"Son of a bitch. Son of a bitch," Cross Dog began to practice in earnest as he listened on the rail.

Lawrence dreamed of his grandmother and his father. Somehow he would have to get his younger brother back to his father and mother who still had their small ranch at the northern edge of the reservation. The actual worries of life and duty permeated his dream. After leaving his brother with an uncle in West River, he saw himself marching off to war in a red-and-blue Marine uniform. He saw his little brother wearing the same uniform and fighting, too, but he was in a strange looking airplane and was dropping rocks. The rocks turned to bombs just like Cross Dog had said. He had to laugh at his little brother flying an airplane, and it was a big one, too. He would have to get him out of that flying machine and return him to his parents.

A loud rising rumble like roaring wind filled his dream. Cross Dog flashed so vividly before him. "Thanks to you, Brother, you kept me from starving." The full-blood spoke in a soft, reassuring voice. "I'll make it up to you some day. I'll look out for you and that is a firm promise." Cross Dog was elevated and reached out to touch him.

The ground shook as the freight train raced full steam into the steep grade. Lawrence bolted from his resting place, forgetting about his dream. He yelled at Kyle who was already awake from the clamoring noise of the slowing train, its engine huffing and puffing to make the grade. Lawrence grabbed up the gunny sack with one hand and his brother in the other. "Cross Dog!" he yelled as the pair stumbled toward the track. Red-orange daylight was just beginning to crack out from the rim of Badlands to the east. "Cross Dog! C'mon, let's catch this son of a bitch!" At the spot where he had last seen Cross Dog, he could make out a severed arm and a leg; the rest had been swept on up the grade. Cross Dog had fallen asleep.

Several hours later on a Monday dawn, the bleary-eyed boys hailed a rancher on a gravel road. Before they could speak, the rancher rolled down his car window and yelled, "Looks like you boys heard the news. Japs bombed Pearl Harbor! We're goin' to war!" He looked at Lawrence with wide-eyed respect. "Hop aboard, son. Bet your headin' into West River to sign up. All the young guys are enlistin' and gettin' their papers started."

Life changed abruptly. The War Department declared the northern area of the reservation as a war emergency aerial gunnery and bombing range. Kyle's parents had to vacate their ranch and moved to West River. Lawrence joined the Marines. The runaways never had to return to the boarding school.

3 SCHOOL DAYS

I had a pleasant life being raised in Rapid City, South Dakota. My older brothers and sisters, the oldest ones were grown and some were starting to marry. Most of my brothers had gone off to fight the war—five all told. I had heroes, real live ones, my brothers all saw combat except one. They would fight what propaganda told us were 'bad people' especially the treacherous 'Japs' who mostly had big front teeth, poor eyesight and were sneaky. We knew nothing about what was happening to the poor Jews. One brother, Russ, was injured in training so he was medically discharged but nothing overly serious or handicapping. He became a second father for my formative years and bought my parents their first home away from the makeshift tent city hastily erected for Indian families working at the new air base.

It was an exciting time, those war years. Practically all of the displaced reservation bombing range Indians were quite content despite living in tents close to Rapid Creek where the children loved swimming in summer times. Jobs made the difference. It was such a clean mountain stream then that the Indian Camp Indians drew their water from it. Eventually, the families did as we did. They made enough money to put down payments on houses and those with sons in the service sent extra money to move on into houses. We bought quite a spacious place in North Rapid and soon a garden, an orchard of plum, apple and even a cherry tree began to thrive. We planted a large lawn, and since our home was at the bottom of a valley there was rich black earth to grow our 'Victory Gardens' (as they were called and promoted for the war effort).

Patriotism

Everything was patriotism and focus on the war effort. Our home grew; flora and fauna, too. My brother Russ was a skilled carpenter and we kept on building additions and living improvements. The brothers in the service kept sending money home to my mom who took care of the financial administration. Our water began being piped in. It was fairly simple at first. My dad and brother dug a trench to the new city waterline and an iron pipe connected to our kitchen. It stood straight up with a faucet on the end, one you could attach a garden hose to. Oh, how proud we were of that four-foot-high iron pipe with a simple faucet jutting out at the top. We didn't know about sinks, and counter sinks yet. Outside, another faucet provided water for some Indian families living close by to fill their water pails. Eventually we got more modern. The outdoor toilet came down when I was in the eighth grade. A telephone line came quite early with only four numbers. 1579. Then it became 1579W. The natural gas company laid pipe nearby and we hooked onto that; no more chopping wood. Electricity was available when my brother first bought the house. One nice thing about having an outdoor toilet is that the household organic kitchen waste from our meals went into a big bucket and was thrown upon the ground a few yards above our spreading strawberry patch. It became a reservoir for angle worms and night crawlers which spread to our fairly spacious lawn. At night with a flash light, we could harvest all the night crawlers we wanted for fishing. Fast flowing Rapid Creek was within a fifteen minute walking distance, Rainbows, German Browns and even a few pink-meated brook trout lurked. The creek flowed much heavier back in those days because the city had not tapped into it as much as it does now. There was no TV back then which was probably a blessing. A refrigerator was purchased and my sister and I went into business making Popsicles for the neighbor kids. A toothpick went into each square of an ice cube tray filled with Kool-Aid. We made a bit of money on that venture. As kids, we were constantly outside which meant we had plenty of exercise. Swimming in Rapid Creek which roared through town became our summer mecca. Various swimming holes along the creek, segregated according to one's age group, drew us. We had almost half a city block—land was cheap then. We had chickens and a big red-orange, mean rooster. He was so big and mean he could whip dogs and chased us kids.

Eagle and the Rooster

One time we went down to the Badlands on the Rez and came across an eagle caught in a rancher's coyote trap. It was very weak from hunger and thirst and put up a feeble resistance against my father placing his Mackinaw heavy coat over it and we tied it down with our belts. We brought it home and placed it in the chicken coup that had a big iron-barred grate you could look through. Needless to say the chickens all vacated and stayed in the trees from there on. The eagle looked at us and drank some water but would not eat the cottontails we threw into it. Mom killed a chicken and put that in there but it still would not eat, not even a jackrabbit. The Hill City Zoo got word and came down and offered $100. We were poor and needed the money but Dad held off, Mom, too.

Dad's Scar

Well the old mean rooster strutted around and would crow at the eagle. There was a small doorway at the bottom of the coop for chickens to go in and out but too small for the eagle. The rooster decided that since he could whip anything around he needed to tangle with the eagle and foolishly entered to engage him. We kids were playing and saw the rooster strutting and crowing abnormally, it wasn't evening yet when he normally crowed. He entered and all of a sudden we heard a commotion and saw a bunch of orange feathers seeming to cloud up on the gate bars. The eagle ate every bit of him except for his feathers, beak and feet. Afterwards he would gobble up our cottontails, even a couple of rats and one garter snake. Dad said it was time to turn him back to his freedom. That night my brother and dad with a flashlight went in to bind him up with a tarp and some rope. My dad got a big gash on his forearm that he was ever proud of thereafter—left one helluva scar. It was Saturday night and the Indian hospital then was closed on Sundays and Dad had to work on Monday. Being Indian you often have a different life than a White Man. Mom said it would be bad luck if we ever sold the eagle to a zoo. She taped the gash to hold the cut together and it healed without infection. Dad put some kind of juice from a plant on it before she taped.

They put the eagle out in the same place they found it. Russ had it fixed that you could just pull two ropes and the eagle would get free. It worked. Out came the eagle standing up tall. It walked sideways to us, not away, always staring directly at us, mainly at Dad. It spread its wings a few times and was in no hurry. Finally it turned directly toward us and lifted into the sky. It went up high right over us and circled around several times and then headed away to the Badland buttes—free. For several years later, my Dad could go down there and stand out waving his big cowboy hat. Sure enough, here would come the eagle and fly several circles over him.

There has to be a God.

TB Hospital

Work was plentiful and my dad and brother were always employed. Even my mom worked for a while at the Public Health Hospital at the western end of Rapid City. They were short on help so she filled in for most of the war. My oldest sister, Mildred, worked there, too, and she drove my Mom. Neither of my parents could drive a car but both could handle horses and were raised riding them and hitching up a team. Women were starting to enter the military back then. The Public Health hospital in Rapid specialized in tuberculosis-afflicted Indian patients who were dying right and left. I was confined there also, as I had a serious pneumonia lung infection and almost died. One lung to this day is a bit smaller than the other. The congealing of phlegm and mucous pushed my heart several inches and I had a weak heart for my early childhood. I could faint at the drop of a hat. Once a bit fat and chubby kid, I wound up fairly skinny all my youth. Anything too exciting and I would pass out. My older brother Russ was very protective of me and beat up the last brother next to me for placing a big green caterpillar on my shoulder. Naturally I fainted dead cold.

The brother four years older than I was, was a bully to me because he was jealous imagining that Dad gave me more attention although my father certainly did not ignore him. He tried to be fair to all of us. Russ, however, kept an eye on him and he got punished every time he would pull something on me to scare me and make me faint, which he loved to do. Even after I grew out of my sickness and began to succeed 'Boob' forever remained jealous. His problem, not mine.

I was skinnier than most kids. The TB doctor told my mother that I could die quite easily after my second bout with the pneumonia. He said I could be sheltered and I might make it but would be sickly. The best advice he gave her was a second option, "Let him run, Julie…and he might come out of it." My mom still had the old natural Sioux instinct and took the latter option. "Better he runs free. He might pull out of it," was her pragmatic remark. I was set free and obviously I made it. I was too active not to. I still remember looking down from my hospital room in the TB hospital at the hearses that would pull up below, late at night and load up a body or two of deceased TB patients. It was a rampant disease for quite some time among the Sioux; all tribes actually. Probably worse than the diabetes epidemic we have now. The TBs died quicker. Pneumonia, a lung disease, qualified me for free hospitalization in the Public Health hospital. My folks said I was nice and fat when I came out of there the first time. I do recall, it was a good place to eat.

Not long after I was released from the hospital I cut my hand pretty bad on a broken glass pane. It severed a bit of thumb palm muscle and some nerves. My typing to this day is mostly with my right hand even though I have failed some Mavis Beacon typing courses. I just do not have the left hand coordination but have managed to publish over a dozen books.

Addiction—A Good One

Regarding diabetes; that is why I play pickleball so much now—five, six and even seven days a week in the winters and often twice a day. You certainly do not look your age doing it that much but so many of us are addicted to it. At least it is a healthy addiction. Most do not even go to church Sunday mornings, instead playing pickleball. It should be called Wiffle Ball. It is very similar to tennis, just on a smaller court. I won a gold medal two years in a row at the Minnesota Annual Senior Games. It is a big state with no pushovers. Swedes are fairly athletic. Veterans Administration doctors can't believe what great shape I am in. P-Ball (www.pickleball.com) on the Rez could save a lot of lives. Go and check it out.

I do have fantastic dexterity with my right hand, however. To fly a Phantom F-4, especially in combat, when the enemy is shooting at you, you had better have. It hasn't kept me from winning that coveted Gold. They even drape the medal over you like in the Olympics. My partner was a tall Norwegian named Orv Askeland. He was as thrilled as I was. It was hard to lob over him and I was pretty fast on the bottom side. Minnesota Senior Games Gold, two years in a row now, yes, what a thrill. It is the fastest growing sport in the nation, but can be very addictive. Many of us play five to six times a day and often twice a day since other suburbs are offering it on outdoor converted tennis courts in summers and newly painted gym floors for indoors come winters in Minneapolis. Seven adjoining suburbs offer it in western Minneapolis and now the St. Paul suburbs are getting into it, and we can all play now, seven days a week if we want to. A resort in Florida has one hundred and ten P-Ball courts that are full of players.   Despite my advancing age you can smash a ball up close to me and I often can deflect it back at you. Not every time but enough to amaze my P-ball friends who often remark to me about my reflexes. It makes me laugh with confidence when I do it. Age does not seem to delete reflexes and adrenaline still happens. When I step on the court, I can turn and spin as good as a much, much younger player although I must admit that as each year passes by, I am not reluctant to have them get the lobs more. I wish they would name it 'Whiffle ball' instead, because that is what we use and it is about the size of a baseball. It is plastic with dime-sized holes to allow it to slow down after hit by an oversized, more solidly built ping pong type paddle, and it sails across a shortened tennis court and net. America's fastest growing sport, it is; especially for the retired and extremely addictive. I had a T-shirt stamped by an embroidery shop in bold letters. PICKLE BALL on the front. Back:

Die Young
Avoid Pickleball

You have to have sharp reflexes to be a fighter pilot but mostly in your right hand. The Marine Corps never knew about my childhood injury and most certainly would have barred me from flying the F-4 Phantom had they known. I had no problem pushing both those throttles with it (my slightly handicapped left) and was commended by my squadron commander several times for my bombing accuracy. Obviously it is often best to keep your handicaps to yourself. My left arm is a little bit smaller and shorter than my right, even a slight difference in color but not much to be noticeable. Lack of dexterity in the left fingers force an odd typing style that Mavis Beacon typing classes won't approve of, but as I said, I have managed to type over a dozen books. Surprisingly, including this Bio, nine are still current.

Rapid Creek

The rest of my youthful life was quite pleasant, as I can remember. We swam in Rapid Creek all summer not far from my house. The mountain runoff-generated water was cold but as kids at mid-July and August, 100 degrees and more, you never noticed. A packing plant was nearby and we would often go over and ride pigs. No one was around on weekends. Far upstream where I still fish for wily trout, I definitely notice how cold the water is. Trout were plentiful. Bullheads and suckers, too. Brother Russ took me down to Rapid Creek only a few blocks away when it used to run more wild than it does now. He showed me a large trout that stayed under a tall cottonwood with some of its roots in the water. You could look down into sort of a washed out cavern and there was a large trout waiting for food. He told me to never fish for him and tell no other kids. I would peek at him at times when I was by myself, which was often as I would then fish upstream and always came home with some. A big flood came when I was in college and killed about two hundred and some people. You can imagine how many houses it took out since it ran right through town. Now it is just a serene stream much smaller because of the growing city tapping into its source— Cleghorn Canyon Springs. Designated as a flood plain, a paved bike trail now courses for miles next to it. We hunted not far from home for cottontails and jackrabbits within walking distance from our neighborhood. We were firing .22 rifles by the time we were thirteen or so. We got cars at fourteen and hence cottontails for our folks who liked them. They are pretty tasty.

Later on, I had to hunt deer for my folks using my brother's Jap rifle which he had captured in Saipan. I never enjoyed hunting deer but my folks needed meat. They never wanted a big buck deer, aka the White man's trophy buck—yah, the one with the big antlers. It was too 'rutty' and not as good to eat as the lesbian doe (what we called a female deer that never had little ones). She is often as big as a buck and quite tasty if you ever become a connoisseur of deer meat. "Don't shoot no bucks!" were my orders. We were re-buying up our old ranch back then through my white brother-in-law's wages as a railroad engineer, so had quite a spread to hunt in down on the Rez. Additional land leased from the tribe also added to the acreage. There were quite a few trophy bucks there that no one was allowed to hunt according to my oldest sister. I would place quite a few into my sights while stalking a choice doe but never pulled the trigger. The older buck prevents wasting disease, which is obviously immune. The herd remains healthy when you allow the strong, large bucks to stick around and mate. Just plain Indian common sense which trophy-hunting, all-knowing White Man has never figured out.

Cedric—A Close Friend

Cedric was an all-around type farm dog and I consider him a great dog. He deserves a place in any book I write about myself. It just wouldn't be respectful if I left him out. After all, he was my first bird dog. The ring-necks were so abundant then, we got our share. I didn't overdo my hunting of them. There were too many more exciting targets like the rats and mice in the granary and corn cribs on my brother-in-law's farm where I spent several summers. The rats were the most exciting, way more exciting than shooting the pheasants which you avoided come summers, even the roosters. Hens were off-limits and not knowing biology much at an early age, I just assumed that the roosters were, too.

One big rat I shot came up in the crib toward me. I about fell out of my high perch on the rafters, such was my fear. I always carried several rounds in my teeth on those sojourns and managed a quick reload to dispatch him. He was about as big as a cat and it was a real scary situation. Actually, as an afterthought, I do not think he was coming at me, as my later experience with those creatures was that they avoid humans as much as possible. He must not have seen my location and was simply trying to avoid whatever was inflicting his sudden wound down below. He just happened to come my way. One never knows, I guess, but he certainly gave me a shiver. Can you imagine a big rat the size of a cat coming at you?

It wasn't much fun shooting gophers after that big rat incident in the corn crib. Nothing is exciting about plinking a cute little gopher wandering out of its hole when you compared a not-so-cute old ugly rat with much bigger teeth. I had one of my first close calls with one, however. This was before the Corn Crib Rat Incident. I shot this poor little innocent gopher and it was kicking away in its death throes. I had reloaded the single shot .22 and did not place it on safe. I picked up my rifle by the barrel just below the sights and brought the butt of the rifle down hard on the gopher's head to end its misery. *Wham!* The gun fired and my baseball cap blew off with a hole in the visor. My ears were ringing and despite its small caliber, the round created a breath of wind past my face, barely missing my nose. Yes, kids are stupid around guns at times, although I did learn to never try that again.

Grumman Canoe

Years later, I would get shot closely again. That time it would graze the back of my neck, drawing blood. It stings like hell when you get shot. My ears rang, too. Worse was that the round went through a college girl I had been dating. It is kind of difficult to explain—how you can shoot a girl and wind up shooting yourself. We were in a canoe, a fairly good size Grumman cargo model, four of us floating down the Salk River in Minnesota. It was Ascension Thursday so we Catholic college students had a holiday. She was shot on that Thursday and back in school the next Wednesday with her arm in a temporary sling. A Ruger .22 pistol was dropped and that model did not have a safety device other than a trigger release to prevent the hammer from igniting the cartridge. We were both standing up in the wide-bodied canoe about to switch positions. Another couple were sitting in the forward seats. The revolver was dropped and *Wham,* went off. I felt a sting at the back of my neck, my ears rang and reached to place my hand on it and warm blood from the harmless graze trickled on my hand. It does sting, however. I bent my head forward and noticed a small blotch of moisture on her St. Benedicts College sweatshirt. It was dark blue and hence the red blood didn't yet show its color; just a small blotch about the size of a nickel. She was fairly small in height, about five feet and I bent her forward to look at her backside and sure enough there was a hole there too. The inside white cotton fibers of the sweat shirt were sticking out, drawn through by the bullet's passage. I damn near went into shock. *Bone splinters,* I thought.

I told her, "Caroline…you'd better sit down. Looks like you're shot." She saw the blood on my hand and examined me and just for a moment we had a slight argument as to who was shot. I can still visualize her saying about as calmly as one can be while holding her hand up to her chest, "I don't feel anything."

In the bow was a St. Johns University wrestling team member and Korean War vet, strong Jerry Hudrlik. He leaped into the water and dragged the canoe to the shore. We had Caroline lie down on the grass with her legs propped up on the canoe. Caroline remained totally unexcited. Her classmate and longtime high school friend sat beside her and held her hand while Jerry and I ran to opposite farm houses to call for help. My slight neck wound did not bleed for long and I recall coming toward a barbed wire fence and clearly sailing over it. A young priest came with the ambulance and was more excited and nervous than my three companions. Caroline just did not bleed much. Miraculously, the bullet went through her at her breast line and came out her back to graze me. We were both in a bent over position to get past each other. It was a clean wound, missing everything vital. She spent only a few days in the hospital for observation. Spirits were with me and since she was pretty much Catholic, angels, I guess, had to be with her. Was one helluva close call for both of us.

I had a helicopter pilot friend in Vietnam that experienced the same episode—sort of. He got stitched by an AK-47 rifle. His last name was Harper so he automatically got dubbed, I.W. for the semi-famous whiskey brand. Harpo, as we often called him, caught three rounds right across his chest: connective tissue only, no nerve centers or blood vessels, just like Caroline. He wasn't in the hospital long and went right back to flying after a short hospital stay. Miracles do happen.

Rats Again

My second summer on the farm, the rats would come out en masse come evening, usually down by the hog yard where they would feed on spilled grain and the undigested corn from the cattle and hog droppings. Rats are practically extinct on most Dakota farms now due mainly to the effective warfarin anti-coagulant poison. Back then, these rats were getting a bit numerous as my single shot could not keep up with their reproduction. Maybe they belonged to one of those certain religious groups that zealously believe we humans need to overpopulate our planet. The more I shot at them, the more cunning they became. The slightest movement from the house toward evening and they would scatter back under the foundations of the storage structures. I had grown a bit by my second year there at the farm and my brother-in-law suggested that I try out his Ithaca pump 12 gauge, Model 37 with a lighter load shell than the normal pheasant load. It didn't seem to kick as hard as I expected when we first tried it out. He had me fire in succession several times, working the pump which was a first time thrill for me. It was sort of like when he had me drive the hand clutch John Deere tractor for the first time. I admit *that* was a much bigger thrill.

This time I had to sneak up on the rats and had to leave Cedric in the house, which was situated between the west and north shelter belt and faced east toward the farm structures. The rats lived under the granary, mostly. It was the first building you passed when you came into the driveway from the newly paved blacktop road east of the farm. It was the first time I heard Cedric whine with disappointment as I closed the back door with my Ithaca pump in hand. My brother-in-law always kept that gun loaded. He had left the low powered skeet shells in it—I noticed when I checked it. I cocked it open and rammed a shell into the chamber. I took a shell out of my pocket and placed that into the tube. I checked the safe and headed north, crouching low. I had sneaked out the back door so that the now educated rats would not see me. I sneaked back through the north shelter belt and then east into the farm structures from the north and on toward the east side of the last building, a machine shed before the granary where the rats would be feeding and we had earlier spilled a little extra corn purposely on the south side. I pushed the gun's safe off.

Around the corner I flew, my pump gun blazing at the first sign of the rats. Big ones and little ones went scurrying. I wounded quite a few, was my guess, but only three were shot outright dead. Some hopped and jumped but made it back to their dwelling. If I would have had Cedric, I figured I would have got at least a few more as he would always run in after a .22 long shot and finish off a wounded one.

For several days there were no rats. Mark said eventually, if I kept at them, they would move to another farm. Mark didn't waste words but when he did speak he was usually always right. He sure was smart to give me those lower powered shells. I was a skinny little thing when I was that age. I had another brother-in-law that would load you up with a high-powered shell just to have a good laugh when it kicked hell out of you. It was good for a young kid to have a thoughtful adult around, especially one that would turn you loose on a tractor after some careful instruction. John Deere developed my motor skills early. Maybe that is why I had few problems learning to fly in flight school, especially formation flying and eventually stepping into the top fighter of our times—the Phantom F4B. It had so much power that you could climb straight up with it.

The Lone P-51 Pilot

Once, Mark told me about a lone P-51 pilot that saved their lives. He said they were returning to England all shot up in a crippled B-24. On the way back a flight of Messerschmitt's ganged up and formed an attack formation. They would line up abreast on a crippled bomber and then flick in one by one on the attack. Just as they were about formed up a lone P-51 showed up and without hesitation attacked the flock of German fighters, breaking them up from attacking the bomber. He said they had no idea what happened to that 51 pilot but it was the bravest act he saw in the war. Whatever happened to that American pilot we will never know until we reach the Spirit World where my religion believes all acts are recorded—good and bad. That pilot should be honored. It would be a good painting to have, a lone P-51 attacking just above the B-24 at a flocked up stack of Messerschmitt 109s about to roll in on the crippled bomber. Maybe then and there I wanted to be a pilot someday, or at least try. I never dreamed I would be one, let alone a combat one. What a glorious happening it would have been to be a World War II fighter pilot but I am not complaining. Noel Dunn, a well-known artist from the Maplewood suburb of St. Paul did the Phantom in this book. I am going to commission him to paint that P-51 pilot saving my brother-in-law's B-24. He has to be honored and no doubt is in the Spirit World now but he will know it. Honor was so important to the Sioux…and still is. We Vietnam warriors were honored by the tribe when we returned. So many white soldiers and white combat Marines were not. Such neglect had a bad effect on them, most everyone agrees. We still honor our older veterans as well. I recently was honored at the big Sichangu Rosebud Reservation Pow Wow. Took over an hour to get around the arena shaking hands with the tribe and being hugged by the women after a rousing speech from the chief Holy Man Crow Dog who presented me with an Eagle Feather. Many of the women cry while they hug a combat veteran.

Fantasy and the Rats

As I said, Mark was usually pretty right about a lot of things but I was hoping that he could be wrong regarding the rats leaving, however. They were much more thrilling to stalk and shoot than the silly pocket gophers that were also fairly numerous. I imagined the rats as Jap soldiers that were going to capture a bunch of Marines and put them in a prison and work them to death. Cedric and I, of course, had to prevent this. Afterwards we would rescue the already captured Marines. Several times I explained this to Cedric. First, eliminate the Japs. He would sit and listen attentively, staring at me face to face with his big brown eyes.

In a day or two after their seclusion, the rats returned. While the animals were hiding, I worked with Cedric to obey silent commands. I wanted to get more rats and Cedric figured in my plans. No one taught me how to do it and I had no book to read. I just did it out of sheer common sense and Cedric responded out of his sheer dog common sense, like he already knew what the heck I was up to.

We repeated the sneak up procedure with him at my rear. I'd signal him to stay (sit) with hand signals and with words initially and then advance when I motioned to him with a come-on gesture. Never would I let him get ahead of me, although he would come up beside me and I would give him a pet and tell him how smart he was. Maybe, way back then, I was cultivating my own teaching skills. Dogs love to know that they are being appreciated. People do, too! Soon he was doing a good job with my no-word training. I never hit Cedric nor yelled at him nor was otherwise mean to him. At my age and size, it would have been quite foolhardy. To this day that is my motto or official *modus operandi.* You do not hit a Golden! Be surprised by how quickly they learn when they are totally relaxed in your training presence. I don't like arguing with humans. Why should I argue with my four-legged hunting companion? Since I never attempted to intimidate him, he always responded in a confident and willing-to-please manner. A relaxed atmosphere certainly speeds up the learning process. I follow that procedure to this day in the training of my Goldens and have had abundant success with them. I do hope that some of you readers pay serious heed to what I have just related. Mind you, I have little experience with the other breeds of dogs. I cannot speak for their effective training methods.

I took the shotgun way out into the slough, about a half section (half mile) from the house and the rats. The slough had a pond that was home to ducks and those funny little skitter things we called coots or grebes. It was summer and full of various birds. Some roosters lifted as I approached. A momma duck with her little ones following behind went quacking away into the cattails. I never gave them a thought, since I was so focused on my dog training. Cedric was happily out front sniffing away. I called him to me and we went through our stalking procedure as we drew closer to the pond. Before we got to some cattails, I had him stay. I advanced slowly and just as I came closer to the open water, I put on a burst of speed and opened up with a couple rounds into the clear water. I figured I was far enough away so as not to disturb my main quarry—the rats. Cedric needed no signal with the burst of gunfire. He was right there immediately after I fired and went into the water to retrieve whatever I had fired at. He swam around searching futilely for a minute then came back to shake water on me when he came ashore. Maybe he was telling me to hit something when I fired.

We employed our technique the next evening. Later in life, several decades in fact, I would be employing this same successful technique road hunting with my Golden Retrievers. Then, it would be wily roosters as our quarry. A well-trained Golden Retriever will stay behind you as you sneak up on a pair or more of pheasants. He won't bolt and run ahead of you when he gets their scent, not until you rise up and pump some rounds at them. It worked. Cedric killed or finished off a few wounded rats each time we attacked them. At least for a while.

I think that the rats eventually employed scout rats for they seemed to be always resourceful. Soon they would vanish when we sprang around the corner. We tried coming around the west side and that worked a couple times but then they had a sentry out on that side, too. I noticed that we were affecting their population, however, on those two successful encounters.

Next, we crept down to the hog house for a frontal assault and when we had to crawl over hog poop I had to pretend I was a John Wayne Marine. The hog yard was just a road's width across from the granary with low boards to conceal us and peek through slats that were slightly higher to fire from. Off to the side of the slats there was an opening large enough for Cedric to jump through and charge to get wounded rats. Cedric didn't appreciate this stint but he stayed with me and didn't go back to the house. Maybe he fantasized, like me, that he was a combat Marine, slithering through a tropical swamp to get at the Japs. I bore-sighted them that time after a careful and long crawl with Cedric patiently crawling behind. We had a convenient hole in the wooden slatted hog fence. I hammered my final rounds into them as they fled under the granary while Cedric burst over the side to grab wounded ones.

With that encounter, every last one of them departed. The farmer nearby complained to my brother-in-law that he suddenly had a noticeable jump in his rat population. Mice hunting just wasn't fun anymore compared to the rats. They never bunched up and Cedric wouldn't think of picking one up after I had dispatched it. It is strange to admit but we both dearly regretted the departure of the rats.

The Indian Gym

Grade school holds fond memories. I was a pretty good student. My teachers sensed that I was bored so gave me extra projects. My last two teachers in grade school even had a special table for me where I could do my extra lessons. I could out spell the grade ahead of me and she often took me to their class to embarrass them. I skipped a grade which was a handicap for sports although I was probably one of the top two regular players on our American Legion baseball team if you didn't count our all-star pitcher. I played a lot of basketball as well. Sports gave me an avenue to meet the other athletes in my high school. I became close friends with probably the best one in my grade and also made another friend, a tall lanky basketball player, who befriended me mainly because I had the right credentials to get him, a white kid, into our supposed to be all-Indian gym staffed by the missionary Jesuits. I convinced the other Indian kids that we needed a taller center, which he was. We played other Indian teams and lied that he was a Cherokee from back East. No one put up a fuss about it. I would come down the court and feed him. Often he would pass the ball back and I was a fairly dead shot from what is now three point range. We won most of our games then and went on to make B team and Varsity.

Stan Curtis was nineteen by the time I was seventeen, but we were both in the same grade. He could whip anybody else in school (our grade anyway). Two ranch kids were bouncing me off some hall lockers once. They were angry because I beat one off the B team. Stan and I had just cemented our friendship by his getting into the Indian gym. Also my parents and quite older, childless and married sister, Mildred, the oldest, who lived next to us, doted on him. She made his first birthday cake. Stan's mother was a bit mean and not affectionate whatsoever. His father was a traveling salesman and a nice guy but too afraid of his wife to ever say anything. Poor Stan never had a birthday party or even Christmas. My family changed all that. Anyway, Stan came around the corner during my episode and promptly laid one bouncer out cold. He had beaten that one out for a position on the B team. We took the other one and bounced him until he started crying. I never had any problems in that practically all white high school from that day on. I never saw a Black person until the Harlem Globetrotters came to town.

Puberty

Back in my time, in Rapid City the upper grade kids, especially after puberty, were not very friendly to Indian students. Grade school, they didn't seem to care one way or another. Hence most Indian youth back then elected to go back to the reservation schools where they could have a semblance of a social life among their own peers. My sister two years ahead of me was shunned by her former playmates, and when she was in the eleventh grade, she quit going to school. She worked at menial jobs for about a year and married early. Kids in grade school couldn't care less what color you were or what church you attended but when puberty arrived, as I said, they changed. Can you imagine how powerful peer pressures or acceptance can become? Indian youth would put up with acceptance of their peers over non-acceptance, even if it meant attending a boarding school. That is something the psychologists can study.

The most sought after male in my grade by the girls was Jimmy Aho, a Finnish blood kid who, despite skipping a grade as I did, was still a star athlete. He probably changed my life more than anyone.

We had graduated from high school just barely seventeen years old. We were both working construction that summer and had no problem getting hired. Believe it or not, I was pushing my Dad's mud for the bricklayers at age fifteen and also hauling bricks to them—five bricks to a carrying tong. I would shortcut my trip to the bricklayers by walking the steel beams over the new gym. That was probably why I was fairly adept at becoming a high steel ironworker in my college years. Construction was good money for a high school kid. Stan Curtis worked with me on other jobs at times. After working we had evening baseball practice for the towns American Legion Baseball team. My reflexes always kept me batting in the first three of the lineup as I could get on base with a single or a double. My dad, who was skilled at leather making, made extra padding for my left-handed glove. Somehow, a terrific sting would issue if I ever caught a fast ball over that big scar but extra padding took care of it. When I would forget my special leather glove tailored by my dad, I would borrow one and simply put my billfold in next to my palm. It worked. You have to be resourceful in life.

First Crush

The cutest girl in my grade, Gerie Monger (she had a younger sister named Janet) came to watch me pitch one of our games. We used to walk together at times to attend Sunday church. I had a terrific crush on her but not much I could do about it. She had to be at least a year older than me, yet she wanted to see me pitch a game. She disappeared to Tulare, California before we graduated. I thought about her a lot when I was off in Korea. I had heard that she married early. A young crush can last a long time.

I had gotten to practice early. The mayor, Ike Chase, showed up and was fidgeting around the grounds, putting out the sacks and home plate. He had a couple of city workers raking and picking up pebbles, smoothing the grounds. He liked me and gave me some jobs working for him around the city. Sports can open doors, I learned. Jimmy Aho showed up and said the words that changed my life forever: "HEY MAN, you wanna CHANGE YOUR LIFE?"

Life comes in a strange bundle if you are so fortunate!

"Like what?" I answered, nonchalant and yet unconvinced. I had absolutely no idea as to what the hell I would do come that fall and many kids were going off to college—the rich ones who could afford it.

"We'll be pros! Hey, man. I just came from the Marine Recruiter. We can get in for two years. We'll be nineteen, man…and we will be bigger! We'll be pros, man!" Jimmy Aho's dream was to become a professional athlete. He had the goods to deliver it for himself and he knew it. He believed it! He was the high school quarterback. First Five in basketball and as good a baseball player as I was. He also had size and had not stopped growing. The young man changed my life. We joined and Mayor Chase raised holy hell along with our coach, Pev Evans, not much less an athlete than Jimmy, because we would be leaving before the state's Legion Baseball tournament. The Marine recruiter, in turn, gave us hell after a very hostile mayoral visit that went all the way to Headquarters Marine Corps and wisely moved our embarking date back to after the State tournament; such is the power of sports especially considering a baseball conscious mayor. Curtis came with us also into the Marine Corps.

Jimmy Aho is now a wealthy retired chiropractor in Carlsbad, New Mexico. He was a walk on at Colorado University where he became a star linebacker and was drafted by Weeb Eubank of the Baltimore Colts. Stan Curtis, deceased, but a few years ago, introduced me to my later life love, pickleball and was a retired high school principal with a Master's degree.

A Date—Sort of

I have often stated that I never had a date in high school. Well that is not exactly true, maybe—maybe not. Jimmy's mom was adamant that he take a girl to our senior prom. She threatened to take away his car, a 1939 Plymouth coupe. This we could not allow. The year before, he and I and Stan Curtis went camping in the Black Hills of South Dakota our junior year prom night. Jimmy was so intent on becoming a professional athlete that he swore off any romantic association with the opposite sex. He firmly believed that associating with a girl could lead to going steady and possibly pregnancy and—one's professional athlete quest would dissolve in smoke. Can't say he was stupid. It happens. I have had a couple relatives that had athletic promise and blew it big time with a high school sweetheart and had to head for the altar. He was right, my opinion. I had no such problem. No girl would consider dating me back then. I was a year or two younger, a bit skinny and had crooked teeth and was an Indian in a mostly all white school. My senior prom date was arranged. The girl was dating an ineligible prom prospect, an Air Force enlisted man and she wanted to go to the prom. Jimmy's mother had scouted several prospects for us as my loyal friend bluntly confronted his mother with the statement, "I ain't going unless he (me) goes." I love loyalty. A real cute girl, who was always polite to me, corralled me at a weekend sock hop and also helped with my arrangements providing I would coach my loyal friend that she would be his chosen date. She threw a party before the prom, my only party (besides one other interesting situation) that I was ever invited to. We went to the prom and had a good time.

The other party I was invited to was held by a pretty breed Indian girl, same tribe as I was. I also had a crush on her even though she was a couple grades lower. Her dad was a fairly wealthy white man and that helped remove the Indian stigma attached to we few Skins who went to Rapid City High School. She was even elected as a sophomore to the Homecoming Queen's court. We had met at a roller skating rink and got along pretty well. It was during my last semester as a senior. Eventually she threw a party at her home and I was invited. Everyone there, except for me, was a grade or two lower. When I rang the doorbell she was real happy to see me. Things went very well at first. She ran me around, happily introducing everyone. Her mother came around the corner, a breed as much as me and had dated my handsome older brother Mick, I later learned, when he was a star baseball pitcher. "What relation are you to Russ and Mick?" she asked with a stern voice. After my reply she took her daughter around the corner and she ignored me the rest of the party. I didn't stay long—always never one to push anything going sour still to this day. My brother, Russ, had just gotten out of jail and had his name in the paper. An altercation with some Mexicans at the Rainbow Ballroom landed him in jail for a few days. The local newspaper always printed such events. I had been in that place a few times as I got older and working summer construction, but college and the women I could date in comparison revised my taste considerably. My interest in the Rainbow was short lived. Handsome Brother Mick was respectful to women but not one to fall all over them. I learned that he chose to move on from that mother's relationship when they were single. Well revenge is sometimes sweet and as I look back, it was probably best I never got too involved, but at least I would have had two girls to fantasize and think about during a year in Korea as a M-1 rifle packing Marine. I wrote her a couple letters and even one when I got out and went to college. No answer. She married some guy that was such a deadbeat that her three children took her maiden name after their divorce rather than his.

I did date her a few times after my divorce. When I was a Marine Captain with gold wings I looked pretty good to her and some others as well. Straightening my teeth and a few pounds helped. Later, at the reviving Sun Dance, where I was a pledger and had to speak before the growing crowd, her mother came with her and was totally positive and respectful. That was good. Life was moving on for me, however. In summary: Romance was fairly sparse in my young life and no doubt best that it was. I never got anyone pregnant nor did I have to get married at too young an age. My adventuresome life would have come to a screeching halt. I went on to some terrific adventure and some treasured accomplishments. My second wife was an absolute winner. My first one wasn't all that bad, either. We still get along well, and I get along with her husband, too.

My second wife is now deceased. She was a very good athlete and the kids benefited greatly from her talent and attentive sports interest. They are now a grown up family of skiers and tennis players and gather mostly at skiing sojourns which is great for the grandchildren.

Not All Blondes

I guess, for the curious, I have to add that I was divorced for quite some time. I have met some very good women, not all blondes but probably the majority. I never met one in a bar that I would wind up dating, although I am not a teetotaler but I never smoked. I just do not handle bar talk very well. I don't think I could last long with a smoker, no matter what other positive credentials, since early sports started me out against it. I probably would never get started with a fanatic regarding any religion and seem to have met so many outstanding, positive women (not just for dating or romance) that were well into the Natural Way Spirituality.

The Necklace

I met my second wife through selling her a necklace that I made the night before I boarded a plane. My first wife was a good woman but is better off with her second husband. He was a State Lions club governor, a Rotarian leader, and an outstanding speaker in Toastmasters where even I learned the rudiments of public speaking which I wound up doing a lot of: first for the South Dakota Republicans about my Vietnam experiences and then later for Indigenous Spirituality. Those latter audiences were mostly Democrats (or otherwise liberally minded). I used to give many, many speeches, but not so much now. I doubt if I could make it to doorman, however, in the most noted business clubs or fraternity type organizations. My first wife and I still get along quite well, her husband, too. One reason is I usually drop off six or eight pheasants as she doesn't mind entertaining. We never had a problem when I would pick up and keep the kids like so many divorcés do, making needless trouble for each other. Bob, her husband was good to them, too, and sported my two beautiful daughter's pictures on his office desk.

I was on an airplane en route to an all-tribe Indian gathering as a speaker. I sold a necklace to this pretty blonde Western Airline stewardess. I had several that I would sell at Indian conferences and this particular one I wanted to show off at the conference. I was showing them to a rancher sitting beside me and he bought one. She came along and scooped up my prized one. I kicked up the price so she wouldn't buy it but she turned and went forward with it and returned with a check. She was twenty-nine, never been married, very athletic, University of Wisconsin Graduate, former teacher and engaged three times before meeting me. Probably should have been four or five times by then since she was such a prize. We married when she was thirty-one and she never had a child until she was thirty-six. My kids became her kids and we took them all over. Ask them how many times they were in Hawaii and they will answer, "We don't know." She became the world's greatest step-mother and was constantly playing with them, which they well remember and miss her to this day.

Pete's Pistol

I mentioned old Pete's pistol in the Foreword. Well, I had dated the Indian girl I had once held such a crush on. This was after I had been in the Sun Dance. I had been divorced and not ready yet to get too romantically involved, but we got along fairly well. We were in a nightclub and had dinner, and this one guy kept coming over to our table and wanted to talk to her but she brushed him off. She told me that she used to date him a bit but ended the relationship. He stupidly followed us to her house and insisted on coming in. There was nothing else for me to do but simply deck him with a hard right to his jaw. My left prohibits a decent jab but my right has surprised me a few times. Down he went and when he got up again I had to hit him again. It was a good thing he left because I had fractured my hand. He staggered back to his car and drove off.

The next morning I had to speak at a men's business club and Doc Lemley came in just as I began. He was quite a well-known figure in the town and the club's leader quickly pushed a chair in front for him. He waved to me and told me to continue. Afterwards I had to shake hands with the members and he noticed that I was shaking hands with my left. He asked me and I briefly told him only part of the story, but enough for him to pull out his pistol and wave it, exclaiming that it was a good thing he hadn't been there. This startled the hell out of the business club members but he was such a known and successful figure, having started the town's major clinic that they definitely would never object. He put his pistol back in his pocket and made me ride with him to the clinic—from which he'd retired—and had my hand x-rayed. They put me in a splint while all the older nurses ganged around him, having not seen him in the clinic for years.

With all the gun regulations we have nowadays, I thought that this mere episode is worth noting. As of this writing, South Dakota is still fairly loose regarding guns. We can carry a rifle or a high caliber rifle on a gun rack right behind us in our pickups. They keep the predators down that go after our prized pheasants. So far we can carry our shotguns in our vehicles, no shell in the chamber but available in the magazines for road hunting the ring-neck. No gun cases or covers required either. Of course we cannot shoot pheasants off the Interstate but gravel roads we can. This will probably change, however, in lieu of all the new regulations.

Doc Lemley

Doc liked me a lot and was always happy to see me when his son Bill (my age) would bring me home with him. He would have us into his study with a big Bengal tiger rug on the floor and tell us stories, mostly about his father and the many Indians he had known. Maybe that is what started my quest to write my history book about Sioux leaders. When I came back from Vietnam, Doc and his wife Margaret had a huge social party honoring my 'Nam service at their abundant dwelling and many of the town's business elite were there. I didn't know most of them but it was Doc who probably made them attend. Like his dad he was a pretty forceful guy and respected, too.

Adventure For My Own Kids and Others, Too

My kids will attest that I played with them a lot. When my second wife came along, as I mentioned, she was twenty-nine and never married before. She had to have loved kids because she was a constant companion to mine.

Each child brought their best friend or two into our lives and they were welcome to go along with us on our many sojourns. My wife Mary most often had extra airline buddy-passes saved up and the kids were thrilled to go along with us to Hawaii or an inherited condo from her deceased parents. My sons' friends got to go along to neighboring South Dakota on a nearly annual summers coming-of-age prairie dog sojourn which they still talk about now in their thirties.

We would head for the reservation with each bearing a brick of .22 caliber shells. That's five hundred rounds which, aside from a few target pop cans, would be spent on a live target. We would stop by the Missouri River and practice on the normal shoreline gar or carp. These are rough fish that even ardent animal rights lovers disdain. Then on to the Standing Rock Sioux Reservation (Hunkpapa and Minicoujou) where several Indian ranchers remembered me well from my Sun Dancing days. Their lands are as wild and remote as our Oglala Sioux Badlands. Way back in there, we'd plunk a pheasant or two or several cottontails for the evening meal and look for a couple rattlesnakes which would come out hunting toward evening. We were always successful getting at least a couple and, along with several cans of pork-and-beans and baked potatoes, have quite a meal. Naturally, it would be a First for these city kids to have their first taste of rattle snake. They are easy to prepare, skin easily and taste between pork and chicken.

To this day, those extra kids are still quite close to me. As a grown man in his thirties, one saved my life (which I will relate in due time).

4 CLOSE CALLS

Adventure can become costly. If you are fortunate to have Spirit Help—my personal term—then you often escape what could be tragedy. Maybe those protective Spirits want you to fulfill some unknown task down your road of life. It is all a mystery but I would be lying or be ungrateful or both, if I did not acknowledge that I have had considerable help. Maybe it is important to set the stage if you would want to seek their protective favor.

Speaking of Untruth—lying, exaggerating, spreading falsehoods, creating dangerous rumors, practicing what you know is unethical, immoral, hurting innocents (and that includes the *Wamaskaskan*—animals—except for sustainable food) and believing in what is obvious superstition, all this and probably a few more is contrary to Creator's Truth. The Spirit World no doubt rejects such if Creator is All-Truth. Pretty simple! Don't go there if you want to advance in that place we all eventually journey to—every last one of us.

Well, enough philosophizing, let's get back to how in the hell I am still alive. I have had more close calls than most men and women, it seems, and not just in actual military combat. Yes, I have had some extremely hairy experiences in that category. Later, I will cover several combat missions in some detail but first let us look at several early encounters.

Not many overly exciting happenings occurred in my first quarter of life. (I am simply thankful that I have approached into the last quarter.) I hope I can go out as my dear dad did. He came upstairs from the basement one morning when my mom was making coffee. He made it into the kitchen before falling down dying on the floor. "They're killing me. They're killing me!" were his last words. No prolonged suffering, no caretakers needed. What a great way to go compared to so many others. He was in his early 80s and never been a patient in a hospital. The closest he got to the medical field was an occasional dentist to pull some teeth. I wish I could say the same but I can't. My mom went a few years later and close to the way he did.)

I was just entering my second quarter of life. The Navy Chaplain rang the doorbell to my married officer quarters while I was sitting down for breakfast before driving off to flight training at Whiting Field which was a part of the Naval Air Training Command, Pensacola Florida. I had married a beautiful farmer's daughter from South Dakota. They are known for their parental attentiveness and of course could butcher and cook an elephant if they had to. Needless to say, I was having an excellent breakfast.

In the military it is an automatic assumption when a chaplain unexpectedly comes to visit: Someone has died in your family or is about to die. I flatly stated, "Someone died. Right Chaplain?" He nodded. I guess I should back up a bit. That was the military I was used to. Nowadays, a knock on your door is usually not because of a death in your family. The Christian chaplains have formed a society that they think allows them to come and proselytize to military families. The military academies are becoming rife with proselytizing. Many of the higher-up officers are grading fitness reports according to how much into Jesus you are. This is chasing many needed and talented free thinking military soldiers, sailors and airmen out of the service and costing our retention programs millions of dollars.

(Worse, you get enough of those fanatics into a nuclear weapon carrying aircraft or just two of them to punch a few buttons in a launch silo that have been converted by a Pat Robertson or similar nut who believes 'the rivers will flow like blood,' and we can have World War Three.)

I sat down. Looking at the floor, I said, "If it is my mom or dad…" I looked up at him. "I hope it is my dad."

"Yes," he replied. A feeling of relief swept over me. My mom could move on much easier than my wonderful, dedicated father. In his later years, although quite healthy, he was more dependent on my mother who, right up to the end, never quit fighting her Martin Luther King flavored battles for Indian Civil Rights. She had one of Rapid City's biggest funerals—White and Indians came by the hundreds.

My mother was quite interesting. Judge Foxx was the Municipal Judge in this small growing town of ours. (Back then about 30,000 people, and the third largest in the whole state. Now it has a population around 100,000. We have always had plenty of room and no traffic jams like I experience in the Twin Cities just to play Pickleball. It is a poor place to winter but the players and the western suburban indoor facilities are what draw me. Community centers there are like country clubs). On Monday mornings the judge would call my mother from his court room. "Julie, I have Martin White down here," and then he'd go down the list of mostly full blood names. A full blood name is like Broken Rope, Swan, Low Dog, Stabbed, etc. Subjective names, I guess you could call them. Rapid was a small town so the list wasn't too long and the crimes were usually misdemeanors, especially drunk or disorderly. Many were Indians from the liquor-banned reservations of Pine Ridge or Rosebud and therefore those Indians would come up from the two reservations to Rapid to drink. My mom could speak good Indian and those days most Indians knew of each other. She'd tell the judge, "Well, So-and-So is a good man and is raising his kids and treats his wife good. It's those damned construction workers, Judge, who get him drunk about once or twice a year that need to be put in jail." She'd then go on and condemn some other accused, "Now So-and-So is no good. Every time his parents get some money he takes it from them and gets on a holy terror. He doesn't work and yet he's got kids strung all over the reservation. The longer he's put away, the better the reservation will be." Well, then Tuesday's paper would have one guy getting a five dollar fine, no incarceration, and the next would get thirty days incarceration—sixty if he was a repeater and inconsiderate of others. The judge was never heavy on fines since he knew most didn't have much money anyway.

When Mom and I would walk downtown, she often liked to stop in at the Virginia café and have a treat, and my sister and I would get a dish of ice cream. White people would come over and talk to her and out on the street quite a few Indians would stop and talk to her. Indian men that frequented the bars on Saturday nights were obsequiously polite to her, which was understandable. When you have a mom like that, even at a young age, you

71

realize there is a lot of existent prejudice. You realize that your Mom has got more important things to do than coddling you. It never bothered my sister or me. The mayor even had Mom on some kind of 'Mayor's Committee' which we didn't understand but figured that was why White people would come over in that fancy café and talk to her.

After the state Legion Baseball Tournament in which my team came in second, my friends and I boarded a train for San Diego, Marine boot camp. It wasn't as bad as the exaggerated stories we had heard. Granted the drill instructors (DI's) imparted a degree of discipline, but as long as you kept your mouth shut, I don't remember receiving a single blow or 'love tap' from the drill instructor's swagger stick. Others were not so fortunate, but in most cases when they were straightened out, they deserved it.

We fired the M-1 rifle considerably at the rifle range where we slept in eight-man squad tents, the same as in Korea. With liners, they are quite comfortable in cold weather. You have cots that keep you off the floor and warm sleeping bags. At the rifle range on qualification day, the DI approached me and a guy named Woodell. (Odd, how one's memory can reach back accurately to those times and yet leave us cold for yesterday's or last week's memory.) He handed me and Texas Woodell some extra 30.06 extra shells. "You two take your positions on each side of Curtis. After you shoot your quota on your target, put some rounds in Private Curtis's target." You do as you are told in the Marine Corps and never ask questions. The DI had a hopeless shooter next to me who wasn't going to qualify. Stanbury was that poor guy's name. He was the platoon shitbird and later was dropped out of the program. People like that can get you killed in combat. The M-1 holds eight rounds. Out pops the metal clip after the last round. We had been practicing for almost two weeks. That is why the Marine infantry is so deadly with their rifles. You learn how to drop in your ninth and tenth rounds without allowing the heavy spring bolt to smash your thumb that pushes and closes on the incoming shell. I fired at my target and then took out my extra rounds and unloaded on Stan's target as did Woodell. When the pit boss complained that Curtis had too many rounds in his target, Stanbury caught hell for firing at the wrong target. He was so bad that he had only a few holes in his and Curtis got a sharpshooter badge. (I have an M-1 and take it down to the Badlands to fire at a few targets. Nostalgia, I guess, but I do like the weapon.)

I was sent to Marine Corps welding school. I had played around with it before the Marines and put it down as about my only skill. It was another great break. I came in first in my welding class. There were only two overseas openings and I picked Korea, avoiding a boring stateside assignment. The war was over by then but I realized that Korea would be much more exciting. Also the talk from the veterans claimed there were R&Rs to Japan. Peacetime Korea allowed more than one R&R if you had built up $300 on your payroll records. We went on board a troop ship out of San Diego and came back on one.

I received orders to go to Camp Pendleton, California to join a staging regiment—men bound for overseas shipment. About a week before we left the States, the master sergeant, nicknamed 'Punjab', was in charge of us. It would be suicidal if you ever called him Punjab to his face, however, as he was as big as the huge protector of comic strip *Little Orphan Annie*. He formed us up outside our barracks. A full colonel was in charge but Top, as a master sergeant is respectfully called, gave us our orders. He made a short presentation. "At ease," he commanded us from our attention position. "All right you people, listen the hell up." He held a .50 caliber swagger stick about two feet long. The gold plated casing was separated from the bullet by a walnut dowel. "Just got word that some Marines in Korea got their balls blown off by a mine. Minefields all over Korea." A murmur swept through us. "One guy lost a leg." He let the words sink in. "Technically, the war isn't over." He pointed his swagger stick toward the ocean. China comes in and a lotta you are going to be pushing up sayonara flowers." (Meaning good-bye funeral flowers.) He pointed the .50 caliber end at us. "Some of you won't come back if the war breaks out." Again we let out a murmuring groan. "A helluva lot of you, probably." He pointed to the headquarters Quonset hut. "The Old Man (meaning, respectfully, in Marine Corps jargon, the colonel) has decided because of this incident, that pay day in cash is Friday, buses will leave here this Saturday morning for Tijuana." He paused. "Lotta you troops ain't been laid!" Giggles, as most of us looked accurately accusingly at each other.

Yes, giggles and some squirming by the guilty or the chaste—whichever you choose. Among the lower ranks, a goodly number, the same as me, never had yet had a bona fide sexual encounter but damn well would not openly admit it. What the hell, I was still yet only 17. What girl would ever look at me twice in Rapid City, South Dakota? If she did and her Dad would find out, he'd unload, "I don't want you with no Injun!" How life would change eventually, at least for me but not yet as the Top Sergeant continued. "Buses will operate to return you up until midnight."

When our troop ship docked in Japan, we were given a two-day liberty. Japanese females (aka business women) knew the ships' movements and very attractive women were happily waiting at the Sasebo docks. Very attractive to a barely eighteen-year—olds loaded with cash. In the cabarets, small bars a few blocks away, more attractive, government-inspected Japanese females awaited. That was the Marine Corps back then. "Some of you won't come back if the war breaks out," rang in our ears.

In Korea I was stationed up near the front lines just behind the real grunts who manned bunkers. I was in an engineer battalion. Some of our troops accidentally stumbled upon a claymore mine and set it off. It was a bouncing-Betty type and hit the hillside as it went up at an angle. It bounced away from a couple troops and scared the hell out of them. We were responsible for making our fighting troops increasingly more comfortable with generators, better roads and shower points out of the many fresh water creeks that flowed from mountainous terrain. We even had hot water. With telescopes you could see the enemy troops staring back at you. We all carried our M-1 rifles and slept with them loaded beneath our bunks in our eight-man squad tents. We ate well and stayed clean. What few Korean civilians around that far north were busily employed in making our lives more comfortable. Momma-sans, older non-sexual offering women, got relatively rich doing our laundry and pressing our utility uniforms. Cleanliness among the troops is almost a Marine religion. Being well fed, too. Pheasants were everywhere and somehow never set off any mines when they landed in the fields surrounding us. Once in a while a distant mine would go off and that was about the only military excitement we encountered. I welded on tanks, bulldozers, cranes and heavy equipment. Even our jeeps and trucks could be welded- such was the thickness of their steel. I was always happily busy. I was fortunate to go on two R&Rs to Kyoto, Japan for two weeks each. The last R&R I got extended to a third week as the Marine Division had orders to return to Camp Pendleton. Shortly afterwards I was attending my first year of college.

College

I started out at South Dakota State. Stan Curtis was my roommate. The most important course I took at this A&M school was welding. I got certified and my brother Russ, got me into the ironworker's union. I was making journeyman union ironworker wages the following summer. If you could climb and weld; fifty, a hundred feet in the air under a dark welding hood while perched on a narrow steel beam, that made you certified, besides 'job security'. Not many men care to or are capable of doing it. Many welders tried but they froze once that hood came down and it was suddenly dark and they were way up in the sky. On more than one occasion we would have a new guy come on the job and they would freeze on the iron. They'd throw off their welding hood to shatter down below and clutch the I-beam tightly and hold on with a wicked grimace on their face. Two times I got called on to help. The crane would take me aloft with a steel choker—a cable with two loops on each end. I'd approach the guy with the cable, telling him to stay put and assure him that if he reached for me, we might both fall to our deaths. You'd be dealing with a real crazy looney at this point. One guy's teeth were clicking and he was making jerky, spasmodic movements. I draped the choker cable over him, ready to leap back instantly if he made a move. I looped it over him, passing one loop through the other and then around the frozen nut. The crane operator dropped his hook to my side and I put the opposite loop on the hook, always cautiously keeping my eyes on the nut. By now everyone was watching. Dropping the loop over him is when you have to get dangerously close. The hundred foot fall, more or less, is going to kill you no question. I wiggled my bottom free foot off the I-beam with an upward toe motion to give the crane operator the high sign. He gunned the motor and plucked him off. Last time he ever sees high iron. The boss was down below with his pay check. I backed off the I-beam and waited for the crane operator to come back and pick me up. You sure as hell will have some drinks that night with your fellow ironworkers.

Author Ironworking, St. John's University Church

(Odd that I often use the expression, "Sure as hell.") We traditional Indians don't believe that a Hell exists. At least not the fire-and-brimstone type with all the tormenting Demons, Devils and Satans brandishing hot pitch forks. I guess that I just like that expression and will continue to use it regardless. Proves that no one is perfect. We believe we all go into the Spirit World, but separate according to our own kind. Bad with the Bad and Good with the Good; Real Bad with the Real Bad and Brave and Courageous Good with their like peers.

Need for a welder that could climb—meaning you could throw a welding bead fifty or more feet up on a tall hangar, tower or iron structured framework—got me a phone call at college every spring, telling me where to report.

Years later, Curtis and I would marry girls from the same hometown. I

76

met mine through riding a Brahma bull in a college rodeo. That is a misstatement. The bull let me stay on for about four seconds and promptly dumped me. Not really a ride. It was my first and only time but at least I gave it a try. It was really a Brangus, half Brahma and half Angus, but quick as a cat. I was fairly scared as I slid down on it in the chute. It banged my legs against the sides but they are so big that your leg simply sinks into the bull and you don't get hurt. About six months after college graduation, I was sitting in flight school in Pensacola and all such foolish activity is banned if you want to be a Marine Corps pilot.

Romance

I guess that the reader is probably curious about my romantic life up until entering flight school, at least. Well, once I entered my freshman year at South Dakota State, I was quite free, as was my roommate Curtis. Asian culture had opened up our young minds enough to educate us a bit more so than the average freshman coming straight out of high school. Japanese professional women are pretty as can be and quite accommodating. Like I mentioned, I went on two R&Rs. As veterans we must have appeared more confident than most and we did not have much of a problem securing adequate dates. My being half Sioux did not present any drawbacks regarding dating cute freshman girls or even sophomores. Curtis was the same age as the junior and senior girls so began dating some of those. My ironworking brother, Russ, was away working on a new Air Force base in Thule, Greenland and insisted that I take his late model Chrysler to college, so that was also a lure for prospective dates. Curtis and I were having a reasonably good time but we both attempted to be serious students as well.

My first romantic bombshell came into my life. I met this cute little blonde at a Newman Club meeting. She remained in my heart for a long time and I must have also in hers as we met many years later. Newman Club is a Catholic social group found in colleges and universities. We started dating and had a wonderful relationship. We fell in love but she got sick toward the end of our freshman year. She had to return to her hometown to recuperate. Her mother was quite dominant, similar to what Stan Curtis had to suffer. My girlfriend had dated some guy in high school pretty heavy and her parents were relieved that she had dropped him for me since he was not going to college. She invited me down to Sioux Falls several times to stay at her place for weekends. Her parents damn well knew I was part Indian and it did not appear to bother them since I said I would probably major in Biology and become a pre-medical student. That pleased them. I also told them that my brother was getting me into the Ironworker's Union and that with their pay scale working summers, I shouldn't expect any financial hardships. My girlfriend was financially dependent on her parents, however. Eventually the mother stepped in and decided that we should break up as she had also demanded of my girlfriend's older brother and his girlfriend. No reasonable reason, just a damn controlling whim. Haven't we all met those types on our life's journey? Worse, in my case, the mother decided that she did not want her daughter to go with an Indian.

I transferred to St. Johns University, a prestigious school in Minnesota. It was probably one of the most important moves of my life. My initial romance was probably also a good happening— it kept me single all the way through college. Years later I would meet the South Dakota girl again. She said that she had read all my newspaper articles and saw my pictures in the Sioux Falls paper. Once I gave a speech on Memorial Day and I was pictured several times. One picture was of me with my attractive wife sitting in a convertible and my small son, wearing a miniature Marine Corps camouflaged flight suit, sitting on my knee waving an American flag. In the back seat was a Marine amputee in dress blues, Perry Shinneman. Surrounding us was a group of hippies waving placards and the police driving them away. Those were interesting times.

I met her again years later with her daughter, still cute and pretty as ever. She was dying. She already had one breast removed and the second one was proving fatal. She said to me, "You will always be my hero." It was pretty touching. Once she asked me in a melancholy moment, "What would it have been like...had we...made it?" I disappointed her with my too pragmatic, practical answer, "I never would have been the fighter pilot that you envision. This I had to be but we would have no doubt married early, too early." I could tell that I had disappointed her with the absence of a romantic, wishful reply. Fantasy! "I had to be that warrior which you see now. I doubt if I would have made it."

Quicksand—Deerfield Dam

I have a favorite fishing spot in the Black Hills of Dakota, it almost cost me my life. I was trout fishing. It was early fall, the grasshoppers were still out, nice good-size ones, so I put a fake hopper on my line, a Joe's Hopper to be exact. I reached into my hopper container and pulled out a live one and smashed it on my fly imitation—pretty good trick. A trout smells the real McCoy and hits your fly harder and you have a much higher percentage rate of his not backing off at the last mini-second before hitting the fly. An imitation grasshopper trout fly does not pop off after a few long casts either the way a live one does, therefore allowing longer casts and less spooking from your quarry.

I caught a few trout and moved downstream toward the quicksand area. The mud is washed down to this particular bend and settles at the turn of the stream. Across the quicksand pit, some big fat trout were jumping for flies. Hard to resist. I cautiously stepped to the edge of the pit and made a lucky cast across it and into the pool. *Wham!* A big guy hit and stayed on. I played him and luckily he made several runs up and down and began to tire. He came back right across from me and jumped. I gave a gentle tug and he flopped into the quicksand pit. With fly fishing you don't just haul a fish in as your leader is tapered to two-to three pound test at the hook end. You have to play a big fish, keeping pressure on your line but not too much. The quicksand was slimy with about an inch of top water, enough for me to attempt gliding him to me. The mud and slime were suffocating his gills, subduing his fight. I fingered his gill slot and unhooked the fly out of his mouth. He wriggled free and back into the slime. I reached down to get him and he wiggled free again, by now covered with black mud and sand. He was making it difficult for me to get a hold of him so I yelled at him to quit wiggling away if he wanted to go free. When I finally pinned him down I was starting to sink at the edge of the pit. I picked him up and hurled him as hard as I could to the open pool. He landed with a big splash and apparently was okay as he didn't float up to the surface. I lost my balance and stepped into the quicksand. I threw my free leg toward a lone rock projecting out into the pit. My trapped foot pulled free and my momentum carried me closer to the rock.

The sun was going down. The high elevation would bring a cold night, enough to cause death from exposure, especially stuck in wet mud. No fishermen would come along at this time to discover my plight. A paved highway was above me with an occasional car or pickup passing overhead but unable to see me. I was in serious circumstances. I began to slowly sink.

If I could wriggle out of my chest waders, I felt I had a chance to use them as a mini-raft atop the slime to slow my sinking and use them as enough buoyancy to stretch and grab the rock. I had a difficult time wiggling my feet out of my wader shoes. It had to have been help from the Spirit World once again when I'd been in a hurry while lacing my wader shoes. I'd worried about a pair of fishermen upstream from where I parked, 'bait chuckers' fishing downstream with their spin poles toward where I wanted to start. Had I laced my wader shoes as tightly as I usually do, I doubt I would be typing this story.

One foot came out of my ankle high wader shoe. Although slowly sinking with each wriggling move I now managed to get my leg free from that side of my waders and flop the wader over toward the rock. I then fell onto the wader and managed to get my body turned despite the quicksand holding my other shoe. I stretched and barely grasped the rock. Twisting and wiggling I managed to get my wader bottom and foot out of the shoe. I can still hear that sucking motion as I came free. A cold breeze began to blow. I pulled myself to freedom and my boots remained down in the quicksand. I would surely have died from exposure that evening. Chalk up one more near death 'cat's life.'

Close Call Rex

'Old Rex' became his 'nomer' after the younger one, Rex IV, also known as Puppy, came along. 'Nomer' is my own private invention for a name. 'Magpie,' is another one for smaller kids and on up through high school as long as they are dependent on you. Their beaks are always open for you to drop various items into and not just food. Self-explanatory.

I never dreamed that I would have a better hunter than Rex III. Oh, he had his faults as just about every dog with a personality has. What faults he had were not overwhelming enough to be seriously detrimental to his hunting. If I wanted to be picky, I'd complain that I didn't like it when he spotted the waiting pickup as we returned. Usually you walk the ditch back up to your vehicle, which often can serve as an efficient blocker for any birds you happen to be driving ahead of you. Usually there were no birds but once in a while you got lucky. Rex, would almost quit hunting once you got within fifty yards of the truck or car. I tried to break him of this habit by purposely walking past the truck but to no avail. He would head for the truck.

What he did for me however, on one wintry day, made any and all faults immaterial, insignificant and out and out unimportant. All in all, this Golden Retriever rescued me from several life-threatening situations. In one particular situation his size helped.

He was a bit larger than most of his breed. The following is excerpted in part from my book: *Dakota Pheasant and Iowa too!*

My new son-in-law, from Queens, NY of all places, was on his first Dakota pheasant hunt. A big storm was about to roll in and he had to leave early and get back to his new job in western Dakota. I always like to hunt with him because if there is such a thing as luck, (which I honestly do not believe in) then he certainly brings it for me. I have uncanny shots when he is close by. So much that he erroneously thinks that I am one hot shot bird hunter. The ground beneath me never crumbles just as I pull the trigger, no roosters lift into the sun, the dog seems to point more and flushes up easier shots more often, fewer hens rise for me in comparison to roosters and I rarely fumble with getting the safe off. The gun never jams either. I hated to see him leave.

Well, the winter storm rolled in early. We were still in October and most often that close to opening day we are in our T-shirts. The guys I hunt with near Mitchell were comfortably playing cards in the Hunting Birds Garage.

I was fortunate to know a group of locals from Emery, South Dakota, just east of Mitchell that I wound up hunting with for years. I had Rex II way back then and he was a good pheasant finder. One day I came across a group of local hunters while out solo. Two of their group were nephews of my brother-in-law and they were having a bit of trouble getting out some downed roosters hiding in tunnel grass. Rex II found a couple birds for them and I have been hunting with them ever since. It pays to have a good dog.

The Marsh

While they were all crunched around the table playing cards, I went out to a restaurant and ate some lunch, waiting for the weather to lift. By mid-afternoon I was a bit bored and decided that I would go out to some public land and see what I could scare up while the wind howled. It wasn't a very bright decision and several told me to stay put, but to no avail. Rex was waiting in my van and his wagging tail coaxed me into thinking I had made the right decision. I had a five day out-of-state license and wanted to make the most of it. I had left my native state for Minnesota and hence was now a non-resident.

We started out east of Emery. I parked at a public hunting site after passing a white house with a fairly large barn. The public land was loaded with sloughs barely frozen over and mostly slushy ice at that, enough so that you could not cross them. I walked into the area which was loaded with ponds. It was a waiting trap. Worse, there were no other hunters dumb enough to be hunting in horizon blotting weather fast approaching.

Rex got a rooster up right off the bat, to make my situation worse. I downed it and another got up and dropped farther into the area away from our van. I felt pretty good about my shooting and watched Rex get up some hens. Farther we went into the slough which was actually several sloughs and ponds. The snow swirled down heavily and, weirdly, sheet lightning rumbled. I looked up at the swirling grey and the sky seemed like it wanted to crack open with the blue grey sheet lightning.

I thought how a swimmer must feel when a man-eating, Great White shark would be circling him. I had a spooky feeling that a Great White would mysteriously flow down out of that threatening, ominous grey sky and attack. Of all deaths that I can imagine, I always seem to come back to a Great White as the most, most…I cannot even describe how fearful. (As I write this, my sons have arranged a trip out to a Pacific Island for this fall and we are going down to take a look at sharks close up. Will be a good family outing.)

All of a sudden things went one dimensional. I held that stupid thought. I imagined the great big shark still coming down out of that grey, ominous, swirling sky. I even held up my Benelli to dispense with such foolish wandering of my mind. I thought how odd it was for thunder to accompany a snow storm. Maybe it was the powerful roaring of the thunder coming out of that deathly grey right above me that was leading me to such foolish and actually idiotic fantasy. It certainly was not a boring situation—that was for sure.

The snow pelted down and it wasn't long before I was completely turned around and disoriented. It was getting late and sundown was coming earlier every day. When I realized I didn't know where I was I looked every which way and I seemed to be blocked by water. Visibility was down; I could barely see the cattails at the pond edges. The sun was getting lower. I stupidly had no matches or compass. Had I had matches or a lighter, I would have tried to wade across a pond, as most are shallow, and started breaking down tree branches from a shelter belt, especially the fallen ones or dead ones. Build a fire and sit out the night would have been my strategy. That is what most lost deer hunters who wisely have matches or a lighter do. But what pheasant hunter expects to get lost? Find a fence and it will usually lead you to a road or a dwelling. But swamps don't have fences. I was beginning to get myself into one helluva predicament. I almost started to panic. I had some degree of panic or muffled thinking because I failed to realize that the storm was coming in from the northwest. My left side was being covered by snow. If I turned slightly right, I'd be facing north toward the highway that ran past the swamp, running east/west. I was too muddled to realize that, however; such was the overpowering enrapture with my disorientation that brought me to near panic. I was flat lost!

I did have sense enough to get lighter. I threw my two roosters out of my vest. The second one was still warm so I put that one back into the front part of my vest. My glove had frozen wet and I threw that away for the temporary warmth of the pheasant. I started to empty all the ammunition I was carrying. I thought about leaving my Benelli as well and if it were not for its sling, I would have. I didn't eject its shells. Keep calm, I told myself as the sun started to shrink. I remembered back when I was crashing a Phantom. *Concentrate, concentrate*, I told myself and did the right procedure to save most of the airplane and myself along with it. I wasn't cited for any pilot error.

Something made me think of my tracks. *Your tracks. Your tracks*, sang through my mind. Rex came over and rolled on the snow playfully as to reinforce the newfound phrase. *Your tracks. Your tracks*, sang out. I looked down. Rexie rolled. I walked on, getting colder by the minute. Then I suddenly stopped and called to my dog. "Rex!" I yelled against the storm. "Let's go home, Rex. Find the car, Rex. Find the car." Rex put his nose down to our fresh tracks. I started to backtrack to encourage him and kept on going while the swirling snow was rapidly covering the tracks. He started out ahead of me and kept on even after they had faded from my vision. It looked like we were heading back. Then, all of a sudden as we approached the edge of a pond, a car slowly drove by. I damned near jerked my shotgun out from my shoulder and blew a hole in the car's back end to get it to stop, such was the life or death, desperation situation. It was just across the pond; that close! I jerked on my Benelli and as I did so the wind let up and to my right at the edge of the pond, on my side of the highway, I spotted a fence line. We turned and at the fence line crossed over to the road. To our left, west, where we had parked our van, there was the more conspicuous barn and the white house, vaguely in the distance. Rex had gotten me out. I shivered almost uncontrollably when I started the van.

Lost Again

Up in the north woods of Minnesota, Rex repeated what he had done for me in Dakota. That time, my son-in-law and I went out for some pine grouse, what we mistakenly called prairie chickens although the forest types are smaller and rise much slower. I am not a big fan of trying to shoot around trees as a straight shot out of a cornfield is tough enough for me but my son-in-law talked me into grouse so off we went. I remember back in my college days when my roommate, John Nordlum, from International Falls, Minnesota, the nation's cold spot, took me out after some Spring season walleyes. Back then Rainy Lake was loaded with that delicious fish. We used to feast on those delicious walleyes and feasted also on ruffed grouse. Up there they are referred to as spruce hens. You could get so close to them we took them with rocks or a .22 pistol. Not so, the much larger sage hen or prairie chicken. In the North Country, we had a goodly plot of land to hunt on from one of the hockey player's dad, Jim Gehrke. I had taken his son, Chris, with my middle son Kyle, both hockey defensemen, out on a prairie dog/Dakota rattlesnake excursion and his land offer was a form of reciprocation. His son came back all aglow from the excitement of shooting, cooking and eating his first rattlesnake along with firing a brick of shells (five hundred rounds) at the elusive and grass consuming prairie dogs.

As I mentioned, we managed to get briefly lost in those big woods. We started out in a circle out from the cabin and got up a few grouse. The highway was about a mile away to our south but in those dense woods it seemed a bit farther. We started out southwest from the cabin and took a few birds and then started our circle back. We were about a half mile from the highway and you could hear occasional traffic. Evening was approaching and after we started on our return orbit, we overshot the cabin and came up against a large swamp. We were fortunate to know that behind us was the highway and we could still barely hear the passing traffic. I told Rex once again, "Go find the car, Rex. Let's go home, Rex. Find the car." Rex took us straight to the cabin which was behind us and a bit farther in within our circle. We would have been able to see the glow of lights from the distant passing cars eventually and been able to find our way to the highway but this was another example of Rex III's ability to get us back safely.

Dangerous Waters

The next close call episode with Rex was a bit scarier. This time I fell through the ice of a lake while attempting to cross over to an island where several pheasants had landed. The ice parted and down I went. Rex was close by and he went in the water also. It was an odd situation. There was a shelf of ice underneath me. I could touch down onto the ice below and bob back up. Rex came over to me and I grabbed his collar. Heavy with a hunting vest loaded with ammunition I could not stay afloat. The shelf of underneath ice was a life saver and of course big Rex. He kept me afloat and dragged me around and back to shallower water. I had dropped my Benelli in the water and we later retrieved it by dragging a weighted bungee cord with hooks over it. By the time Rex got me back to shallower water my son came running over. Just a bit further out on that top layer and I could have drowned. When he was dying years later, it was no bullet-to-the-head relief for him. He was taken to the veterinarian for a humane passage.

Number IV

Rex IV (also known as Puppy) and the Author

Rex IV (alias Puppy) became my last adult Golden Retriever…but Puppy was his early name and it never got changed. I guess I should have called him Rex after his predecessor passed on but I never got around to it. The exceptional way he hunted for me and others, as well, we really didn't care what his name was. Like Cedric, he didn't need a fancy name. Mind you, there are much better dogs than mine, were we ever to be challenged in a field trial. But for an overall companion, I was more than satisfied with that little bundle of fur I picked up one March day at a kennel near St. Cloud, Minnesota.

All puppies and kittens are cute but I believe that Labs and Golden Retriever puppies are almost spellbinding with their cuteness. This little fur ball was playing with its brothers and sisters. I had a thawed out rooster which I had placed in a weed patch. We placed pups downwind and watched the tumbling playmates gradually approach the weed patch. Suddenly one male pup stood rigid, sniffing the air while the others continued unaware. The little guy seemed perplexed but started to follow his nose. At the edge of the weeds he actually trembled; afraid to enter but something was drawing his instincts and he came upon the bird. He jumped back in fear but then after a minute he had to move closer and grabbed at a tail feather. I picked him up and put him back with his pack and moved the pheasant to another location upwind and the same scenario was repeated. Again, he was the only one that showed the initial interest or the ability to make the first detection. I picked him up and told him what a great life he had ahead of him.

Unlike the rescuing ability of old Rex however, the following is a related episode that I believe is worth mentioning, regarding Puppy and me. Yes, pheasant hunting can be outright dangerous, not just from weather alone. One does take a risk, especially out hunting by yourself. Maybe it is the old fighter pilot that still lurks within me but even after the following, I still go out there with just my dog. Puppy did an almost unintentional fatal number on me when he was less than two years old. One dog had saved my life, the next one almost took it.

We were hunting down in Iowa during the holiday season. At that time of year my hunting companions were too tied up in the usual season's social events to go out with me hunting on that particular day. Right beside my motel, which was at the edge of the city limits (it is a small town with only one motel) a shallow drainage ditch courses through the northern edge of the town running west to east. I frequently stay at this particular motel and had always noticed an abundance of birds going in and out of it about a hundred yards from the highway crossing less than a block from the motel. Being by myself, I thought that this was as good a place to hunt as any.

I had hunted the week before with my local hunting friends beginning at a bridge farther upstream from the motel, just outside the city limits. So I walked on the frozen ice at the bottom of the fairly deep drainage ditch to the bridge crossing for the gravel road farther west and began hunting. The depression of the ditch was about eight to ten feet, enough to hide a walking man, and almost immediately we got up a flock of hens lifting from the gentler sloping sides of the ditch (in comparison to the usual sharper slant of most Iowa drainage ditches I have experienced). As we walked, the narrow frozen stream spread out to frozen pools. Nothing but hens seemed to be rising as we walked along. Finally a rooster got up just out of range and since that area's slope was easily accessed, we probed the thick grass for a possible extra rooster. After a while, I went back to the bottom of the ditch and headed upstream. I usually stay with my dog when he is poking around searching but the area did not look productive and I figured the dog would soon join me.

A couple of hens bursting out of shallow cover were the reason why he had stayed yet I kept on walking. Finally after I began to cross a larger frozen pool, I turned and called to my dog and added a beckoning pat of my knee to join back up with me. With this signal, Puppy leaped with his young energy and started to run toward me. Mind you, this was a frozen over pool that separated us. I had a few yards left to go to the edge of the pool and turned and kept walking. This was a very big mistake. All of a sudden, my world turned into a half somersault. Up into the air I went heels high up over my head which went crashing onto the ice and fortunate was I wearing my very winterish, Mongolian Marine cold weather hat. Despite the fur padding, I went into darkness with my dog licking my face when I woke up. How long I was lying there I had no idea. My Benelli was lying on the ice about ten yards away. My neck was sore and my head hurt and I was staring up at my dog who kept licking my face. I do love my dog…all of them, but at that moment I remember saying slowly, very slowly, out of my stupor, "Puppy…you…son…of…a…bitch!"

I wasn't angry at the dog. It wasn't his fault. But I still said it.

What had happened was when he hit the ice at full speed, he could not stop. He went sliding, crashing into me and with his size hit me right at the back of my knees with almost eighty pounds of fast moving force and up into the air I went. I was thoroughly checked as if he was a hockey defenseman. For a long moment as I lay there, I wondered if my body was still working. My neck was darn sore and my head was throbbing. Still in my stupor, I started to panic. Nothing moved! This was a very poor place to be paralyzed. For that matter, any place is a helluva place to be so restricted. Slowly, as I began to focus, I began to be afraid to even try and find out if I was okay or not. My arms did not want to move. Slowly I went to my legs and wondered fearfully if I could feel my toes wiggling. What a relief. Then I could move my legs. What another bunch of relief. I could imagine myself lying at the bottom of this drainage ditch and no one would find me, not until it was way too late. I had a terrible headache but ignored it. Not being able to move made it moot. I tried to move my shoulders and they moved. And then my fingers and hands could move. It was one scary experience. I rose slowly to my knees and crawled toward my Benelli and began walking after I retrieved it, downstream this time, back to the motel, headache and all. Spirits again!

Like Rex IV, Pupp' will stand out within my many hunting excursions, a couple I will divulge here. One example is when we were all getting assembled for a cornfield walk and it was a genteel resort crowd, sixties and upwards, and mostly over-and-unders. (Those are expensive, genteel shotguns.) Those experienced folks don't miss many shots. While the dogs were being let out of their kennels from the resort bus, Puppy, who always rides free in the client bus, ambled over to some heavy weeds by the nearby cornfield, obviously drawn by the fresh scent of a bird deciding to exit the bus parking spot when we drove up. I never saw him leave but there he was, looking for me with a live rooster in his mouth, standing among the startled and exclaiming hunters. All the rest of my memories are very positive about this dog who turned out to be the most outstanding hunting dog I ever had despite his defenseman-like ability to knock me down on the ice. It could have been a pretty tough situation back then, but I sure as heck would hate to do my passing-on in an old folk's home. I plan to keep on hunting, and often with just the dog and I, as long as I can! My middle son and I are now raising Rex V but I call him Weed because he seems to be growing so fast. Hopefully I can avoid what so much of America winds up in—the old folk's homes. My advice, get out and hunt and keep that body moving.

Helen

Puppy had a good friend, an elderly lady that lived next door to him. Her name was Helen Neitzel. Every dog owner should be so fortunate to have such a neighbor. She fell in love with Rex III when he was a pup and mourned his loss right along with the rest of us when he passed. She insisted that she pay for half of his veterinarian bill including the cremation. He is buried by the lake in back of the house, and now Puppy is, too. Puppy would go to visit her often and at times stay overnight, sleeping at the foot of her bed as did Rex. His picture and Rex III's graced her nightstand. He also had the run of her land that borders the lake. Incidentally that lake is loaded with ducks and geese that come up to her backyard bird feeder that often holds corn as well for the larger birds. Both my dogs got rather used to them and learned to tolerate their presence, especially when the big Canadians stood their ground come Spring when their young arrived.

Helen is gone now, too, and her loyal husband Ken lives alone in the house overlooking the lake. We would take Puppy to the hospital to see her as she began passing. He was a most welcome guest by all. A pair of married nurses were so impressed with his human-like demeanor that they wound up purchasing a Golden Retriever from his blood line. Helen was always so happy to have him come visit.

I will include one more incident involving this tremendous 'finding' dog. You would knock a pheasant down, and it would take off running with maybe only a broken wing. Puppy would be in fast pursuit. Maybe a woven wire fence would slow him down or heavy brush would give the bird a head start and he would have to track the bird in dense cover. Often he would be gone for ten to fifteen minutes. It seemed like the longer he would be gone the more successful he would become. Eventually he would walk out of the cover with a rooster bobbing out of his mouth. A bird dog usually carries a rooster back so that its spurs are turned away from its chest or throat. The rooster always seems to go remarkably placid and bobs its head to the dog's movement as if it is enjoying a free ride. You reach down while praising the dog, grasp the ring-neck and wring the bird's neck before placing it in the compartment for bird hauling sewed or zippered on to your hunting vest. You do not do an adequate job of execution and eventually, while you are walking, the bird comes to and takes off out of your vest. I have had that happen on more than one occasion. Often an inexperienced hunter will not have a carrying vest and will give you their bird to carry. Their bird hops out and sometimes gets away.

Ahlmans Gun Shop

Cabelas (national chain outfitter) sells a lot of guns and sends you to Ahlmans Guns north of Owatonna, MN to get yours fixed. Puppy and I went up in the air on a broken away ice chunk down at the watery bottom of a Northern Iowa drainage ditch; landing in shallow, sand and mud filled water—my Benelli, too. I had to take it to the gun shop to get its butt spring cleaned. I came back a week later to pick it up. It had a note on it. 'Manager wants to see customer.' I sat down and waited about ten minutes and was just about ready to leave when he came down and shook my hand. I told him there was no reason for my credit card to bounce. He waved me off and asked me if I was a guide. "I see you are from South Dakota, lots of pheasants!" My Benelli is only twenty-four inches, not for ducks or geese, and sported a sling which most hunters don't use. I bought it when they first came out and those days they were on a waiting list for almost a year. I think hunters believe a wobbling sling will throw off their aim. Never bothered me and I find a sling damned handy. A twenty-four incher turns around much easier than a twenty-eight or thirty incher in a pickup cab when you are road hunting. It also comes up much faster out in the field. Your hands are free with the sling when you walk back to the pickup, especially with a full vest and your group has got its share of birds or some guys don't have carrying vests or want to keep their guns at the ready in case some action comes up. I told him I was just an ordinary hunter but nodded that I hunted the Dakotas considerably. He said, "I've seen many a Benelli but yours is one of the most used. I just wanted to see who you were." In the pheasant hunting world, I considered that statement one hell of an honor coming from Ahlmans. They now send me personal Christmas cards, which makes me feel good.

Iowa pheasant hunting you get to hunt over their deep drainage ditches. Creeks not just tiny streams are flowing below you. They are too steep to walk but a good dog will hunt near the flowing water's edge. You cannot see your own dog but can see your hunting partner's dog walking the other side and likewise he watches yours. When a pheasant does leap up you get at least an earlier warning for your shot as it rises below you and often drops in the water and not heavy brush or holes where your dog can more surely retrieve it. Once in a while the dog will spring out a coyote also.

Drilled

It was a Sunday. The season started the day before. We had some hunters from the East. Puppy was up ahead of me as we approached a cornfield end where blockers were waiting for the birds to rise. This particular field held quite a few birds and we had shots at them as we made our drive. Four blockers were waiting a few yards back from the end of the corn. This is a very exciting time in the annals of pheasant-dom. Birds are going to be springing forth and action, I mean, extreme action is going to be happening.

I could see the surgeon, up ahead, at the end of the cornrow, probably twenty feet back from the corn's edge and just beyond a sagging barbed wire fence. I had hunted with him the day before. A good friend of mine, Daryl (son of the hunt-master) was also a doctor, a cancer research type. He had invited the surgeon, Doc, out from the East, where they were employed somewhere near Baltimore, back to his home town. Doc had a very expensive and beautiful 12 gauge over-and-under. Although I preferred my four-shot paltry price-wise Benelli, 12 gauge, (only a thousand dollar range) I had to admire that two-shotter'—two to three times more expensive. Anyway, Dr. Daryl and I had taken Doc to a choice place the day before and set him up to drive birds to him out of three miniature choice—usually loaded with birds—sloughs and he missed almost every bird flocking out as we drove the slough with Puppy.

Back at the cornfield, Puppy paused up ahead and lifted his paw to point. A rooster lifted low and rose in front of me. It stayed lower than half the corn's height and flew straight toward Doc. I can still see him coming up with the expensive gun—it became a Civil War cannon. Its open maw, rather two maws, pointed death and doom straight at me. The pheasant closed. Puppy leaped futilely into the sky. Those barrels seemed so much larger. Any more height and my great gracious dog would have had his head blown off. The dog leaping, the pheasant closing, the over-and-under, the deadly barrels and the world froze. The retort! It now became as deadly as the SAM missile back in 'Nam. Only…this one fired! The trigger was pulled. Time stood still. Then the impact. My right shoulder flew back, turning me, driving me backward. A yelp came out off to my right where a young hunter, in his early twenties, had been walking about ten corn rows over but had come much closer. The shotgun's pellets had spread and caught him also, scissoring off part of his ear lobe but not detaching it completely. "Owww," he let out. I turned to him, forgetting my own hit.

Doc passed out. We all thought he had a heart attack. The kid with the ear became secondary. Me? No one knew it. I didn't check until I got back to my motel. A bunch of heavy welts. I had had my hunting vest shoulder pad reinforced due to aching from probably too much 12 gauge shooting. (I still have that problem to this day and this past season was why I did no shooting and missed my first season in years. I could not sacrifice my pickleball playing for any other pastime.) I also had my flight jacket on under the vest. Pea sized welts were all I suffered.

The kid was down on his knees holding his hand to his bleeding ear. His older brother Todd came running over. Todd was one of my son's close friends and we had spent years hunting together. "God damn! Eric. You get a fucking Purple Heart! It ain't all that bad. Think of all the good looking chicks you can impress in the bars!" I could have never uttered a more healing passage. The kid beamed appreciatively. "Yeh! Yeh," he replied trancelike. Then a big ass smile. "You Goddamn right, Ed."

Someone yelled: "The Doc is dead!"

Someone else yelled: "He got shot!"

Another: "Yeh, someone shot the Doc. He's fucking dead!" They all looked accusatively at me and Eric.

Daryl ran up and put his ear to Doc's chest. He is a big, tall, good looking guy, and like I said, a doctor, too. He stood up. "Shut the fuck up! He ain't dead and he ain't shot."

Doc started to stir and they went back to the pickup trucks where we started. We took Eric into town to get his ear sewed back up. We sort of glued the ear piece and semi-reattached it with electrician's tape on the way into town. The Doc went into his motel room and never came out until his plane ticket carried him back East on a Wednesday. He told Daryl at a medical reception that following Spring: "I don't want to talk about it. I will never hunt again."

Black Ice out of Des Moines

The casino Indians had a Dodge Ram V-10 for me and a nice house I stayed in. My good friend was a Mdewakanton tribal Sioux member, Joe Brewer. We did a lot together. The truck was his but I always used it. Coming from a workshop near Kansas City I had a load of books in back.

I hit ice and went skidding, spinning helplessly two and a half times toward approaching traffic, across the middle part of the freeway against that scary oncoming traffic. It was night time on a Sunday and a lot of cars were heading home. I was so worried I was going to hit some little car, demolishing it with that big V-10 pickup. Luckily (probably Spirits) they all dodged me. Then came a big semi with big wide bumpers. I hit it head on but to the side. The truck kept me from going off down a steep ravine. (Spirits again.) I bounced, spun.

Wham! I bounced off the corner and swept my box underneath the trailer which contained a load of sandwiches bound for California. The driver told me all about it with his wife who was watching also. I took out his reefers so he had to return to his loading area and left me off at a motel. The Highway Patrol told me to park my pickup at a truck stop after I had picked up my books strewn alongside of the freeway. Part of the box was sticking out and with a rope I tied that projection back in and continued with my journey the next morning. That was a close call but it helps to lead me to an interesting scene with the casino Indians and several other related adventures I had completely forgotten about.

Judge Miles Lord

My phone rang. "McGaa, I want you to come down to my courtroom. How busy are you right now?" For a federal judge, you get unbusy, especially when one personally calls you. Within the hour I walked into his courtroom, led by a U.S. Marshal. Several months before, the judge had called me in the middle of the night and told me to go to St. Cloud Prison to help settle a prison standoff of mostly Indian prisoners. "What kind of car are you driving? The Highway Patrol will be looking for you. Get up there—*Now!*" I heard a phone ringing in the background, "Don't worry about the speed limit. Get going!"

For that one I tucked two small bottles of rum into my flight jacket pocket, not knowing how long I would be in there. My wife was away on a trip and usually we had a few of the small airline bottles. Half way to St. Cloud from West Minneapolis and at about ninety miles per hour, the State Patrol ran me down. They came up to the side of me with a window rolled down and signaled, *Follow me!* The warden was waiting, it was raining and past midnight. No one searched me. They took me to an auditorium and turned me loose through a door. I walked down the aisle and there was a group of Indians, up above me, on the stage, mostly, clad in choir robes. It was a cold night and the robes were handy.

They gave me sullen stares as I walked toward them. I cursed myself for not bringing cigarettes. These were younger prisoners and not in a happy mood. I have never smoked and that late, I just hadn't thought about

94

stopping somewhere and buying some. (Cigarettes were a godsend with the Max Security prisoners I will briefly tell you about later; another Judge Lord assignment.) The stage was dimly lit. They were eerie-looking standing above me. I took a front row chair, sat in it and looked up to address them. First, I pulled out a rum bottle. "Anyone got a coke?"

This was the last place I'd ever expect one, but the leader made a motion and a guy went back stage and brought me a can of Pepsi Cola. I opened the can and told the prisoner to take a swig and then another. "Take it down to half," I politely suggested. All this time the audience was staring quietly with no emotion. I mixed my drink, dumping the bottles' contents, took several swigs and asked my coke provider if he wanted a taste. He looked at the leader and declined. I took one more drink and introduced myself and told them who sent me. (I hate the hard stuff, now, but I was younger then.) "Any Siouxs here?" About a fourth raised their hands. These were young guys and at that time, not many of the young knew much about the Sun Dance like they do now. A couple standing side by side held their hands higher like they wanted to say something. I offered them a nod. "We saw you at the AIM Sun Dance." That broke the ice. It took only a day to settle the situation. It wasn't a revolt, riot or what have you but initially was pretty tense.

Max Security

Odd how one forgets as you get older. As I write this, just now I recall Judge Lord sending me into Maximum Security at the State Prison. And then, as I started writing it, I remembered the St. Cloud incident. I guess that is old age for you. It is a good thing I have written down most of my experiences quite a few years ago. These last two I never wrote down. These two were not life threatening although the guards didn't like the idea of me being left alone with some actual murderers when I had to do the Maximum Security mission.

My order from the judge was to "find out what the hell is going on, McGaa." It is kind of handy being an Indian and looking like one to some degree. I had a law degree. That was probably why a congressman wanted me in to negotiate at the Wounded Knee American Indian Movement (AIM) takeover. Maybe this prompted Judge Lord. I never asked. (My experience, it seems that the rank and file trust you. Governor Al Quie once asked me to head up the parole board but I turned it down.) The State Prison Warden didn't like me, I sensed, but I could have been wrong. I was given carte blanche to go anywhere on his turf and had a letter that said so. "Take mental notes, interview them face to face and get back to me." I ate with them, went into their cells accompanied by a couple guards. Judge Lord gave me another letter and this time I would be alone with Max/Sec types, out of the guards' earshot. The warden balked and I agreed that he keep the guards where they could see me in case I got attacked. It was an agreeable compromise with the warden shaking his head as if I were some kind of an idiot. He could have been right. I wasn't worried about it. What the hell, I was loaded with cigarettes. It was interesting: the guard would bring a handcuffed prisoner and another guard would be giving me a quick rundown on the prisoner as they approached. "This guy has killed several people, etc. I'd keep the cuffs on this guy—killed his wife and kids." "This guy's a psycho nut." The guards would bring in the prisoner. He would back up to an opening in the bars and the guard now on the outside of the bars and me inside would unlock his cuffs. I had a small desk in an adequate sized barred room.

The prisoner would sit across from me with his back to the guards so they couldn't read his lips. They would drift off in the distance until I would wave to them as far enough. I didn't want to piss off the warden. I'd introduce myself and somehow just about every one of the Max/Secs knew who I was and what I was up to. All but one smoked and sucked down my cigarettes. I couldn't blame the guards for being so edgy. If I got attacked they probably figured they might lose their jobs or somehow, innocent as they may be, it wouldn't look good on their record. I didn't have any problems. After Vietnam and all those missions, I just never worried about anything.

It was the same with AIM. (AIM's main leaders and I have become friends for life.) Initially I probably should have been at least been uneasy but I never was. Maybe that is why a beautiful missionary's wife was so impressed with me. I never batted an eye and spoke fluently and openly. She was once again in the front row granting me some wonderful, attentive scenery. Damn shame she wasn't single, or widowed or divorced. She was enough to relax anyone. And then the highly serious meeting afterwards with the AIM leaders. I'll touch more on this important event later. What happened at that meeting made a terrific change in the Indian world. My mission from Chief Fools Crow accomplished that one. We beat the Missionaries. We won!

I finished the task for the judge. Wrote it up and he was satisfied. My last assignment was started in the courtroom. There was a group of Mdewakanton tribal members who were about to get rich in a matter of a few years. They knew me and I knew them. I had worked closely with the tribal liaison, Joe Brewer, as an undercover casino manager. There was a group out of Miami who posed as 'Cuban Mafia' but it was all bluff. They had started the casino but were corruptly raking them off as happened so often with impoverished Indians trying to get their casinos started. Joe and I kept records and pretended to be at odds with each other to keep my cover from being blown. I Xeroxed the copy of my nightly take before wiring it down to Florida headquarters in the mornings and also did the same for the Bingo manager's nightly summary, unbeknownst to him. He reliably got coffee at the same time every morning when we would bring our casino records over and his Xerox machine was right there. I made copies while Joe stood look out. We never got caught. In time we found the right FBI agent—oddly his name was Pistol—and got the 'Cuban Mafia' kicked out through Judge Lord. They were not paying the rightful percentage to the Indians: Greed!

The 'Cuban Mafia' would often drop a veiled threat as to what would happen to anyone crossing them, but I considered them mostly bluff. Mr. Pistol thought it a good idea for both Joe and I to carry weapons, however. I preferred a snub nosed, .38 Special, similar to my 'Nam weapon. We wired up Joe, and they offered him a bribe. I was wired but they fired me. They tried to threaten me but they were just too flabby and soft to take seriously and besides I was armed. By then we had enough evidence on them. The judge said: "McGaa, you are going back to the reservation and run their casino for them until they get on their feet with it." That was my last assignment from him.

Two more driving close calls and the last one is pretty funny. Sioux humor demands that we at least lighten up this chapter.

Approaching Okabena, Minnesota Turn-off

Rex III and I were on our way pheasant hunting. I fell asleep on I-90 heading west. Down to my right I go and start to climb up the steep Autumn grass embankment. *Thump! Thump!* I wake up. Just miss a culvert and at a high

97

angle, my passenger side is much higher. My tires are so kinked that they pick up grass squeezed into the rims. I am awake enough to grab the wheel and bring us back to the base of the rise. A steel post whizzes by. Another obstruction and I manage to get back to the shoulder, just missing a highway sign and Okabena Turnoff sign. I drive up the exit shaking. I turn to the south on the county highway. Still quivering I shut off the car and sit there and talk to Rex who is sitting behind me. I tell him how damn close we were to getting killed or hurt. I see a movement through the front window. A quarter section of picked soybeans ends at another small ravine and three pheasants have just lifted, crossing an east/west gravel road and landing. We drive down, park a ways back and sneak up slowly, Rex so obedient and experienced right behind or beside me, never bolting when he gets their scent. They lift suddenly but within range. I knock one down over the road. Rex gets another.

White River Turnoff

I had a similar experience later while pheasant hunting again. I fell asleep off Highway I-90 again, this time much farther west in South Dakota. We had just passed the White River turnoff heading west. Down I go to my left into the mid-section again missing posts and dodging culverts. I awaken and get back on the freeway.

I had stopped at a liquor store earlier. I bought a bottle of rum, probably some coke, too. I could never drink it straight. Pheasant hunting, you can get pretty stiff come evenings. You check into a motel and have a drink or two after supper to kill the aches and pains. Long day walking and not in shape, believe me you have pain, especially as you get older. Not being former Marine fighter pilots, most hunters drink whiskey or bourbon or beer. Young guys have the stamina to go into the bar and stay a few hours. Not me. After the dog is fed and watered, he and I hit the sack. I had put the rum in back, unopened naturally, and went looking for birds.

I was so scared and relieved that I turned my truck around to the White River turnoff, knowing that there was a picnic area not far away where a bridge crossed White River. I had to give back something to God for sparing my life and my dog, too, or maybe the Spirits, either or both.

There was a man sitting in the picnic yard. This was Indian country but he appeared to be a white man, older than me. I got out of my truck, let Rex out and took the rum bottle and walked toward the man who was sitting beside a large garbage can. He looked like a wino: scraggly beard, unkempt hair, ruddy, red complexion, soiled clothes and watery eyes. I started unscrewing the cap. He lit up with a huge smile. He gave forth an enormous grin when I was only a few steps from the open garbage can. He sat up straighter, grinning, his hands tucked into his belt like a starving man about to enjoy a huge meal. I held the bottle above the garbage can. He mistook this as a friendly offering and stood stiffly, chest out as if to expect me to deliver the bottle but instead I began pouring its contents into the refuse container. "Wha…wha… what are yah doin'?'" His mouth gaped with disbelief as the contents gurgled downward. Rex showed up and took a leak on the garbage can. I dropped the empty bottle into the container. "I don't think you'd understand," I answered solemnly. I called Rex and we walked back to the truck. I don't think I have bought a bottle of the hard stuff since.

Early Ocean Experience

I have been in shark waters often since we Marines are most always near the oceans. I could easily lie and make up a real humdinger of a 'Shark Story.' In the Caribbean, my squadron was stationed ashore for about three months and of that time, on an average of two early evenings a week I was designated the squadron longusta (lobster) hunter, especially on Fridays. Longusta kill their prey with their flashing, cutting long antennae and have no large clamping claws like the more commonly known species found mostly in the Northeast coastal area.

I had a pistol-sized, rubber band fired spear gun which was more maneuverable than the longer spear type for shooting the lobster coming out of his protective coral hideaway to start his evening hunt. That is also the same time the sharks start to patrol. The most aggressive were the hammerheads. One had even killed a Navy SEAL who attempted to rescue his girlfriend. Investigation, however, led to the belief that she was swimming with her menstrual period, not a good idea even if you are with a SEAL. Hammers are actually quite passive when compared to Great Whites. The latter is rarely found in the Caribbean. I dragged a small tire about twenty feet back just in case a hungry shark wanted my longusta. It was loop tied so in case of attack, I'd pull the tie and not get dragged backward.

I'd shoot the lobster and break its back so it cannot swim away and pitch it into the web-netted tire. After catching six or eight, I'd take them to the officer's club and the cook would grill them for the squadron's Happy Hour.

On several cruises this was my enjoyable pastime. The squadron commander would always have a jeep for me come around three p.m. If I had to fly a training mission, it was scheduled for morning mission. Happily for me, I never saw a big shark. I did see plenty of barracuda but all I had to do was point the spear gun at them and they disappeared in a flash. About ten minutes later the barracuda would be back again, watching curiously, but I always considered them harmless.

5 SHARK TRIP

Great White Shark

Departing from Ensenada, we dropped anchor off a Mexican island, Guadalupe, within a designated sea park with no fishing allowed (except for a few Mexican fishing boats anchored distantly). The island has about one hundred inhabitants on the other side of the island, which is nineteen miles long and eight miles wide.

I had flown to San Diego from South Dakota (that may have had megalodons—giant prehistoric sharks—in the huge ancient inland sea that once covered the Badlands just east of the Black Hills).

Most of us, about twenty-nine Nautilus Explorer tourists, suffered seasickness on the boat ride from San Diego. I thought I was immune, having spent fourteen months at sea, mostly on aircraft carriers in the Caribbean and Atlantic and about a month and a half going to and coming from Korea as a young Marine. Back then I laughed at any of the poor miserables down with seasickness.

The ship is about a hundred and twenty feet long and thirty feet wide, with three passenger decks. The middle passenger deck has portholes, closed for travel. Several passengers were dead out; lying prostrate on the floor of their rooms or in their bunks. Toward early morning I started to get weak in the gills. I felt like vomiting but made it through the day. The ship pitched at times and there was some rolling, occasionally a slight shudder. I was thankful it was not rough seas. I went to sleep that first night and slept until noon. Longest I had slept in years. After a tasty lunch I felt much better. We docked at 8 p.m. in a calm, welcoming sea.

Passenger Commentaries—First day of going down in the shark cages

> The first day was so amazing! We were both thinking we would be scared, but we were not scared at all! We were the first ones in the 30 feet cages at 8 am. We got to see 3 white sharks that came really close to the cages. They were super curious about us in there, but we never felt threatened. Great experience, with a great dive schedule all day; time to eat drink and reheat in the spa before your next dive. We didn't really get cold until the 3rd and 4th dive of the day. We both wore 3mm shorties and our 7mm suits with a hood. By the last dives we saw up to 5 sharks around us. SO COOL! The crew is so friendly and helpful. The food is awesome. We are having a great time and can't wait to come back someday with the rest of our families!!
>
> -Lexi Warren & Laura Kiker—Passengers aboard the Nautilus Explorer.

Author's First Entry

I have had many, many adventures, mainly because I am so damned old—latter 70s—but this is one of my best ones. Another poor devil aboard, Dale Miller, whom I bonded with, is also my age, a bit taller, a few months younger; which makes me the oldest person on the boat. He was agile as a cat and had his own wet suit and had scuba dove around the world. He looked like he was in his fifties. He had led an active life and kept in shape. Diving is akin to my addictive Pickleball sport. Once I put my wet suit on, the adrenaline set in and I could move as if I were twenty-one again.

I am so fortunate to have three stalwart, considerate, successful sons who paid for my Nautilus Great White adventure. At first, I didn't want to go, especially considering the cost to them, but their persistent begging made me reluctantly give in. How they complained it would be less fun without me was a bit difficult to understand but at least I paid my airfare. I don't think anyone can say my kids don't like me unless they have some ulterior motive in mind. I did admit that I wouldn't mind seeing a Great White up close. Be careful what you wish for!

I am somewhat Spiritual (not religious) and I seemed to have some connection with the Great White, and was thrilled when the first one swam casually by our cage. My sons had brought two friends who I have known since they were boys, when I'd taken them out in the Badlands to shoot prairie dogs. Now here we were in a beautiful secluded bay with a wonderful crew and fantastic food. How fortunate are we to go forth on another adventure.

Rob Brown is a family friend from Edina, Minnesota. He has quite a memory, often recounting funny incidents or bringing up statements I had made on our many trips. Little did I ever imagine that this young boy who sat wide-eyed beside my son out on an Indian reservation, eating Rites of Passage rattlesnake, would someday be a very large, strong man accompanying us on another adventure on the Pacific Ocean. His strength and awareness proved of considerable value on my last dive. Yup! He and the first mate dragged me out of the Jaws of Death!

Read on:

Rob Brown's Day 1 Entry

First day after a rough 20hr. boat ride from Ensenada to Guadalupe. Many of the passengers fell ill with seasickness as the boat made its way. After a good night's rest I woke up to the cherry pickers dropping the cages in the cobalt blue water. We descended 30 ft down in the cages. As I panned the scene I spotted the first Great White coming toward the cage to investigate its new neighbors. Within minutes we had been greeted by two more! I'd like to think they swam by us with reciprocated wonder. They got so close you could even see their eyes move and the sinew caught in their teeth! Some of my fellow divers were fortunate enough to get a cage bump and the captain of the ship came within a foot of a large male.

It was quite a sight! As the day went on they seemed to become more comfortable with us, came closer more often, and stayed in the vicinity for longer periods of time. We wrapped up the day with an evening dive just before sunset. The Great Whites are in good company and so are we! Looking forward to day two!!!

Rob Brown—Day Two

We entered the cage for the second dive of the day. The group consisted of Mark, Jessica, Kyle, myself, and JJ the dive master. We entered the cage as usual expecting another adventure with the Great Whites. The water was clear and luminescent with the bright sunshine fostered by the clear sky as we were lowered 30 feet down suspended by an inch thick cable. Four large Great Whites were on the spot within moments! They circled around with the same curiosity as the previous day, going back and forth and around in a patrolling fashion. About five minutes into the dive a sea lion joined us to see what all the fuss was about. He started down from the surface, nose down and rear flippers up. He had to make sure he didn't get on the great white's menu. He stole the show by swimming into the foursome of whites and showed the massive apex predators his agility, speed, and bravery. It was brought to our attention that sea lions often harass the whites when territory is being encroached upon. The sea lion took off into the blue and the sharks reclaimed the floor. The whites became very, very aggressive, perhaps from the frenzy inducing chumming of nearby boats which visibly picked up on our 2nd dive day. They came by buzzing the cage like there was no tomorrow! Snapping those massive jaws on the steel cage.

Bruce was a large 16 ft male who snuck up the side of the cage vertically right next to JJ the instructor/ highly focused watch dog. Instructors often stand at the top of the cage to feed and attract the big fish. When he (Bruce) reached the top of the cage he snapped at the steel chains that come together to give more balanced suspension from the cable. He rose slowly upward to several feet further to the air supply hoses that gave us the ability to explore their habitat. With a swift chop and a quick tear he severed all of the hoses that delivered our air. It was surreal to look up and see this giant beast jeopardize our lives. I had just exhaled at the moment he cut the lines. In a frantic scramble I made my way to one of the four air tanks we had as reserves. My best friend Kyle had already opened the valve and gracefully shared his air as Mark and Jessica shared the adjacent tank. JJ soon arrived in a bold dive and took the regulator from my mouth and began to take in the air with haste; he had held his breath the longest to get down to us. Initially, four of us were quick sucking on one hose. In the corners of these deeper descending cages there are air tanks with regulators that you turn on for just such an emergency. You have to be scuba licensed to go down in these cages. He had been without air the longest.

We passed the regulator back and forth like a bunch of hippies passing a joint at a Phish concert, but with obvious serious eagerness and conviction. I took on quite a bit of water while gasping in anticipation for the return of breathable air. I took many deep breaths and was able to calm my nerves. Looking around I saw that all my comrades were ultimately okay, but a considerable amount of desperation set in until the pressure release in my ears told me we were making our ascent. I couldn't wait to surface and get out of this cage that had become our prison and almost our death chamber! As we made the ascent the adventurous side of me said "you'll live to make another dive!"

Nicole Hersey (Alien)—Day Two

I (Alien) was in the surface cage with Kevin (The Undertaker) and Ed (Chief). From this cage we could see the 40 ft submersible cage towards our right. Joel was the dive master standing on top of the cage baiting the Great Whites. Three brave girls were in that cage. These sharks were all males and enormous. One of the Whites swam towards the top of the submersible cage. I kept a close watch as the shark got closer and closer to Joel. This Great White swam directly towards Joel. Instead of ducking back and down into the cage, Joel punched the shark in its lower jaw. Not only was Joel the diver master bait man, he was the photographer/shark puncher. First he butted the shark with his camera, the shark paused, Joel butted him again—a pause but it continued slowly onward to Joel, it was so close that Joel was getting into in-fighting range and threw a solid right into his nose. The nose actually snapped upward and the shark sort of wallowed with the punch and into the cage's 4 support chains. Then its lateral fin caught some rope. Sharks are not supposed to go backwards but this one seemed to. The shark jerked a bit and backed off. Within seconds the shark returned for round 2. This time, the Great White swam right *on top of Joel so he was not visible. Then the Great White's mouth opened and exposed his jaws. He began to chomp on the cage's chain. His mouth opened and closed a few times as I watched in search of blood. Thankfully there was none. The shark spit out the chain, no doubt losing some teeth, which would not be unusual, and swam off. Joel was untouched.*

(Nicole was termed 'Alien' because of her small size. A humorous pun attempt by me since the movies always depict aliens as usually much smaller (and brighter) than we humans. She didn't mind her new nickname.)

I was in the same cage with Alien and the Undertaker. Alien was only four foot ten ("and three quarters!" she hastily adds). She stayed for several hours each time in the surface cage (the bottom is submerged about five feet). It is for non-scuba licensed clients and provides some spectacular viewing. Undertaker, Alien and I were its prime inhabitants. The second day we braved the next cage over toward the port side—depth, fifteen feet. That one had a spooky, somewhat vulnerable portion that even the experienced scuba licensees were cautious about when sharks were patrolling nearby. If they were coming up and the sharks were swimming nearby at a higher speed, then they were extra cautious and would wait until the sharks were swimming away into the blue and disappearing before scooting up the bottom ladder then quickly turning 180 degrees to the upper ladder and into a covering shark guard and coming out on the surface, exposed to some degree, before climbing out on the back of the ship's almost-water-level back deck.

We were right next to Joel's group and had a close view. One of the girls said when the huge White was above her, troubling Joel, she reached through the bars and touched its big belly. She said there was no way that shark could come through the cage bars and her two companions agreed.

Joel exhibited one of the bravest acts I have ever seen. I have seen a lot of combat, in America you get plenty of opportunity if you want to find it. Many brave men I have seen and of course some cowards as well, but damn few Marines in that last category. Joel was the Toreador of the Sea—the Ocean Bullfighter—jabbing his camera initially at that invasive beast, so used to going to where it wanted to go. I do not want to detract from JJ's leaping dive down to his charges in the earlier happening, unfortunately I did not get to witness that one, wherein two of my sons, Mark and Kyle, daughter-in-law (Magnet—blonde Jessica McGaa—she attracts sharks) and almost son, family friend since little, Rob Brown, were involved. That was one helluva symbol of bravery and duty.

The big monster slowly kept coming yet Joel stood his ground and took a prize fighter's crouch at the top of the cage. He could have easily stepped backward and dropped down to the three girls crouched down below, one reaching up to touch its eggshell colored belly. Wham! Joel delivered what would have been a knockout punch to a human. His distance from the shark's nose was the perfect proximity to deliver a maximum blow that actually changed the contour of the shark's nose, pushing it upward to a peak for a brief second and raising the shark's neck despite it being the biggest shark I had seen. What an awesome sight. Long ago there was a prize fighter named Jersey Joe Walcott who temporarily held the world heavyweight crown. *Life Magazine* showed him getting hit in the side of the face, moving all of his features for a brief moment. I gave Joel the Indian name—*Hogahn Eyahh* (Shark—Scary fish) *Iwo taka Wichastah (Eewoe tahka Wee Chah stah)* 'Shark Puncher Warrior'.

My Third Day Encounter

We took a close-to-shore excursion in an eight-passenger boat to about a mile of rocky island coastline lined with thousands of swimming and sun-bathing seals. Only a few young ones were visible. Within a few weeks the newborns were scheduled to appear. An occasional sea lion and the weird looking, large elephant seals were among the seals. The half-hour trip assured me that these seals were safe, guarded from any extinction by the sharks simply through their sheer numbers. They were unconcerned with our presence, some coming up close to our boat. They reminded me of a bunch of frolicking prairie dogs playfully oblivious to a lone eagle circling high and a pair of coyotes hiding behind a Badland butte.

Odd about the sea lions, they are so much more maneuverable than the sharks that they will come at times and harass the Whites, boldly biting on their fins. I guess they will at times gang up on Great Whites if they feel too invaded by them in the sea lions' own territory. Hard to believe, I know, but they are extremely maneuverable. Seals are, too. Some of them cavort off the boat's fantail. One even hopped up on the back by the fifteen-footer ladder and sat for a while. The ship refrains from feeding them as they don't want a crowd of them coming and going because it actually might drive away the Whites since they too nip at the sharks, especially if there are a gang of seals. Hard to believe, I know, but there they are, right in front of you. Like I always say, direct observation. I am starting to suspicion that it is only the old or the inexperienced young that make up the White's diet. One sea lion relaxed on his back on the surface while several Great Whites were below it. I expected a big splash from a rising shark but it never happened. Great Whites were constantly below us as tuna, mostly tuna heads or tuna in a gunny sack, were offered and being swarmed by ten to fourteen inch mackerel pecking at them. The tuna would seep through the gunny sack and mostly get consumed by the small mouthed mackerels, but its smell would keep the sharks interested. Sharks would come up and make constant false passes but turning off at the last closing second on the head. They must have been hooked by fisherman before to be so wary. Once in a while they would take the head.

I went down in the fifteen-footer cage. The 'Baby Cage' (Surface Cage) was to my left as we faced aft. I had not bothered to get a scuba qualification so was confined to just these two cages. No big deal, you could see sharks, sea lions, seals, mackerel or what have you from either cage. Besides, at first I felt the pressure just before touching down at the fifteen-foot level, hanging on to the ladder several rungs trying to clear my Eustachian tubes (inner ear passage). I forgot to articulate my jaws and had finally touched down at the cage's base, my ears still not completely cleared. At that moment another diver came down the ladder and hooked my air hose—knocking it out of my mouth. I panicked and grabbed for it but bubbles blocked my vision. I found the hose and all I had to do was push the back button which blows the sea water out and put it on. Instead I shot to the surface coughing. Most of us newbies were quite apprehensive with all those sharks around so such a simple correction was neglected.

The next time down I was fairly tense, but by now I had finally figured one's exaggerated, sort-of rotating jaw hinges did the trick. The first ladder has a back shark guard as you go down but in reality a shark could come in and get a piece of you if it really wanted to. Even the experienced divers that went in the thirty-foot cages went up and down those two ladders rather quickly. Half way down, you had to turn and grab onto the bottom ladder.

Both had eight or nine rungs. Where you switched ladders we called it no-man's land. No one went through there if sharks were nearby and definitely not when they were approaching. You waited until they approached and swept past then made your move. This portion of the trip was not for the fainthearted, especially when more than one sixteen-footer was patrolling. I wound up on this last look-see as the only diver down for what seemed a long while with two big sixteen-footers patrolling and, knowing I was the only 'seal' down there, they constantly were studying my cage in not too wide circles. Kyle went with me initially and another diver was there taking pictures of the crowd in the thirty-foot dive basket to the port side. That bunch started to ascend and took several pics of us. They are hauled up by a crane and do not use a descent ladder. Seems a lot safer but fifteen feet is all you want as a newbie, at least This Newbie.

An emergency air bottle is in one corner of the fifteen-foot cage and Kyle helped me practice using it. I turned it on, took out my regulator, pushed the bottle's regulator button, bubbles blew, and I placed it in my mouth for a couple breaths then switched back to mine and shut off the emergency valve. Kyle gave me the all-OK sign. By now I could take my regulator out of my mouth, clear it by pushing a button on it and put it back in my mouth while keeping the button depressed and resume breathing without swallowing any water. And then he demonstrated clearing fog from the inner glass portion of his mask by tilting his head forward, letting in some sea water and swishing the inside of the mask, and had me do the same. By this time, I could do that, too. It all seems pretty simple but at first one is so damned apprehensive of those big monsters shadowing overhead, under or out in front of you that an ordinary person gets nervous as hell. I certainly was not the only one but by now quite a few were using it (the fifteen-foot cage) for picture taking and often there would be an experienced diver with their cameras down there.

Kyle had gone down with me without a wetsuit between his deeper dives and was limited due to the coldness of the water, which wasn't so bad with a wetsuit. He indicated he was going to go back up and I waved goodbye to him. He stopped half way as did the other experienced diver who was wearing a wetsuit. The regulator is on a fifteen-foot hose so they were okay as they waited just below no man's land (between the somewhat non-protective guard bars as the pair of giants seemed to patrol a bit faster). The sharks maneuvering held them for about five minutes. I was at the bottom staring off into the darkened blue hoping a sea lion or two would come by attempting to touch a few close by mackerel or two who at times would enter your cage. Cage bars are pretty wide down there. A small shark could slip through but I think the big ones scare the smaller ones away. I did see one six-footer or so who seemed almost like a baby by then and he was just traveling through and certainly never paused to hang around. Any other time, I would have been scared of that size but not after viewing the monsters who had shifted gears and were constantly patrolling. After about five minutes, Kyle and the other guy were gone. I then realized I was the only 'seal' down below on the port side. The starboard thirty-footer cage was down and they were feeding tuna in a gunny sack, but my two huge companions seemed only interested in me. 'Alien' (Nicole, the 5 foot 4 Rhode Island math teacher—a cute thing in her forties) was watching me from the 'baby cage', the surface cage just inward from the starboard thirty-footer. Her cage reaches down about five feet underwater and offers excellent, comfortable safe viewing. Its bars seem to be just a bit closer together. Worse, the tuna sack got a hole in it by then and pieces of tuna started floating out and down into my cage. At first, I thought, *What fun!* and tried to grab some bigger pieces to get the swarming mackerel in closer, even inside my cage. Then it dawned on me that the big guys might just attempt to come in, too. A nice piece was floating by and I had reached out for it then saw a big shark and quickly withdrew my hand. I blew some bubbles at it to send it away. A mackerel almost slapped my face. Several were inside my cage by now. The tuna seemed to stir up the two monsters who would come just above close to no man's land then split into the darkening blue going away from the ship then quickly appearing 180 degrees opposite from their gloomy, dark blue departure as if on signal or some sort of related Orca Telepathy and come through no man's land again in close formation. Round and round they circled, moving much faster than usual. It was no question: in my mind that they knew that they had a seal trapped inside that cage. It became to be one helluva feeling.

No sense panicking in this situation. What the hell good would it do but I started to get scared as hell. What a drama! But this was one of those real ones like spinning upside down in a Phantom after getting an engine knocked out by a SAM missile. Round and round you go and the ground coming up and you can't move your arms to eject because of centrifugal force. Pretty soon you won't be able to eject downward. My close calls were here again—

right back on me. The quicksand, crashes, jets, choppers, Ram pickup bouncing off the semi bumper. This one had a lengthy addition, it was a drawn out one, stark ass fear and to put it bluntly, not very goddamned pleasant. Such a pause on this one. Others were so much quicker. This one was getting too damned drawn out, unnerving as hell. These sharks cannot wait at a seal hole the way a polar bear does. They have to keep moving. That is why they speed up then slow down coming toward me. It gives them more opportunity to be at this seal hole—me. Was one of those Great Whites finally going to get my adventurous ass? Maybe! This could be it!

Here I was in the midst of this new situation; those two big 'Phantoms' circling in sync. I was getting colder despite the wetsuit. No question, they were stalking only me. If they weren't, I sure as hell would never be convinced otherwise. Fear was in my moment—round and round. Seemed quite a while. The damned chills were going to move me out. When the hell was that other aluminum barred basket coming back down? At least the tuna had floated off followed by the mackerel swarm.

Ahh! The timing of the circle slowed down. Oooh! What a welcome happening. Round and round they had gone. It was almost like some crazy ass movie charade. Under the water in a totally new element makes it all so much more eerie. After their split aft, they appeared a bit later. Damn! They are still reappearing at the same spot—port midship and coming right by the no man's land. Then a bit longer again. Split. Blue gloom. Gone Right turning oval for Port Monster and left turn oval Starboard Guy. It is silent. Just like the same kaleidoscope pattern over and over. I could almost hear the whine of torpedo engines as they came by. That blip, blip of radar sonar ping in the submarine movies. Remember, they do eat seals and right now they assume I am one—worse, a scared seal and they damn well know it and sense it. A scared seal down in the rocks has to come up for air, sooner or later. That's how they understand it. Even worse, they are working in unison and talking, telepathing? Communicating? Meeting back again and swimming formation, over and over with each other in the same location as round and round they go. I thought about little Alien looking down from about ten feet above. She looked more like a seal than I did but had no damned ladder to worry about, let alone the dreaded no man's land crossing to get the hell out. They are thinking I have to come up for air sooner or later. They sure as hell are not departing, looking for greener pastures. Hunger will keep them in the same 'green' pasture. My vibes are letting them know I am vulnerable.

Ahh! They made a longer blue gloom run before re-synching. Then another just as long. "Fuck it." I was getting too damned cold. I blew bubbles and sucked in air. "Now or never." Just before that moment, I noticed the tuna sack starting to be hauled in from its position almost straight aft of Alien's cage. I shot up that ladder, switching, half spinning quickly in a turn facing aft for the top ladder rungs. No man's land briefly and now it's gone from my life—never to be revisited again. Blessed relief, but not yet total, which I was about to find out. At the top there was some guy in a snorkel only, no mouthpiece. Thinking he had some protection from the ladder. What the hell was such an idiot doing there? I brushed him aside to port as I broke surface. Had I brushed him to starboard he may never have made it. I didn't know it but aft the blue gloom monster was coming up on the sack. From what I could piece together that shark had to turn away from the sack and came toward us, torpedo style, with me being the closest to its course. I still did not see it and pushed myself back against the ship's edge; my waist weights just above the surface as I could now feel their weight more. Two pairs of strong arms grabbed me under my arm pits and hauled me roughly, yes very roughly, up and backward, dragging me, weights and all onto the ship's deck. My observant saviors! The first mate, handsome Shawn, and Kyle's close friend, Rob Brown. They had been watching that surfaced monster turn into a speeding torpedo—right at the ship. Ship's modus operandi: *Keep a close watch at all surface activity especially near the ship's fantail.* I barely saw the shark's broad back and huge fin before it disappeared under the ladder. Maybe it came to investigate the brief commotion or maybe he was after that 'trapped seal'? Who in the hell knows?

Later, in South Carolina where I religiously go at least once a year, to catch delicious stripers, I came across quite a few Megalodon teeth at a good wholesale price. Megalodon is a prehistoric monster shark that waited at river mouths flowing into the sea for food. Consequently its teeth are found by divers. South Carolina is a source as the ocean retreated and its teeth are found further inland in river bays. I made up quite a few shark teeth necklaces and sent them to my kids and the Nautilus Explorer.

6 BELIEFS

"The old Lakota was wise. He knew that a man's heart away from nature becomes hard."

Luther Standing Bear, Oglala Sioux

Mentors

Ben Black Elk

Bill Eagle Feather

Fools Crow at the Custer Battlefield National Monument, June 25, 1976, the Centennial of the famous battle on the Little Big Horn

I want to know about this person. What are his beliefs? However, one may go so far as to state, "If He (or She) doesn't believe my Way, what is there worthwhile to care, to know anything of value from that person?"

Fantasy

If you want to lead yourself to big trouble and begin to block your God-given mind from leading you to True Knowledge and spiritual, philosophical advancement, then start loading up on simple-minded fantasy. Fantasy is what you wish would happen or what you have been told by mere man and if it sounds or appears good, then you believe it and let it lead you without searching out its possibility through Creator's True Laws of Creation.

I am not one who delves into fantasy. I believe in a Creator yet will not allow myself to condemn those that don't. Pragmatically, they have a fifty percent chance of being right or wrong, no different than my mathematical chances. So why waste my time condemning them? I do believe this Maker, Higher Power, Supreme Being, Great Mystery, *Wakan Tanka* (*Wah Kahn Tahnkah*), Great Spirit, Ultimate Entity is obviously benevolent. We Sioux deeply respect *IT* but are not afraid of *IT*. Does it have a gender? We don't know so it is closer to real Truth (at least for us) for us to state, "We don't know for sure, hence we Traditionals use the term—*IT*."

And since it has allowed we humans a degree of 'humor,' I might add, that my atheistic or more casual religious friends may take the liberty to proclaim IT as Mumbo, Jumbo, Bwana, Sahib Lord Big Jim or possibly, from the feminists, Momma, Bahwana, Big LuLu Queen. Who in the hell knows for sure? I suppose a Wall Streeter may want to call it, 'CEO, Emperor, Fattest of All Fat Cats—No Limits.' "Oh Great, Holy Insatiable," begins their lead off prayer followed by, "Give us more." Mathematically, they also have a fifty percent chance of being correct.

Creationism

A Mystery

Mystery to us means we don't know for sure or it is beyond our capability to know for sure. This attitude gave early missionaries fits. Their attitude, which they tried desperately to brand upon us, was that they knew who Creator, Great Mystery, exactly was—including gender. Thanks to Martin Luther King's Civil Rights movement, the missionary-lobbied ban by Congress upon our innocent and fruitful Spirituality that served us for thousands of years was finally lifted and more than half my tribe, especially the young, have gone back to our old Way. I could be in error but of the thousands of people I meet, especially in the summer tourist season— numerous representatives of our country's rank and file and foreign tourists—the average person believes closely the same major precepts that I do. The constantly heard propaganda that 'America is a Christian country' may not be all that accurate. At least, it is quite apparent that the extreme right wing is far outnumbered by the much more open minded folks that travel and observe. Crazy Horse Mountain has more than a million visitors per annum, therefore I get to meet a broad perspective of interesting, traveling, observant humanity.

I have three major precepts regarding my personal concept of this Benevolent, providing Maker: It is All Truth, All Knowledge and is a Mystery. Nothing more, nothing less. I refuse to argue over It, and refuse to impose, threaten or condemn others who deem contrariwise.

Benevolent?

Creator allows all of us taste. Such a wonderful treat. We see in color wherein we could survive if only observing in black and white. When you cut yourself, it heals eventually. When you break or fracture a bone, it heals but also exhibits pain so that you will not attempt to use that part of yourself until it mends itself. Creator does not want you to use it and once mended the pain goes away. How thoughtful Ultimate is to us. When one is in extreme pain, Maker allows us to faint and avoid the pain. If you have ever had the need to utilize that mechanism within, you deeply appreciate it.

Hold forth a bouquet of flowers; several varieties. Besides their calming, pleasing beauty, you can even enjoy their varied fragrance. Who designed them? How can that designer, maker be a wrathful, unfair entity? I think not. There is a myriad of thoughtful gifts bestowed upon us that one will not find or read about in the white man's Bible or Koran. Probably because they are common sense observation and direct from Creator's Nature. Will Creator ask? "Why did you ignore so much knowledge that I placed before you and went to Man's words instead?"

Bad Spirits

Some folks believe there are all sorts of Bad Spirits floating around, ready to do harm. Maybe, maybe not. Being of a pragmatic sort, I think that Creator gave us all a brain to attempt to figure out the puzzles of life. I have deduced, as said earlier, in that area of wonderment that Creator is All Knowledge and hopefully, All Truth. IT certainly exhibits through Its creations that moral, truthful and honest Spirits would have to reflect their Maker. Wouldn't you think? What is it inside of us that wants to be appreciated? I can take a bit of correction, especially if I have an experienced teacher attempting to have me learn a certain puzzle of life, especially one that I may go on and make such study to benefit my occupation or a favored path. Constant condemnation, however, especially if uncalled for, this I frown upon.

If that is a correct supposition then it seems that IT will allow only Truthful existence in Its Spirit Realm, the Other World, so to speak. That is why the Indian in me rebels at the white man's Devil, Satan, Evil Spirit concepts. I simply refuse to buy into the white man's concept that Un-Truthful entities are allowed in what most will presume is an All-Truthful Creation (if, however, one believes in an afterlife). My fish-in-the-water example. You have to be in a certain modus to exist in that realm. If you are not so equipped, you don't exist—at least not in the realm where you are deeply satisfied.

My life is far more comfortable believing that only a real Truth-bearing and respecting Spirit is allowed to exist. Sort of like those fish swimming in the ocean. They have to have certain characteristics, design, and physiology to exist in that habitat. Well, for me, an All-Truthful entity would certainly reject Un-Truth, would it not? I know that the organized religion types will come up with all kinds of arguments refuting such a hypothesis and that is their right as long as we abide within a democracy. It is too difficult for them to interpret through Creator's Nature. Such is their mere man reliance and follow-the-crowd encouragement. Who makes the fish? Who makes the ocean? What teaching could possibly lie therein? I will state time and time again that I refute Man-composed teachings especially when they come up against and disregard certain Truths that I deduce from Nature—God's realm! Many teachings? This is my personal belief and it well satisfies me.

I do not believe in so-called evil spirits despite the obvious fact that humans love to harbor superstition. Superstition does not exist in Creator's created Nature. You cannot come up with a verifying example to contradict that statement.

Of course, these thoughts, however, never entered my childhood. The higher-ups, those with control over me, mainly due to my size then and of course dependency, those folks wouldn't allow such contrary thought to come out, or at least have it exhibited by a child. This child did as they said, as they taught and I went on to make Holy Communion, never allowing any deplorable accusations overheard to penetrate from an evil agnostic (or was it an atheist?) to another, laughingly joking that holy communion was a bit cannibalistic. I promptly told my mother and she assured me that I was on the right track, and that those two jokesters were surely bound for hellfire and eternal damnation. Of course, I believed her—heart and soul.

Life of Pi

I regret that I did not have the foresight to think as Pi did in the book, *The Life of Pi*. He is the main character shipwrecked onto a lifeboat that has an unusual set of passengers: Pi, a zebra, a hyena, a female baboon, a rat, some cockroaches and, *Lo!* a four hundred and fifty pound tiger. They are bound from India to Canada. In the beginning, Pi comes across as a fairly spiritual youth. He sees positive aspects in the three largest religions—Christian, Muslim and Hindu—(Or was one Buddhist?) and attends services or ceremonies in all three. He is quite content with all three. He does arrive at a conflicting situation when all three religions through a leader attempt to claim him and exclude or purge the other faiths from his interest.

I was fairly deeply indoctrinated as a child regarding Jesus, his Mom, Mary, and God, who I was taught was his Dad although I understood that St. Joseph was a sorta' dad as well. I pretty much believed everything the teachers were saying. The Protestants, they said, were errantly wrong to start their own churches and the Jews would be going to hell eventually if they failed to repent and join the True Church. Nothing was ever said about the Moslems. It was all a bit difficult to understand but what the hell, they were adults and I just accepted what they told me. I wasn't about to have a bunch of religious puzzles befuddle me. It would interfere with more important matters, namely playing games with the neighborhood kids and later hunting cottontail rabbits for food and the wily, tasty trout for which I would receive comforting praise from my parents.

Soul Saving Trout

I went on for quite some time, in the first third of my lifetime, with shrugged shoulders, regarding who JC really was and how a man could turn into a God. It never bothered me when I would hear the cannibal comments, for it was always in jest although quite sacrilegious from the devout communion takers. Whatever JC had said contrariwise to my few questions, then that is the way it was and it would be a mortal or a venial sin to think otherwise. We had all kinds of these two sins to attempt to step around to save ourselves from some real trouble in case we died early. I made sure that I caught a lot of trout just to guarantee that my family would not all go to hell if our house burned down on a Saturday and we were all killed before the absolving holy communion at Sunday mass. I always breathed easier after that sin-dissolving wafer of Jesus's body was passed out. The priests would drink his 'blood' just before we got the 'flesh'. Can't blame the agnostics/atheists, non-believers for coming up with their cannibal stuff. Catholic kids go to catechism instead of Bible study like the Protestants (who we are taught may all go to hell or at least do some time in Purgatory a sort of halfway house). Nowadays it seems the RCC is laying low on a lot of the rules they laid on us. Venial sin, Purgatory, Friday fish only, hooded nuns not much different than the Arab's burka, to name a few.

I prayed extra hard one Sunday for JC to forgive whoever ate the two cottontails and slab of deer ribs that were in the refrigerator Thursday night and disappeared by Friday eve when we gathered for a trout supper. Can you imagine a little kid trying to send up such a critical message to the Supreme Power over a couple of dead cottontails and a side of deer meat?

I suspected a couple brothers who had stopped by or my brother-in-law next door. He was a sort of Protestant and definitely not a Catholic, if he was anything. I knew they had different rules. I prayed that it was him and not one of my brothers or—God forbid!—my oldest sister who was always hovering over my folks, taking my Mom everywhere and buying ice cream cones for us last two at home. "Oh, Dear Jesus, do not let it be my sister, Mildred!" I sure as hell wanted the ice cream cones to keep coming! I did suspect that God or was it Jesus who was sorta' God, too, that he was supposed to be so kind that he would cut through some of the white man's bullshit and let some of us slide a bit, since we were poor Indians. I never worded it that way but it was what I at least thought. Then there was Mary who was the Mother of God and she had powers, too, mostly to get you out of hell, one way or the other. Later on, the Catholic High School kids thought she could win football games. I did ask Mary if she could make cute Gerie Monger like me but realized that I was too young for her and had crooked teeth. Oh yeah. I was an Indian. I should never forget that. Nothing the Mother of God could do about that.

I began doubting back in college, a Catholic one at that. It was subconscious doubting, not an all out, *I Quit* type. I had to go to confession and tell the priest what I did wrong. At least, I figured, I might get better grades if I did, and took communion when some teachers might be watching since most of us lived on campus. Actually, I doubt the monks there were concerned at all. Anyway, we were going to go out and chase girls one Saturday night but I detoured to the church with my two companions, Harry Dodge who was a sheer genius and got mostly A's and handsome John Nordlum who was so pretty he actually doubled for Jack Lord on *Hawaii 5-0* and on Tom Selleck's show. He got paid for it. Not only his looks but he was built like an agile weight lifter from hard work in his dad's International Falls creamery and also Northwoods logging. Similar to my high school friend Jim Aho but more so—I got more than one date from college girls that wanted to go out with him and would conveniently scare up a date for me.

World's First Hippie

Hippies had not been invented yet back then but Harry Dodge was maybe the first. I asked Harry why he never went to church or confession yet got such good grades and wasn't he worried that the priest teachers might come down on him? He said belligerently that he would sue them if they didn't give him his grades. I eventually stopped going to confession. One priest gave me a hard time. He always wanted me to come back to him only and said he knew who I was despite that little curtain which I thought kept you kind of halfway hidden.

Harry said, "Goddamnit, Chief, That old son of a bitch wants you back because you date a few women. He wants to live vicariously over what you tell him." I always admired Harry for his knowing some fancy words back then.

"Vicarious? What does that mean?"

"What you are doing Chief, or what he wants to imagine you doing, he is placing himself in your shoes."

"Well he's always insinuating that I am putting the make on every girl I go out with. He's always asking when, where and if I touch them and how do I feel about it."

Harry laughed and said, "Chief! You have to please the old son of a bitch. Next week John and I are going to prime you. We'll tell you what to say and add a bunch whether you did anything or not. You don't have to name any girls' names." Well that is exactly what we did and it was one of the best confessions I ever made. One of my last.

"Now my son, I am glad youse came back to me." The priest jumped right to the girls, the hell with all the petty venial stuff. "So you took a girl, did youse?" He had a German accent.

"Yes Father," I replied. "A couple."

"And… and, you parked your car, right?"

"Yes, Father."

"And youse touched her, right."

"Well, first, Father, I had to kiss her first."

"Ahh yes, der kiss." His accent came on harder.

"Kiss-es, Father," I corrected. "You have to kiss them a lot before you get to touch them."

"Yes, Yes. Jah, jah." He was pleased. "Yes, but you touch her—right?"

"Yes, Father.

"You puh—puh put youse hand on her leg, jah?"

"Correct Father."

"And youse move id up—jah!"

He was getting completely lost by now and muttering some German which I couldn't understand.

"Your hand, you move it up, jah?"

"Yes, Father, but also I am kissing her too!" Goddamn! Obviously he never knew a helluva lot about women. I was no expert but knew a helluva lot more than he would ever know.

"Ahhh, Yes, but soon…you are touching her."

"Well I wanted to touch her breasts first, Father."

"Jah, jah." But the way he said it weakly was sorta like he wanted me to get to the lower part.

"I did start touching her…down there, Father."

"Ahhh," he let out a gasp. "Unh, she gets wet, jah?"

I figured he must have got that knowledge from other confessions because I understood that they aren't supposed to do any of that stuff firsthand. You got to figure I am still a college kid and brought up to be scared as hell of priests, mainly through my mother and my mostly neutral Dad telling me to lay low around them and do as they say. Harry Dodge was making some strong inroads awakening me however. The Marines, Korea, and Japan R&Rs had their effect, too.

I figured my friends out in the car wanted me to get going so we could meet some girls so I knew I had to cut it short.

"Well, Father, she was all wet and gasping, sort of like losing her breath."

He jumped the gun. "Then youse…youse…was going to put id in her…jah," he almost yelled in excitement. Confessionals usually are pretty quiet, lots of whispering. "In her, right? *Achh Himmel*," he went jabbering in German. He was really excited and began rustling around in his box on the opposite side. My space was pretty small so I figured his was, too. The confessional creaked a bit as he moved about. After a lengthy silence amid the rustling, he jabbered, "Come up. Come up. What did you do?"

"Yah, Father. I started to unzip my pants but a car light came up."

"A car light? What?"

"Yeah, Father. It was a sheriff's deputy. He told us we couldn't be parked there."

Well, needless to say, my buddies roared with laughter and I began to take the Church not so seriously.

Overall, Harry Dodge and John Nordlum worked seeds well into me despite my little, protected life before then. When I began flying the Phantom F-4 I had a good Catholic wife, who was quite beautiful, and what appeared to be a promising career in the U.S. Marine Corps. I went to church to please my wife but started to realize their thing wasn't going to last for me. Had I continued in that vein, I could have or would have gone on to become an unhealthy, unexercised retired Marine Colonel at least, retired, right wing as can be and voting for the 1%. "Who in the hell were Chief Fools Crow or Chief Bill Eagle Feather?" Whatever they did, I wouldn't give a damn. Black Elk and *Black Elk Speaks*—"Never heard of 'em!" "Maybe some goddamn Indians that never had the sense to get the hell off the Reservation...add fin...ent um!" Such would possibly be my outlook regarding Spirituality. I do not want to place any blame upon my beloved Marine Corps but it would be the lack of knowledge that a couple of my older brothers would be echoing within me when they remarked about my desire to endure the Sun Dance. I also had a brother that stayed solidly behind me regarding that mind changing venture. Brother Russ would have supported me, too, had he not been killed ironworking.

"Chief Red Cloud, what the hell did he ever do?" I recall my second oldest brother stating—he who never had a spiritual thought.

Chief Fools Crow

Chief Fools Crow, Oglala, (1890? 1891?—1989) is no doubt, the most famous North American holy man of the latter twentieth century. He lived at Kyle on the Pine Ridge Reservation in a modest cabin. (As all of our Sioux Medicine men and women live modestly; quite possibly one of the major reasons why the Spirit World works so closely with them!) Too much wealth seeking, grandeur, and greed recklessly destroys their needed focus to attract helping Spirits. He, along with Chief Eagle Feather, Sichangu Holy Man, (1914-1979), was responsible for the return of the Sioux Sun Dance in modern times. Spirituality and historic author, Thomas Mails wrote an interesting and revealing biography on the venerable and spiritually powerful leader, *Fools Crow*. Russ Means, (AIM Activist) and I have our quotes on the back cover. These two mentors along with the book, *Black Elk Speaks* would severely alter the early religious teachings put into me as a youth. Eventually, I would certainly become more like Pi, the alpha male of the life boat adrift on the Indian Ocean. I would leave the resolute one-religion-only thinking. Spirituality and not religion would begin to blossom.

First Encounter

My first encounter with the supernatural came when I was a young Marine warrior about to go to war. After this first experience, held by Fools Crow, it should be obvious why I never returned to the White Man's religious indoctrination despite years of catechistic upbringing including a bachelor's degree from the Benedictine college, St. Johns University, (MN) where I was quite content and satisfied with the surroundings of the good Benedictine monks there who were mostly our capable teachers. I never returned to my confessional priest after the absurdity began to sink in. That monk was just another cog in a wheel and an exception. For the most part, it was a perfect school for my background, isolated way out in the North Woods of Minnesota with a pleasant lake, streams and surrounding wild life. It was a disciplined, no nonsense study environment, yet encircling Nature offered so much pleasant contentment for my bloodline.

Father Adelard, Dr. Bryde and Bill Stoltzman—Mentors

I dearly loved my time at St. Johns along with several teachers especially the head of the Biology Department, Father Adelard Thuente who was like a second father for me. Except for one Chippewa several grades lower, I was the only American Indian on campus. Father Adelard was also from the Dakotas and had been raised among my people. Maybe that was why he seemed to show me special attention, mainly by allowing me to do wildlife studies for extra credit since there was so much wildlife and fish around. Probably, I was a connection to his past, his boyhood, therefore his added consideration. Those were wondrous rewarding years there mainly because I had such a comforting and guiding mentor.

Yes, I have been blessed with many good and guiding mentors. Like Father John Bryde, S.J., later Dr. Bryde. I am sure Father Adelard has no regrets toward me now for the spiritual course I have chosen. I never would have been a writer were it not for the historical information I gleaned from Dr. Bryde, a Sioux linguist who spoke our language well. See *Crazy Horse and Chief Red Cloud—Warrior Chiefs*, which is based primarily on Fr. Bryde's numerous interviews in Lakota with the old time warriors who were still alive when he was a Sioux reservation missionary for over a decade. He married a former nun and moved to the University of South Dakota and became Dr. Bryde. As a part-time University employed pilot while I was in law school, I flew 'Doc' to his many lectures off campus which allowed me a thorough education in my tribe's history listening repeatedly to his wealth of rich knowledge. Several years after my graduation he called me up after he had read my *Mother Earth Spirituality* which is quite close now to its 50th reprinting out of Harper/Collins. He said he had cancer and wasn't going to be able to finish his historical book and had chosen me over many writers wanting his notes. Unable to complete the historical book himself he gave me his notes to complete the endeavor. It is my main seller in my home state, South Dakota.

'Doc' Bryde was able to capture accurately our Sioux history much more effectively than most all the other writers whom the old warriors could not and many, purposely would not talk to- Father Bryde, they readily came to tell him first hand. Of about 400 warriors he interviewed in the '40s, everyone stated that the Custer—Little Big Horn Battle lasted "As long as it takes a man to eat a meal." (30 minutes approximately.) The Big Horn Battle Association now declares the same in their daily summer lectures to the many visitors finally putting to rest the raft of fantasy writers who errantly declare an all-day battle complete with "a shower of arrows," flanking movements and all sorts of John Wayne battle strategy. (One shot and five Sioux fall off their horses!) Incidentally, the Sioux and Cheyenne allies had deadly effective Winchesters, 15 shot Repeaters and numerous Sharps 45.70s.

I appear hard regarding the Church but the experiences my people have suffered from missionaries and their overzealous boarding schools wherein my older brothers and sisters were confined for nine long months each school year are adequate evidence. I must add one other priest, however, that has strongly influenced me. Father Bill Stoltzman, now a Diocesan priest in Shakopee, Minnesota. He was also a former Jesuit. His writings appear in several of my other books. One chapter is almost totally his work. Father Bill tells of his positive experiences in the sweat lodge, vision questing and spirit communication. It is all in his book: *The Pipe and Christ.* Read it, especially if you are a bit too spooked to leave Jesus thoughts altogether. My Mom played both ends against the middle, so to speak, and never was in much of a dither about it. I asked Father Bill if he was going to get in trouble with his Church for writing so vividly and honestly of his positive experiences. He brushed off my worry with a laugh. "I am too old and they need me! I'm building a Church for them." What he had seen and experienced with his own eyes (from Creator) he could not and would not alter just to please possible church doctrine. "Truth is Truth and cannot be altered." Father Bill's courage is certainly a shining example of God's Pure Truth.

Early Fools Crow

Like Captain Jonathan Carver, a very early writer/explorer (1700s) who tells about the same ceremony you are about to experience, I too was a Captain, a Marine pilot home on leave. My mother said to me, "Fools Crow is looking for you." Chief Fools Crow was the chief holy man from my reservation and intercessor or leader for our annual Sun Dance which was barely starting to come back. "He said, he wants you to come down to his cabin. He wants to hold a ceremony for you...for that Vietnam you are going to." My mother had five of my brothers go off to war earlier, mostly World War Two. She simply accepted it as a regular fact that all of her sons would be involved in combat, one way or another. She was a strong Catholic and spent much of her time helping at the off-reservation Jesuit mission in Rapid City, my hometown. I saw more of my mother during my high school years at the mission structure after it was built than at home. It was a combination gymnasium and church besides a large facility for the donated rummage sale, hand-me-down clothes my mother spent most of her time sorting and arranging for distribution to the local Indians and some poor white people. I spent many evening hours there and on weekends playing basketball. To this day I have a healthy set of legs for my age. My father did most of the cooking at our home. His wife was happy at the mission and consequently he never complained about her absence. He was a basically happy and contented parent, albeit in his advancing years as a parent yet of a high school youth, his last—me.

My only connection to Chief Fools Crow was that I was a powwow dancer and would dance as a social dancer in the evening time. The Sioux Sun Dance would be held at the same dance grounds in the early mornings when most of the social dancers were still fast asleep in their tents, camped along with those few families who were supporting their relatives in the Sun Dance. Chief Fools Crow enjoyed the powwow social dancing and was always a present figure looking on. My old step-grandmother was there at those early sun dances. You are not supposed to say step-grandmother in my language. A so called step-grandmother is your grandmother. Your step-mom—if you have one—is your mom. That is just the way it is. Your half-brother is your brother. *Mitakuye Oyasin.* It means we are all related. That also is the way it is. There are many differences in our culture and dominant society culture and it will not hurt much if some are pointed out.

In those days there was little interest in the return of the Sun Dance, our primary symbol for the return of our Way. There would be no return if the governmental authorities and the colluding, meddling, proselytizing missionaries had their way. By now they had converted the majority of the reservation—so they thought. They were confident they had destroyed the primary spiritual fires. Too confident, they would later discover.

At the dance grounds, a sweat lodge for the small numbers of sun dancers would be held in the early morning. When I first saw one, my grandmother had to explain to me what it was and what took place inside. Such was the typical ignorance of the younger Indians of my time due to the very effective cultural blotting out enforced by the reservation missionaries. In those days the advocates for the Sun Dance were facing strong resistance from many tribal members who had been converted to the white man's religion. The strongest resistance came from the missionaries themselves, primarily, on my reservation. Certain Jesuit priests from that order came to convert us in the latter part of the nineteenth century. Their successors were most adamant in their opposition to the Sioux who simply wanted to keep the old way of belief. Such pomposity is the *Wah shi chu*—the White Man. Not only does he want to take your land; he even has to take your own very workable religion/spirituality away from you. To draw a crowd, Chief Fools Crow combined the two events, powwow dancing and the Sun Dance. With the heavy resurgence nowadays of the ceremonies return, this procedure would be unheard of but those were different times and Chief Fools Crow knew what he was doing. Know-it-all detractors who have ignorantly criticized him will pay dearly in the Spirit World, is my biased opinion.

Federal Ban of Indian Beliefs (Missionary Instigated)

Fools Crow's Cabin

I picture Fools Crow waiting at the horse gate when we arrived for the *yuwipi* ('they tie him up' or, 'to be bound') spirit calling which the holy man would conduct. My traditional-leaning grandmother's last request was that I attend a *yuwipi* ceremony before leaving for war. In the centuries-old calling, Fools Crow would beseech the spirit people for protection. My mother had been with us that clear summer night as we drove from Rapid to the holy man's reservation home. She was considered quite a church goer and volunteer at the local mission, but my grandmother's prediction that I wouldn't come back if I failed to attend a *yuwipi* was enough to dispel the black magic aura drummed into my mother by the missionaries. For my benefit, she could speak excellent Lakota as did my father. They spoke Lakota often in our home. She would interpret the forthcoming *Yuwipi* ceremony for me. I wished my father and grandmother were alive to attend with us. My father kept his distance from the missionaries yet advised me to follow my mother's way. "Those priests can make too much trouble for you. Don't be following what I believe," was his practical summation. "It's a white man's world and you have to be part of it if you want less trouble." I have to add, once I grumbled about Mom's absence while eating a supper meal cooked by him. "What's the matter? You don't like my cooking?" he growled back. I replied that his cooking was fine with me. "Your mother," he replied after some long minutes of silent eating, "she is doing what she likes to do. Let her be." Then he added, "As long as you're getting something to eat. Don't complain." I seem to have followed his advice down through the years and most generally eat what is put in front of me with no complaints.

The tall, trim holy man held us for a few moments with that mysterious look, the penetrating stare of a hawk or an eagle. Fools Crow was like a Badlands hawk or an eagle—regal, keen, and observant—alone and aloof within his own vast spaciousness, oblivious to the encroaching *Wahshichu* (white man) world.

The straight-postured man spoke from the gate as we got out of the car, "What took you so long? You should have been here earlier."

On the way down to the reservation, my sister drove. She stopped in at a supermarket to purchase a considerable amount of groceries for Chief Fools Crow as is the custom of our people when you go to visit a medicine person. You do not take them pretty rocks with ribbons attached as some think they have to nowadays. As I recall, we did not take them a can of pipe tobacco. My mother may have purchased a carton of Camels cigarettes, as that is what she smoked, and gave them to Fools Crow as he occasionally lit up a cigarette, but the intention of 'giving tobacco' as is the custom nowadays, was not the intention of my mother or sister. The large amount of groceries was much more of a custom back then. To this day I wish people would dispel with giving me tobacco when they first come to visit as I am no medicine man and do not intend to be one. I am a writer and a veteran. Besides, I dislike the taste of tobacco left in my mouth when I rarely smoke a pipe and have seen too many close friends die from it, mostly emphysema, a slow, tortuous death.

We're sorry, Grandpa," my sister Mildred answered. "We stopped to get groceries." *Grandpa* is a common and respectful form of address for Sioux holy men.

Chief Fools Crow had no telephone, so how did he know we were coming to see him? This would be my first taste of the Lakota supernatural, as the holy man led us into his mud-chinked cabin. Kate Fools Crow stood by the wood-burning stove and welcomed us with her warm smile. Speaking in the rich Sioux language, we visited and laughed together as the blue-enameled coffee pot was filled, meat was cut and put into boiling water, dried *woshapi* (berry cakes), were set in a pan of water and fry bread preparations were made. The laughter flowed. My sister, Mildred, my mother, Sonny Larive and his grandparents, and Fools Crow's son-in-law, Amos Lone Hill, exchanged conversation in Lakota Sioux. Blacktop, a bashful eight-year-old, sat fiddling with the damper on the pot-bellied stove near the west wall.

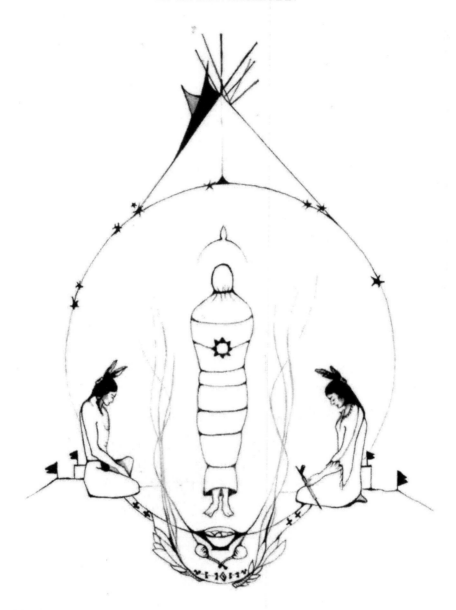

Yuwipi spirit calling ceremony

Spirit Calling

When Fools Crow went to the closet for his medicine bundle, it was a signal for the women to push back the furniture and draw the curtains. Sonny helped prepare for the tying ritual that preceded the *yuwipi*, while Mildred unrolled a long string of tiny cloth tobacco offerings. The four directions were represented by red, yellow, black and white flags, which were placed in earth-filled bowls to form a square before an earthen altar in the middle of the cabin. Mildred wrapped a string of tobacco offerings around the bowls, marking the limits of the spirit area. Sage was passed to all participants, who placed some in their hair and over one ear.

The holy man entered the square made by the string of tobacco offerings to place two leather rattles on the floor before raising his peace pipe to offer an opening prayer. Afterwards, he stood ready to be bound. Sonny tied his arms and hands behind his back with bailing twine before draping a blanket over the Oglala's head. An eagle feather hung from the top of the blanket that covered the holy man down to his moccasin tops.

Next, Sonny wrapped Fools Crow with a rawhide rope, beginning with a noose around his neck and then six more times around his body, down to his ankles. Each wrap represented the seven sacred ceremonies or possibly the Six Powers and, of course, the Ultimate Power. While the holy man was lowered, face down to the floor, Mildred sat at the place of honor with the peace pipe, behind the dirt altar with her back against the stove. The kerosene lamp was extinguished.

Amos tapped a drum and sang a centuries-old call to the ancestors of the Sioux, the spirit beings. They came quickly from the west, rattling the stovepipe and swishing the rattles through the room, as if they had been close by, waiting for the call. My mother commanded me to start praying. Would I return from the war? Would I be a prisoner? We knew the spirits would tell if we prayed humbly. If I promised to live for the people, they would try to protect me, is what I learned later but at the time I was suppressed by the white man's false stereotypes. Startling, tiny blue lights entered through the stove door behind Mildred while I prayed. They flickered and danced with the heartbeat of the drum, then raised to the ceiling, circled the participants and, then, as the song ended, disappeared back through the stove door behind the pipe holder. I sat down in awe at what I had seen. The buckskin rattles that had accompanied Amos Lone Hill's song, now fell to the floor, silent.

The *Wotai* (woe tye) Stone

A stranger's gruff voice came in and began to speak to Fools Crow. "*Changu Taunk ahtah,*" I heard my sister whisper to my mother. I knew enough Sioux from my parents who constantly spoke it to know she said 'Big Road'. The area where Fools Crow was bound emitted a dim haze. The spirit of Big Road, Fools Crow's spirit helper, carried on in conversation with the medicine man. I was experiencing—what I called it then—my first ghost.

Fools Crow's muffled voice spoke out in the darkness, telling us how a stone had fallen to strike the sacred tree at the summer Sun Dance while an airplane flew high overhead. The stone bore the image of an eagle within its grain. Later he had a vision. "I saw the airplane land in a far-off place, and a warrior walked away from it without looking back. He walked toward the sacred tree and stood there with a boy. The stone was brought to the Sun Dance lodge. I took the stone from Eagle Feather and put it in my medicine bundle. It remained in the bundle only a short while and then it was gone." The group waited while the holy man took several breaths.

"The stone has returned and is now among us here. Eagle Boy, you must pray hard so it will remain." (My Indian name then would later be changed.)

I answered quickly, blurting out, "Grandfather, ask the stone to stay with us. Tell the spirit people I offer myself for the Sun Dance. I will live for the people and the power of the hoop." A shrill tremolo pierced the darkness, followed by a chorus of "*Hau.*" The cry came from the women to honor a warrior who would go off to battle. It would be repeated when the warrior returned, or at his grave.

Later on, I would alter that pledge, "I would live for the Way!"

Prediction

Then Fools Crow spoke with uncharacteristic volume and excitement. "The eagle on the stone is for a warrior who will fly with the winged. Eagle Boy, you shall wear this stone as your *wotai*. When you are across the ocean, you shall carry it. As long as you wear it faithfully, the bullets shall bounce from your airplane. You shall see the enemy many times. You shall not fear battle and shall laugh at danger."

After a long pause, he spoke more cautiously. "There is no guarantee, however, that you shall return and become a new warrior to stand beneath the Sun Dance tree with Blacktop, my grandson."

Fools Crow paused with a cough, weighing what he would reveal. The rattles buzzed. Later I would learn that the old man had envisioned that I would see the enemy one hundred times and would vision quest before my Sun Dance…if I returned. The small blue lights flourished one last time. Big Road made his exit. The rattles clashed, each shaking a different rhythm, their discord breaking the stillness.

A concluding song, the untying song was sung. When the lamp was lit, Fools Crow was sitting up untied. His blanket was neatly draped over the stove. The tying rope was wrapped in a tight ball. No one, including Fools Crow had moved during the untying song. The *wotai* stone, oval and not much larger than a fifty cent piece and twice as thick, waited on the cabin floor and was bound in a buckskin pouch. After the pouch was opened it revealed the small stone; an eagle was clearly imaged in its grain. If you ever come to the Black Hills of South Dakota, Dear Reader, go down to a stream and find your own *wotai* stone. The Black Hills streams have polished these small stones for eons and they often bear images of animals or earthly scenes.

Spiritual Connection. Spiritual Communication.

Where, how does Chief Fools Crow have such unusual, inordinate, awesome connection (power) to draw in 'Spirits'—former ethical, selfless, moral entities of obvious predictive and healing power? Quite simple, as I mentioned earlier! Unlike organized religion's leaders, Chief Fools Crow is far more focused and much less distracted. Greed, control and debilitating ego are quite void within his constitution. The guiding spirits would not work with him otherwise.

You must always remember that I am the one on the other end of this ceremony. Those SAM missiles fired in Vietnam, miraculously did not get me. I lived! I cannot dilute this happening and the ceremony leading up to it just to please organized religion with all of its thin-skinned followers and short comings. Oh well! We shall all meet in the Spirit World, in time. We can sort it all out then.

A later chapter will authenticate Fools Crow's/Big Road's predictions.

Before I left for Vietnam, I went down to view the Sun Dance that the two holy men had revived a decade before. There was some increase in the amount of the traditional faithful attending but nothing like I would see in a few short years. The young were noticeably absent. The dancers had pierced on the third day. I had just missed their participation. My sister was there and cried that Father Steinmetz had lobbied the Tribal Council with his following and insisted upon saying Mass beneath the Sun Dance Tree the following morning—Sunday—the Lord's Day, according to the Jesuit. The tribal chairman resisted his plan but was outvoted by certain council members. Hence Chief Fools Crow and Eagle Feather had to give in and curtail the Annual Thanksgiving from four days to three. I slept at my sister's travel trailer which was parked not far from the Sun Dance arena to take electricity from a light pole Bureau of Indian affairs electricians had provided. I got up in time to view Paul Steinmetz say his dictatorial Mass, replacing the Sun Dance. I looked on in my Marine captain's uniform and said to myself as he held up his 'holy' Eucharist, smirking so triumphantly: "You son of a bitch, I will stop your ass when I come back from 'Nam!"

7 FIVE MISSIONS – BACK TO BACK

Pre-Combat

After college graduation I was married and in flight school. A few students in your class get killed going through flight school. When that happens, a few more will drop out, mainly because of the urging from their wives. Some of these 'Drop-outs' would go into flying positions like Radar Intercept Officers (RIOs) wherein they would no longer be pilots yet would be airborne usually. Somehow, that position would be more appeasing to many of the wives or soon to be wife—girlfriends. I never considered dropping out, ever. To me, Flight School was nothing more than a thrilling 'Play-House.' The more acrobatics I could do, the happier I was.

I was assigned into a helicopter squadron after graduation and had a wondrous time. I flew a Sikorsky H-34. It had one engine and could carry 8 combat equipped Marines. We did many maneuvers with them and went aboard air craft carriers along with the Marine battle troops. To me, it was again, a lot of fun, plus I was getting paid to do it. We went to the Caribbean numerous times and when ashore we would do more maneuvers with the ground forces. We would also pick up 'Externals', smaller size jeeps and artillery and various supplies and deliver them inland and bring them back to the carriers and other transports to precisely place them: All that activity and I just don't remember any fatal accidents. Helicopters are fairly safe aircraft in peacetime but not so when real combat happens as Vietnam well proved. Many of my Caribbean comrades were killed or wounded in Nam'. Most all were shot down a time or two.

I did have a couple close calls in Helicopters. One failed engine at 1000 feet was not that dangerous really. I lost an engine; it just quit chugging after take-off when I leveled off at cruise power as I pulled the mixture back to normal cruise speed. The engine lost power by going to idle; not enough power to keep on flying. It would be like you had reached 60 mph on the highway and suddenly your motor went to idle only, despite how much you pushed on the gas pedal. I had taken off in broad daylight from a North Carolina landing strip and reached 1000 feet. At that level on a reciprocating, high Octane gasoline burning aircraft engine (ours was about 1250 horse power) the pilot adjusts the aircraft to burn less fuel so it can stay up longer. Our Standard Operating Procedure manual by the Sikorsky helicopter company tells you to climb to 1,000 feet, weather permitting and at that level do look out for a convenient spot below to land in case your controls adjustment goes haywire, which is exactly what happened. If you have nothing but trees below you then you should refrain from mixture adjustment and fly on to where a safe emergency landing spot can be found or do a quick turn back toward the field you left from and pull your mixture back. I had quite a few corn fields beneath me when I made my adjustment.

I immediately nosed the helicopter over and made a dive for a corn field. One's altitude allows enough lift from the rotating rotors as you sail downward. The air passing over your rotor blades allows significant lift to maintain your controls. As the ground rushes up you are able to pull back on your control stick and the aircraft will briefly rise just above the ground. Your control stick in a helicopter is called a cyclic and what controls the speed of the rotor blades is called the collective. When the engine is running properly you increase the speed of blade rotation much like a motorcyclist increases his speed by rotating his throttle handle. On a Sikorsky the method is similar. Twisting or rotating the throttle on the collective speeds up the blade. The cyclic gives you directional ability. Just as the flare is briefly executed and the chopper starts to drop earthward you pull up on the collective so that the rotor blades will alter their pitch and you have a brief amount of extra lift by the now more tilted rotor blades to the airstream, similar to flaps on an airplane for landing and takeoff. The blades bite into the air and you can gently settle the machine onto the ground providing you have not flared too high or too flat. We practiced auto-rotation considerably and got fairly good at it.

Another incident was quite a bit more dangerous. It was a foggy night and I was sent out to pick up a load of about 8 reconnaissance Marines at a place called Bogue Field near Jacksonville, North Carolina. On the way back as I climbed out, my automatic stabilization equipment failed on me and the helicopter became a bit stiffer to fly but remained flyable. It would be as if your power steering went out on your car. You could still continue on to your destination if you had too. Safety rules however prohibit you from going up into the fog and flying on instruments. I picked out the highway returning to Jacksonville and at a certain junction I planned to turn toward my base called New River field. The fog was at around 1,000 feet and lowering, pushing me down several hundred feet to stay out of it. As I closed on Jacksonville the fog kept lowering and another helicopter closed in on me from the opposite direction and I ducked underneath it by diving toward my right. I did almost a full circle trying to avoid it and banged into the ground and bounced several times going forward. A big lit billboard was coming forward and I flared the machine to barely stop in front of it, my whirling blades almost touching it. It read, Dawson's Motel. I settled the helicopter down and the crew chief from the cargo compartment called me over his microphone after he jumped out to inspect the damage. "Lieutenant, nothing is broke except the tail wheel locking pin." It is about a 1/4th to 3/8th inch thick. "You can shut her down if you want." I unstrapped and walked into Dawson's Motel and scared the hell out of them as I had left my helmet on and in my flight suit they briefly thought I had stepped off a flying saucer. I called the squadron, and they told me to stay where I was at. They came to retrieve us and posted a guard on the helicopter for the night and flew it out the next morning. I was not cited for pilot error on either of the two incidents.

How did a former corporal in Korea become a Marine Jet Pilot, and a Phantom F-4 Driver, the premier fighter/attack bomber of its time?

After I came back from Korea as a Corporal, I was only 19 years old when I started college at South Dakota State along with my friend Stan Curtis. I wound up graduating from St. Johns University in the North woods of Minnesota, a good no-nonsense, you-study-or-they-kick-you-out Benedictine all men school. No student car was allowed on campus unless you were a second semester Junior with a 'B' average, a senior or a Military Veteran.

During my senior year, a Marine Officers Recruiter came to the campus and let me know after a thorough physical that I was qualified to try for flight school. The Vietnam War had not yet started and I would first have to pass Officers Candidate School which lasted 3 months. 50% never made it through; 98 % were college graduates. Having a durable set of legs and being able to conquer the obstacle course was more important than straight 'A's in college. If you never used your legs mainly along with body coordination usually gained from one form of sports or the other you would not receive a Marine second lieutenant's commission. A degree of common sense was also required.

After 50% were weeded out, another 50% would not make it through flight school which lasted; pre-Vietnam era, 18 months before you won your gold aviator wings. To get jets out of flight school, the odds were even higher. Over half of the Marine Corps aviators would go through helicopter training. I was one of those.

I actually enjoyed helicopters. The Jet drivers had more of a prima donna attitude than the more down to earth 'chopper' drivers. I had some wonderful Caribbean cruises with a medium helicopter squadron. To this day, I communicate with them more than I do with my fellow F-4 pilots even though my combat flying was in F-4 Phantoms.

I garnered 2,000 hours flying a H-34 Sikorsky helicopter flying Marine troops and their equipment onto islands in the Caribbean mostly off of helicopter carriers. It was fun duty and during time off and as mentioned before, I managed to get into some enjoyable snorkeling and deep sea fishing. I was involved in the Haiti Crisis, the Cuban crisis and the Panama crisis; none of which involved much excitement. My recall of the Cuban Crisis was a boring following of a Russian freighter alleged to be carrying some missiles bound for Cuba. While in Panama, I received orders to the 'Real Marines,' an Infantry assignment lasting a year. This is commonly termed non-endearingly by pilots and Air Wing personnel as; 'Your Grunt tour.' 90 some percent of the Marine Pilots hate such an assignment. Number One: You cannot expect to get much flying time into your log book. You will be fortunate to fly your required minimum of four hours per month. I was fortunate in that I was based in a battalion and later on regimental staff at Camp LeJeune, North Carolina which is located close to the Marine Air Station where my former helicopter squadron was based at, New River, North Carolina. The full Air Wing aviator colonel at Camp Lejeune was the overall commanding officer for our combined infantry/helicopter detachment on the Cuban Crisis tour and based on our aircraft carrier. Colonel Casey was his name and I was assigned to fly him during several offloading exercises. He was a jet pilot and didn't fly our type of machines. I did a good job for him as an embarkation officer and better yet for me he wanted to learn how to become qualified in an H-34 helicopter while at LeJeune. I got more than my required four hours a month.

When my tour was up I expected to be sent back to helicopters. The 'Nam' war was starting to heat up and the Corps was taking jet drivers to fill their helo pilot needs besides, of course, training more prospective helicopter pilots in flight school. I put down, however, on my 'Duty Station' request: Jets, Jets and Jets—for the three choices. A board of three Bird Colonels would decide my fate and several other ALOs (Air Liaison Officers) as we were termed. Colonel Casey sat on that board. "Chief, you did a good job over here." He addressed me. "We are going to make an example of you." I had no idea what he meant and never dreamed what next would take place and bring such a change in my life. "Chief,..you were one of the few who never cried or whined about your year's infantry tour. You did your job with enthusiasm and stayed up night and day on exercises with the rest of us." I still had no idea and figured this all was just a pleasant 'well done farewell' and I would be heading back to 'choppers' possibly the new gunships at the most. "You put down Jets and we are going to send you to Cherry Point (Fighter/Attack Jets Air Station)." I almost fainted.

In the Corps, certain 'Full Colonels' have their eye on certain subordinates, usually senior First Lieutenants or new Captains that have made regular officer. A Regular Officer is one that generally will make his career in the Corps.

A black man was working for the Federal Overhaul and Repair Aviation Department, that may not be the exact name but it explains it. The facility was located at one end of Cherry Point Marine Corps Air Station. They were overhauling/re-inspecting Air Force, Navy and Marine Phantom F-4s that had acquired considerable hours. He was a simple laborer spraying down an Air Force Phantom as I drove by at a distance. An hour later I returned and the F-4 was shiny aluminum and no markings. My boss, a Lt. Colonel was in charge of a much smaller scale maintenance squadron that had only two obsolete TIA Lockheed two-seater, single engine training jets that were mostly used by non-squadron pilots to get their required monthly flight time. Since I was a former helicopter pilot those two were the only aircraft on the base that I was qualified to fly. I was picking up more than the usual amount of time in them to get my proficiency enough so to go on into a regular squadron flying A-4 Douglas Skyhawks, A-6 Intruders (two pilot) or the F-4 Phantom (single pilot, Radar Operator non-pilot in back seat.) It would be most likely since I had such few hours in jets (not quite a hundred hours) that I would eventually wind up in an Intruder squadron.

I was the training officer for H&MS (Headquarters and Maintenance Squadron), and Lt. Colonel Guy M. Cloud was my boss. He claimed to me, at our first meeting, my reporting in, that he was part Cherokee so we should have some things in common. He had a reputation for being a real stickler. Basically a training officer primarily is to make sure everyone is able to perform the Marine Corps wide Physical Readiness Test and those that shirk exercise start performing by having a readiness chart kept on them. If no improvement occurs one can be told to leave the Corps. I was probably a good pick because I could outrun everyone in the squadron distance-wise except one enlisted man but such a gift does not endear a Training Officer to everyone, especially senior officers. Cloud made me bear down hard on all shirkers, which I had to do. I also could drill troops and could handle a sword in parades which few pilots care to know or do. The year's tour with the infantry also gave me the opportunity to drill or march troops in formation. As an ex-enlisted man, I well knew close order drill. As every morning in engineers in Korea, we would form up after breakfast and march down to our working area. It was just a common occasion. When the Seargent was away, as a Corporal, I'd always volunteer to march the troops so it became 'old hat.' I would never have dreamed that such an example would lead me to becoming assigned to a mighty F-4 Phantom cockpit. That and a black laborer of all people.

Yes! All this gets back to the black man that has cleaned up the Air Force Phantom. My boss was away and I wanted to clean up our maintenance hangar for his return. Old paint of various colors hideously decorated its interior. I asked the black man what kind of chemical he was using to so effectively clean off all the paint on the Air Force F-4. He pointed to a 5 gallon can with a closed pour lid and told me to wear rubber gloves if I brushed it on old paint. "It doan take long to peel, Suh." I asked where I could purchase two cans. "No Suh. You a Mah-rine Off-Sir, Suh, yuh doan pay." He picked up a full can and carried it to my Kharmann Ghia convertible. The second can tilted my snappy convertible on the passenger side. "By the way," I began before driving away. "What do you call this paint peeler?" He put his head down apologetically and spoke to the ground in almost a whisper. "Cap'n suh." He looked around as if someone might hear him. "Suh. We calls it…." Then quickly he retorted. "DFA, Suh." "DFA?" I remarked with a puzzled query. "Yes Suh. DFA. It Doan Fk Ah roun!" I was no doubt the first, last and only Marine Officer the man would ever talk to as he saluted me when I drove away. Needless to say, the maintenance hangar was spotless when my demanding boss returned. That black laborer helped me get into Phantoms and on into some fantastic combat episodes.

Col. Cloud liked how I performed his assignments and of course a few which I came up with on my own. When he was given command of an F-4 Training Squadron he called me into his office and told me that I was going to be his Training Officer for his new Squadron. I almost fainted again. "Chief, how many hours you got in those T1A's?" "About a hundred, Sir." "Well, I want you in Phantoms and will get you in VMT. (This was the Marine East Coast jet re-fresher squadron that used obsolete-for-combat F-9 Grumman, two-seater single engine, no afterburner jets of Korean War combat vintage.) I garnered about 200 hours in it under very capable and envious instructors before receiving orders to Col. Cloud's F-4s. "Chief, we can fly circles around you and would give our left nut to get into an F-4 squadron but Cloud is your Rabbi." Rabbi, means a higher officer sees promise in you and Guy M. Cloud was about to receive his full Colonel rank.

F-9 Jets

After I started in the F-9, I was shooting touch and goes for more proficiency in landing. I came in, touched down and bang went a tire. The F-9 Grumman Cougar, former Korean War vintage fighter lurched toward the runway edge but I had enough speed to add power and climb back into the air. The fire truck personnel were happy below because they had something to do now. They foamed the approach end of the runway and I came in for a final landing keeping the blown wheel off as long as possible. Bang went the other tire. I again added power and now had two blown tires. I went out toward the ocean and circled around burning off fuel. The Fire Department were all waiting with their foam and had a MOREST set up for me. Those are cables stretched across the runway. I came in with my tail hook down and caught a cable which stopped me rather quickly. It wasn't all that dangerous after all.

Once the F-9 syllabus was finished, I checked in on a Monday and Col. Cloud had me solo that big beautiful F-4 Phantom beast, twin afterburners and all on the following Friday—one of the biggest thrills and accomplishments of my life. You ride in the rear seat in the morning as your check pilot takes you up showing you everything it can do including acrobatics, stalls, and slow flight with your landing gear and flaps down. You have been living in that front cockpit all week and knew it by heart. In the air it is simply a bigger truck than the F-9. It really wasn't all that difficult to solo, just remember to get it going at 100% on take-off before you light those two monstrous afterburners. Boom you get a big kick and are now on the forward end of the rocket making sure you stay there and soon you are hitting 200 to 220 knots. That's a bit more than 200 mph and the control stick is already back in your gut and stays there until you decide to lower your climb angle, keep it there without wing tanks and it will go straight up. Lift off, raise your gear and flaps; not all that much to remember. When you land, immediately pull your drag chute. Yeah…and shut the Burners off after takeoff otherwise you will be breaking the speed of sound quite soon -raising hell for the folks down below if you are at low altitude.

I was almost detoured from going to Vietnam however. It was 1966 and the Vietnam War was starting to heat up. I had been down in the Caribbean at Roosevelt Roads Naval Air Station, Puerto Rico practicing shooting Sparrow Missiles at Drone aircraft out over the ocean. After a training mission at Cherry Point Marine Air Station, North Carolina I was called into my squadron commander's office and was told that a Congressman had called for me. "Chief! What the hell are you doin' contacting a Congressman?" My 'Skipper' (Squadron Commander) growled. I returned the call with my boss listening in. It was Ben Reifel who was a long time South Dakota Congressman. He said that he wanted me to come to Washington, DC for a visit. Arrangements were made and I flew a Phantom into Andrews, AFB. The Congressman who was part Sioux Indian proudly showed me off to a number of his peers including soon to be President Gerald Ford. He told me that he wanted me to go to law school and would appoint me to the upcoming class of 1966. It would prove to be the biggest mistake of my life. My wife who was a farmer's daughter from Madison, South Dakota was elated to get out of the Marine Corps and an obvious Vietnam combat tour for me. Most wives were not too ecstatic about their spouses going off to a combat tour.

If you ever saw the movie, Private Ryan, you will remember Matt Damon's reluctance to leave the battlefield because of the death of his brothers. He now considered his comrades as his brothers and in a time of deep need. I felt that as a trained F-4 pilot I could not run out and on into law school. I had to have that combat tour first. I have to admit that the adventure it promised was too much to turn down. The Congressman was disappointed but he settled for my attending law school in the Class of 1967. To me, the Phantom was a 'Dream 'Bird' to fly...and to be so fortunate to take such a machine on into actual combat—what more could a man ask for? This probably sounds strange to many but if one has Sioux/Lakota blood it should not be considered unusual. 'What more could a Lakota Warrior ask for?' Maybe this might be a bit more understandable. As a little boy, my hero was my oldest Marine brother who was at Tarawa, Saipan, Tinian and the Gilberts and probably some others. 20,000 of his division went out into the Pacific and only 5,000 came back that were not somehow wounded or KIA. He was also proud of me.

In Phantoms it was a well-known fact that they were the primary combat expectant bird utilized. No other aircraft was as versatile and effective especially for Close Air Support. In Vietnam, CAS meant you were going to be exposed to enemy fire practically every mission. It had its safeguards and advantages over other aircraft however, but no guarantees. It could come into direct contact with the enemy on a bombing mission much faster than the other models. It could also leave much faster after your ordnance was dropped. It was the only CAS aircraft that would accelerate against gravity once you lit both J-79 afterburners even if you were fully loaded with twelve—500 pound bombs and were close to full fuel in your two large wing tanks and fuselage storage. It held the time to climb record (30,000 ft. a minute) for quite a while. From tree top level over a shooting enemy to 10,000 feet was our main concern and that was but a manner of seconds.

Least time to be exposed to enemy fire especially when you start out right over them is what every pilot prefers. It does raise hell with your ears in later life however, as the ear drums get over-stretched from the thousands of quick pull ups you have incurred.

A typical mission was to come in low, treetop level, over your own troops on your first pass. You are loaded and heavy with fuel. You do not drop on that first pass nor on the second one either if you are not quite sure where your 'friendlies' are. Marine Pilots do not kill their own troops! The 500 pounder is a highly dangerous weapon, Napalm worse. Eventually the Army Airborne troops forbid the Air Force F-4s to drop for them. The Air Force habit of bombing from up high, releasing 6 or more at a time and having little or no training CAS practice caused too many Airborne casualties. Not coming down to tree top level for observation passes only was not in the Air Force repertoire. Hence the Airborne called on the Marines for their CAS needs. Consequently, we were very busy when we were assigned 'Hot Pad' duty.

I mentioned in one of my books the time that I flew 5 missions back to back to help rescue two chopper loads of Marines about to be overrun by an NVA battalion up in the Vietnam Highlands. Hence I will put that episode in this chapter. Those Marines were the 'Hunted'. Our pair of Phantoms became key rescue factors, beginning one afternoon while serving on 'hot pad' emergency response duty.

The McDonnell Phantom F4B was the initial production model from the St. Louis plant. Two F4A's were built as prototypes. One crashed. Over 5000 were to be built, mostly later F4—C, D and J models. These later models had internal 20 mm and the Air Force version had flight controls in both cockpits. I cut a French church in two with one using an external pod-type 20 millimeter Gatling. I got secondary explosions from it meaning the Vietcong were keeping explosives or fuel in it. My gun pod sliced that structure in two pieces like it was butter. The Marine F4B had only one set of controls. The back-seater was not a pilot but was termed a Radar Intercept Officer in case enemy aircraft were about, which was rare in Vietnam. The RIO would detect any other aircraft with his foreword sweeping scope and if an enemy, the pilot would be directed by the RIO toward the intruder and attempt to shoot it down with heat seeking Sidewinders or radar guided

Sparrow missiles. This rarely happened. We wasted a lot of valuable training time on RIOs that should have been spent training dropping practice bombs. Luckily for me I spent a good month practicing on a tiny island off Okinawa.

Close Air Support—providing protective cover for beleaguered troops or suppressing enemy forces that our troops are attacking were the two major roles the Marine Air Wing attack aircraft provided. Douglas A-4 Skyhawks and McDonnell F-4s were our two CAS models. The A-4 was nimble, slower and lighter allowing it to be quite accurate against targets but carried less bombs and had a shorter duration airborne for staying on station and making pass after pass than the much larger Phantom which carried 12—500 pound bombs and two larger fuel loaded wing tanks. Because of its size, the Phantom F-4 could stay aloft much longer than the A-4, although both aircraft had air-to-air refueling capability. Unlike Hollywood movies, however, the refueling C-130s which we utilized were not always available and one had to be critically accurate with their fuel estimate to get back to base in time unless one wanted to risk bailing out over Viet Cong or NVA territory and if lucky or unlucky—spend one's life in Hanoi Hilton. Pilots were the most numerous of all military occupations in the POW camps.

The speed of the Phantom was an important asset; rolling in at 500 knots and leaving faster on pull out after drop allowed only a few seconds to be exposed to ground fire. When you are making pass after pass releasing one at a time out in front of your men, there are situations where you have to get right back to them after your last bomb drop. The F-4 could zip back to base at a thousand miles per hour and more, refuel and reload in about 12 minutes and get back to your troops. Making numerous passes you know where your own troops are and where the enemy is at especially their 37 millimeter antiaircraft (and .51 calibers also). Those you try and take out. Less 'Friendly Fire' mistakes happen when the same pilot returns. You have some very dangerous weapons that you are expending. That is why a squadron commander will keep sending his experienced pilots back into an area that they are already familiar with. We avoid killing our own men. 'Staying on Station' with lethal 500 pounders much longer than the A-4 was invaluable for beleaguered, life and death facing troops down below. Many a combat infantryman under siege has emotionally thanked me down through my trail of life once they discovered I was a CAS F-4 Marine pilot. Accelerating against gravity, even fully loaded was the F-4s greatest asset.

The U. S. Air Force is more concerned with engaging enemy fighters and show little interest in providing cover for the U. S. Army. Consequently their pilots have little or no training regarding Close Air Support. CAS can become quite dangerous for our own troops down below. The Airborne especially had some bad experiences with Air Force attempts to provide needed cover for them resulting in too many fatalities inflicted on our own troops by the untrained Air Force Pilots. Typical Air Force F-4 Close Air was to release six—500 pound bombs from high altitude, most of their missions never coming down low to check where our own troops were at. Eventually the Airborne began to call on the Marines for their far more accurate and less dangerous (for them) bomb dropping. Marines usually would fly their F4s or A4s low, tree top level and make several scouting passes while talking to the forward Air Controller down below or an FAC Pilot (Forward Air Controller), driving a small single engine observation plane also at tree top level. More than once a Marine pilot would dip into the top of the jungle and come up with a vine beating on his fuselage. That is how low you can get at Close Air. A hair lower, of course and you get your name on the black wall in Washington, DC.

The Air Force was slow to realize how efficient a bomber the F-4 could be besides being the premium fighter of its day mainly because of the tremendous power its twin J-79 afterburner equipped engines provided. The Marine Corps realized its capability and happily traded off their prop driven AD (Spad) Douglas attack bombers for cancelled Air Force Phantom orders from the McDonnell Company. Air Force AD pilots, (Flying Commandos) were shot down right and left due to its low pull off speed, especially when dropping only one piece of ordnance at a time.

When the Spad added power for pull up from a close air support bombing run, it would slow down to around 145 knots. That is helicopter speed and hundreds of those whirly birds were hit by ground fire. As mentioned, I flew 'choppers' before I went into jet training. I used to visit some of my former pilot mates at the helicopter squadrons stationed at the other end of Chu Lai. Almost every visit, I would hear of some pilot I knew stateside that had been shot down, forced to land or worse, killed or wounded. 145 knots is not much faster than what a helo cruises at. You are pretty vulnerable to ground fire at such a slow speed.

Having talked to a former Air Force commander recently, I was informed that the Wart Hog (A-10) comes in at 350 knots, much slower and minimal acceleration compared to the Phantom. 500 knots on approach with an accelerating climb vs 350 knots and decelerating! The A-10 would not have fared well in the Vietnam jungle concealing terrain.

Your 'pickle' (bomb drop) button is on your control stick; your throttles (afterburners) on left. Coming in much faster on a bombing run and after hitting 'burner,' you leave faster on pull up with a full load and consequently speed saved hundreds of Phantom crews. The B model had only one set of pilot controls, the radar operator sat in back and it had no internal Gatling 20mm. An external Vulcan two-barrel 20mm which had a reputation for jamming was occasionally carried on the bottom MER (fuselage ordnance hook up). Rockets were also attached externally but were ineffective compared to our main ordnance—500 lb. bombs or napalm. Rockets do support more safety for the pilot as you come in at a higher altitude for delivery. I believe napalm has finally been outlawed as it should be. To my knowledge it was not used in Iraq or Afghanistan, but of this information I am not certain. We carried twelve 500-pounders or seven napalm on most of our missions. From experience, we seemed to receive less ground fire when one bird carried napalm (jellied gasoline). In a division flight of four, at least one machine would have nape. In a section flight (two aircraft) we often, but not always, would have one nape carrier.

Colonel Bill Redel, USMC, was retired and taught at a college in Nevada near Lake Tahoe. Still tall, handsome and muscular in the 70s or early 80s, he had me come for a college Indian Week and speak and lecture to students on the benefits of knowing and being involved in Native culture. He reached back to WWII and did CIA work with the Greeks and their fighting the communists and on into Korea and Vietnam.

He began his introduction explaining our first conversation on the phone. "I knew from his voice that I had spoken to this man before. It was in Vietnam and I was in a dangerous situation. I was trying to get out of the high country with some of my squad wounded. It was late afternoon and our escape route from our insert up north was blocked by a larger sized squad or maybe several of NVA (North Vietnamese Army). They also had the advantage of being on a hill and were going to annihilate us that night. I saw a flight of Phantoms high above and issued out an emergency call on the Guard channel which they have tuned in. No time for formalities. 'This is Colonel Redel, USMC, I am in a precarious situation and about to be overrun.' I called out my coordinates. Over my radio, Captain McGaa came on. 'Hey, Colonel, you got trouble? Looks like we are nearby. What can I do for you?' Well, they saturated that hill with bombs and Napalm. There wasn't much left when we got across it and were picked up by choppers on the other side. The Captain was talking to me, pass after pass."

The Colonel, who had a lifetime of combat back from WWII, gave that introduction more than a few times as I would come back to that college several years in a row. He also had quite a few friends in the Lake Tahoe area whom I met at dinners they held for the two of us and told them the same story. It can be a small world at times.

When you have hot pad duty, you are confined to an air conditioned hut, a small Quonset shaped structure close to a pair of Phantoms that most usually are loaded with 500 pound bombs and Nape. They are hooked up to a starter cart and the internal ladder is punched down below the fuselage footholds to the open canopy. You are waiting for a phone to ring inside the hut clad in your flight gear; your ejection seat harness over your flight suit, your .38 pistol and various survival paraphernalia attached to your ejection harness. Most important is your survival radio in case you are still alive after having to eject. The radio will be your location finder and communication to friendly would-be-rescuers. I stupidly carried two hand grenades as well given to me by a Marine grunt (infantry) lieutenant. When the phone rings you bound out the door for your F-4. The non-pilot in the back seat of your plane takes the phone call, writing down the coordinates of the battle zone you are being called into.

Most missions from hot pad are suppressant missions enough to allow rescue helos in to extract downed pilots, wounded troops or to aid reconnaissance forces or probing the enemy. I may condemn Air Force CAS but will readily praise the brave Air Force Jolly Green S-53 crews for rescuing pilots with their extraction jungle penetrator ball which performed hundreds of successful rescue missions. Other missions are when the enemy is attacking with a larger force against Marines or Airborne Army troops that have come under fire.

Highlands

There were two CH-46 helicopter loads of downed Marines. We fought long into the night, returning at high speed back to refuel and reload out of Chu Lai. Rarely, if ever, does a pilot ever fly 5 combat fighter attack missions back to back, never leaving the cockpit except of course to quickly un-strap and walk rearward over the wide fuselage toward the exhaust to urinate; one engine turning at idle. I learned what the Marine helicopter pilots went through, flying long hours, that day and on into the night. I didn't have to hunt my quarry on those missions. They were right there and it was mostly our bombs and napalm that was keeping the NVA, a suspected battalion from capturing that last helicopter load. We came in so low just to the left of them when bombing seaward that my radar operator said he could see the belt buckles of our troops jumping up and down cheering from the bomb craters they huddled in. After my third mission it was twilight and we were fighting in mountain terrain. It is dangerous enough dropping low pass ordnance on flat jungle at tree top level but in mountains there is added risk and night time it can be close to suicidal. This situation was highly unusual, if you dropped ordnance we figured that the Chi Com .37s could not vector on us if we dropped below them down into the mountain pass. Eventually though, because of our repeated passes and their exposure, we silenced them.

My squadron commander was standing in the loading and refueling revetment when I taxied in. This was usually not a good sign. I knew where I had placed my bombs and usually came in low at times for pin point accuracy which my Skipper (Squadron Commander) had commended me for more than a few times at our squadron morning pilot meetings. Snake Eye bomb configuration allows you to do that without getting your tail blown off from the resultant blast. An umbrella like set of fins springs out from the bomb as soon as it releases from your bomb rack, retarding the big 500 pounder momentarily and therefore allows you to come in real low, drop and get away without having shrapnel take out your rear end. A 500 pounder throws out a terrific blast. Before the snake eye configuration, a large bomb just could not be released safely from the aircraft at a very low level. The lower you are, the more accurate you are, and when dropping close to your own troops, pin point accuracy is critical. Air Force pilots, as I said, usually do not receive the Close Air training that we do and seldom come in as low as we usually do.

I knew why the Skipper was standing there when the plane captain signaled to keep one engine turning to provide power for refueling and reloading. The bomb crews below scurried feverishly with their carts and ordnance. It looked like I was going right back out, such were the dire circumstances the Marines were facing; almost fatally trapped back high on that mountain range. We had already lost an A-4 jet, a Spad AD prop attack aircraft and a Huey gunship. Miraculously, all of these pilots were rescued and were down in those bomb craters with the Marine grunts (Infantry). All three aircraft had managed to crash land at a miniature airstrip cut into the mountain side. Skipper motioned for me to stay in the cockpit, yelling in a loud voice asking how I was feeling—fatigue wise. I was damn well fatigued after 3 demanding missions but I was young and you just do not disobey or get reluctant with a Marine Corps squadron commander. I lied to him however, when I yelled back that I was OK.

"G.D., Chief. I hate to do this to you." He yelled with a relieved tone. Even one Phantom engine running at idle gets a bit loud. The flight surgeon, a full Navy Commander was standing beside him. He forked up a chocolate malt which I knew was loaded with Imodium to keep you from needing to go to toilet. In combat, if you have diarrhea and on long refueling missions where you have to stay in the air orbiting because Marines may be in critical need of you...well... life isn't like the movies. Imodium is a wonderful preventer whether or not you happen to have a case of diarrhea or not. The pilot could urinate at the back of the Phantom, as I said, when we had to go right back out. Pilots, even military pilots who have never experienced extreme combat, find this hard to believe. You simply unstrapped and the aircraft was so big and broad that you walked aft and held on to the vertical tail fin that reminded you of a bull Orca while you urinated into the exhaust below you. Helicopter pilots had a convenient 'Pee tube' for that purpose but I think the pressurization requirements of a high altitude Phantom prevented such a necessity. You zipped the front of your flight suit back up and re-strapped yourself to the ejection seat while fuel was being pumped into your tanks and the bombs secured below. You had about 6 to 8 minutes do all this while the efficient reloading and refueling took place. Fellow Marines are dying out there, killed and wounded is what is on those frantic bomb crew minds.

"Chief, I will lose a pilot if I send a green one in." It was a sort of unwritten rule, only three back to back missions at the most. Mainly you are too damned exhausted (the way we bomb, pass after pass) to do more. He meant that an inexperienced pilot to those mountain passes could easily kill a crew on pullout, especially in the black of night. More than one crew had met that fate. Despite all the Bravado and ferocity attributed to the Marines they definitely do not want to lose you. It is a close tightrope between being expendable or saving the rescuer's ass also—to put it bluntly. We had to come off low to make sure we would not hit our own troops and yet still get to the enemy close by. Often you would dip down a canyon after a drop to be unreachable by the 37 millimeter mounted guns. Night would make it all that more difficult. We had suppressed the 37 millimeter guns but new ones could always be brought up. That Chi Com 37mm is what Jane Fonda sat in—the Bitch! Later on her visit to Hanoi Prison she caused several pilot POWs to be severely beaten for slipping her a note which she traitorously handed over to the prison commandant. She should be put on a naval ship and kept at sea, quarantined for life as happened to a similar figure way back when our country had some needed discipline. Instead she is 'honored' as some kind of sleazy, putrid 'Woman of the Century'.

I yelled back at the Colonel below jokingly. "Skipper, if I get back… I want a shot of booze from that Swabbie (meaning the Navy Doctor Commander) standing next to you." I added, "If I don't… then have one on me!" In combat you can say fairly much what you want in such a situation. In the States you could possibly face a Court Martial if the insulted senior wanted to make an issue of such a derogatory remark. A 'Swabbie' is a slang term for Navy personnel—even Navy Doctors, which our flight surgeons are. No one calls a full Navy Commander a 'Swabbie' or a 'Squid' but I did! Both men gave me a salute out of respect while I attached my oxygen mask back on and prepared to relight my number 2 kerosene quencher—the J-79 power plant that could give 17,500 pounds of thrust and allow a takeoff, fully bomb loaded, almost straight up skyward if you needed it. As I said, without bombs or wing tanks it would go straight up. Power? That baby had plenty of raw power and there were two of those General Electric J-79s attached to it. I wish I could have met some of those trapped troops. This all happened one night in July, high up on a mountain ridge. I knew the return route like the back of my hand, even in the night. As I approached the plateau before the mountains, you could see the glow of combat. Flares were being dropped by a C-47.

Like I said, life is not like the movies. It was almost impossibility, but my Skipper was again standing in the revetments with the flight surgeon when I returned back from the fourth mission. I felt like a zombie must feel if there ever was such a thing. We still had not suppressed that stubborn NVA battalion commander enough to get extract choppers in. He had to be hurting however. One more Huey, a gunship, was added to the planes downed. The Navy flight surgeon was holding a canteen cup. My Skipper was shaking his head disparagingly. His posture made me wonder for my section leader, Major Duffy, who was flying the same amount of missions I was. 'Had Duff been shot down?' I worried to myself. In combat you do fly to your destination initially together but once the shooting starts you take separation and bomb individually. You also return individually. None of this Hollywood formation joining back up; not on critical situation hot pad duty missions, at least. A plane carrying seven napes is going to be empty sooner than a plane carrying twelve 500 pounders and needs to leave the bombing pattern immediately when empty to get rearmed and refueled. Full speed, it can zip back to base saving precious minutes for returning fully loaded. A-4s couldn't match our speed nor stay longer. No other close air support planes had this valuable ability. Those desperate troops below well knew the Phantom could remain in the bombing pattern much longer. (Due to its huge fuselage, wing tanks capability for storing fuel, and its two large external fuel tanks.)

'Major Tom Duffy had been shot down?' I worried as I taxied to a stop.

The Skipper came over and stood below me. The Flight surgeon had been standing beside him holding a canteen cup, obviously my booze I had requested. Skipper punched my ladder release and came half way up. He looked perplexed and began with, yelling loudly, "G.D. Chief, Some more Marines are going to die tonight if you can't make it back there, one… last-ass-time." He shook his head with a tight frown. He had to be worried that I physically just could not do it despite so many lives at stake. Tragically he cried loudly, "We lost the one chopper. I just got word and close to losing the other." I took off my helmet to hear better and with it my oxygen mask. I let out a groan. I was one tired, fatigued Son of a Bitch, to put it all in combat Marine Corps terms. The flight surgeon below added, "That is…if you can make it." The canteen cup below was tantalizing. I apologize to the kids that read, but in combat you simply use more expletive vocabulary which no doubt will make the politically correct wimps wince as it is. We all spoke like General Patton when shells were flying and more so when our troops were on the line being killed and captured by a determined and successful enemy. It is just more precise communication for us and certainly more emphatic. "G.D. Skipper." I replied. "I don't have any choice." I waved to the north. "Folks out there—getting killed…"

"Or captured," he added. "It doesn't look good for the chopper." He meant the one that wound up being captured. (They were shot in the Highlands, obviously, as they never showed up on POW roles.)

I stretched my feet into my rudders and partially rose from the cockpit. I yelled back boldly. "God Damn Skipper, I am one fatigued son of a bitch!" I honestly did not think I had the strength, the stamina to go back out again. Four combat missions, close air, is damned demanding. I just did not have it in me to commit. "Skipper, can I have that God Damn drink?" I retaliated.

The flight surgeon acted like he was about to pull a rabbit out of a hat when he lifted up the canteen cup with a wry smile. The Skipper backed down the ladder and yelled at the plane captain. They brought out the 'Cigar Box' attached to a pole. The plane Captain raised my drink, the canteen cup, up to me. I sat in my cockpit and took a long, deep drink. It went down burning and soothing. Damn. It tasted good. I took another drink. Suddenly, unlike a normal drink, my head buzzed and I came instantly awake. I took another and it was as if you had a shot of adrenaline. Years later, I would receive a similar rush when I would step on a pickle ball court at a much later age. I had had some of the mixture before, but this was much stronger when I had crashed a Phantom on takeoff, due to blown nose tires at take-off speed, full burner and no fault of my own.

Arresting Gear

Lift off? I had already had lifted the rumbling nose wheels minus their tires ending the tremendous shaking caused by rims only, I smelled fire which there was. Had I lifted that 200 knot machine with increasing speed, I probably would have been killed because some of the blown tires went into the engine intakes and they would have surely blown. Something screamed into my mind, "FOD, FOD!" (Foreign Object Damage). I did not lift off but instead reached for the pair of throttles and jerked them backwards. I was over 200 knots by now, probably around 250 knots and the main tires wanted to dance lightly on the runway. I aimed for the middle of the runway, nose up, the plane wanting to still leap skyward- such was my speed.

I banged my tail hook down, hoping to catch the arresting cables waiting close to the end. I kept the nose wheels off as long as I could. I was probably over a hundred miles an hour when I entered the arresting cable zone. My nose rims were now on the pavement and rumbling, bouncing the aircraft violently. Smoke started to come into my cockpit. I sailed past the first wire, heading for the sand at the runways edge and with the cutting rims I could imagine flipping the aircraft over in a blazing ball of fire. I reached for my ejection seat activator loop just above and behind my head. I only got my hands part way to it and they froze with a sudden ending to my inertia. The cleat on my tail hook had caught on the cable and I was brought to an abrupt stop. My back seater popped his canopy open and out of his cockpit in a flash in the few moments the F-4 had come to a stop. Smoke was starting to fill my cockpit. A strange noise came out which was the huge arresting bungees pulling back on the steel arresting cable. I hit my canopy release and unstrapped my ejection seat harness. I punched the release button for my leg strap release but they remained secure. By this time my RIO was running away from the aircraft. I frantically punched the leg strap release with no results. I was trapped.

In many fighter planes, a pair of leg straps attach to your ejection seat. You are trained to place your feet on your rudder pedals when you are about to activate your ejection seat handle. Stateside, about every 4 months you go through 'Ejection seat Training' to habitually develop your ejection technique. Your spine is straightened more so in this position to enable a stronger backbone posture to absorb the shock of the ejection force needed to lift you out of your cockpit. If your legs are tucked more underneath your sitting posture, then you are more inclined to receive back bone damage. The ejection procedure is that immediately after the charge force is activated, your legs are then pulled back enough to clear your feet from being cut off or at least the tips of your feet from being cut off by your dashboard of flying instruments as you sail out of the cockpit. I know it sounds scary but it most often works. You also learn to pull your top ejection handle with your elbows tucked in closer together. Having them wide apart when you pull, you stand a good chance of having an elbow or two cut off from the canopy.

I then proceeded to go backwards in the Phantom, yes, backwards which is obviously impossible on two dead engines. The nose wheel rims cocked and then I was slowly spun around backwards by the force of what would be huge rubber band type bungees. This was impossible and I was into shock by now thinking I must be fainting and into some sort of weird dream. I could see the fire trucks coming screaming down the runway. The rims had caused so much heat that hydraulic fluid was dripping down on them causing the fire and smoke. A firefighter was above me in an asbestos suit and reached for me with a big knife in his other hand. I pointed to my leg strap release button and made a down signal with my thumb. He pointed the big knife at my feet and I thought he wanted to cut my legs off to save me. I pushed the knife away and used the manual method for releasing the calf straps by simply reaching down with both hands to pull the strap ends through their metal tightening loops. They were attached fairly tight and I had to use my survival knife to detach one of them. This done, I came out of that cockpit while the rest of the fire crew were putting out the hydraulic fire blaze. The two engines did contain foreign object damage and would probably have blown soon after takeoff. Two new engines and two new rims and wheels with slight hydraulic repair and the aircraft was back up flying again. I wasn't hurt but such an occurrence does get your attention. Medical alcohol was offered to me in the sick bay clinic right after the crash. The flight surgeon opened a refrigerator door behind him to reveal three plastic containers each with fruit writing on white tape; apple, pineapple and orange juice. I had it cut with orange juice because it is fairly 'wicked stuff.' The commander laughed. "You don't mind cutting it with orange juice? Do you Chief?" We all knew how strong the medical alcohol was. The flight surgeon talked to me for a while and deemed I was OK. I was back up flying that afternoon.

Back at Chu Lai

"S… of a… B," I voiced out slowly in sheer wonderment. What was in that drink was more than just alcohol but at the time I had no suspicion. I could have fallen asleep in that cockpit but now I was beginning to feel wide awake. I could go out one more time to save the lives of our troops.

Combat indeed allows strange things. Rules are broken. Maybe our Skipper knew all about our beloved, yet feared combat General, General Chesty Puller, who did likewise for his troops as a battalion commander on Guadalcanal and then later as a regimental commander in Korea on the Frozen Chosen trail. He would crawl out to a beleaguered and lonely dangerous outpost and give his frontline men a good stiff drink from a bottle of bourbon or whiskey he carried for just such a hairy and dangerous occasion.

"G.D. Colonel, what the hell you doin' out here?" was their most often used and startled reply. Read the book on Chesty Puller; it is all in there what I am relating. If anybody doesn't like what he did—then, 'Tell it to the Marines!'

You never, never drink and fly. Those are the rules. But that night I did. I savored every G.D. bit of it. It hit my empty stomach like a fireball with a warming glow. It was like spinach to Popeye or 'Shazam' to Superman. When the plane captain gave the startup signal for the second engine, I looked down with a fuzzy headed, broad cocky smile. I held a thumb's up and put my bonnet (flight helmet) back on, clicking on my mask. Both higher ranked officers saluted me—a Captain. I went back out feeling miraculously invigorated and we got the troops out after that final mission.

"You don't mind cutting it with orange juice, do you, Chief," rang in my ears as I headed north under power from those big dependable J-79s, oblivious to the black night and the waiting mountains which we feared more than the enemy's anti-aircraft fire. Flying under those flares you have the added challenge of avoiding hitting your own troops thrown in. You have but split seconds to decide whether to drop or not to drop and you have to get in there and drop—and that means right ass on the enemy. It is a damned demanding situation. You absolutely just do not have time for fear or that stupid word, reluctance. Landing on an aircraft carrier is a piece of cake compared to dropping Close Air at night and worse—under flares. Worse yet—in the Mountains. There are Marine pilots still out there; impacted into those mountains. Marine pilots concur—'You just have to do it, man. You have to ass do it!' These new dangerous drones are a joke compared to the efficiency of what a pilot in a Phantom can do. I doubt like hell if that will ever change. Finally we got them out, after dropping our ordnance under the flares which is a fairly hairy, spooky maneuver. I'd take night carrier calls any day…or any night even in rain…over bombing under flares and worse—in mountainous terrain.

With deep regret the other chopper load was captured and just disappeared. No POW list—nothing. Murdered in the Highlands. Success can be bitter sweet. Their names are on the 'Wall' in DC but the rescued lived. Major Duffy was awarded the Distinguished Flying Cross for the same missions I had flown. I was also recommended by my loyal Skipper for the same medal because he knew we were under the exact same conditions, and indeed both fulfilled our challenge placed before us. Major Tom Duffy was killed soon after and I never received my medal because I was getting out and going on to law school. Again—life is never like the movies, life is inexorable. I have told my children, however, that I want that medal pinned to the pillow inside of my casket someday. In my mind I earned it…but life is never like the movies…is it? If I get cremated, I have a small miniature one which I wear on my baseball cap and defy anyone from removing it—throw that in the fire or have it pinned or taped on me when you do it—Cremation. Good way to go—takes up less space in this crowded world.

Marine Close Air

Close Air Support (CAS) is Down, Deep and Dangerous I guess you can describe it but oh so highly effective as thousands of visiting Vietnam combat veterans attested almost daily when I had my book selling table at Crazy Horse Mountain Museum in the Black Hills of South Dakota. Such high praise every one of them had for that effective F-4 Phantom that flew so close over them attacking and protecting. "So damn close you could see the pilot, feel the heat of the napalm or his bomb blast," was a common expression. Actually a helluva lot more dangerous and death defying overall than the glamorized TAS—Tactical Air Support; the MIG chasers who go aloft to orbit round and round for hours, plug into a KC-135 tanker and orbit in complete boredom some more time punching holes in the sky, often plugging in a second time. If you look at the statistics, there were damn few MIGs shot down or engaged compared to the daily encounters we Marine CAS pilots experienced against ground fire, 37mm/51mm AA fire (Jane Fondas) and occasional SAM missiles en route to our targets. Black mountains at night and worse, under flares cannot be omitted. You do not drop your load—'Air Force Style' either. Besieged, often desperate troops are down there. You drop one or a couple and have to go back in repeatedly as this chapter illustrated. More lives than yours are at stake and that is what you are getting paid and trained for. None of this, 'Drop High and too Many' as most every one of the many combat Vets I have had the privilege to meet complained about regarding their opinions of Air Force Close Air. The Airborne eventually banned the Air Force attempts at Close Air after losing troops and called on us Marines to support them. I dropped many a load, one at a time, tree top level just beyond beleaguered or attacking Airborne who were highly professional with their communication and position marking to us.

Close Air on the Deck, Marine Bombing

Airborne 'O' Club

A fellow pilot and I got the CO's jeep for a day after we had taken out a SAM missile site all on our own and did not follow Air Force rules to wait at least a half hour after being fired upon. (Yes, some stupid rules which added up to losing that war). We had a damn good CO who knew what we did and let it pass quietly with no fanfare. We wandered into an Airborne club, a make shift shack complete with different brands of booze. They even had an ice blender so I ordered a couple of Margaritas a switch from my usual Rum and coke—a favorite of Marine and Navy pilots since we trained in the Caribbean and Ron Rico/Bacardi offered us free rum on Wednesday nights at our Roosevelt Roads club down there. Two burly Airborne Captains approached us and growled uncomfortably for us. "You look like a couple of pilots." A lieutenant joined them who looked like a NFL linebacker. "Are you Air Force?" he snarled.

I took a swig of my margarita and replied adamantly, "No fkg way in hell." (In combat, one often is so immersed into pragmatic profanity that it can permeate into the rare moments of social life as well.).

"Navy?" We shook our heads. They looked puzzled but still appeared as if they were about to throw us out of their club. The lieutenant bent his face down to mine, "Then what the fk are you?" One of the Captains brushed him back. "Are you two—Marines?"

"Fking A!" I replied and downed my drink figuring I wouldn't get to finish my second. The ice slush was almost as good as the drink.

'No Shit!" One remarked with a welcome smile. "What you drivin'?"

"F-4s." I answered proudly.

"No Shit?" The Lieutenant's voice changed dramatically. "You ain't from that one with the Eagle on the tail?"

"You got it." I reached for my other slush Margarita.

"These guys are from One Fifteen." The Captain answered the Lieutenant then yelled exuberantly at a group huddled at the bar. "Hey guys, we got a couple from One Fifteen, -that big ass eagle on the tail—F-4 Pilots drivers over here." The bar group let out a cheer. A Major held up his drink, "Goddamnit, don't beat the shit out of 'em like you did those Air Force pilots!" A rousing cheer followed. "What the hell are they drinking?" They held up their glasses to us. The Major yelled, "Drinks are on us!" Needless to say, we spent the night there and the CO got his jeep back the next morning. Usually cantankerous, he wound up liking what we told him. Back then I first heard the phrase, "Too high and too G.D. many." And also, "Marines are down there with us, saving our ass, Tree –top level, dropping one at a time."

The Captain sat down beside me and reached across to shake my hand. "I was in that last operation with you One Fifteen guys covering. "Yeah, I know." We're getting a lot of calls from you folks."

"We were about to throw your asses out if you were Air Force." He said with a growl he wouldn't have had any problem backing up. "We don't have any love for the way they do Close Air. You Marines are a helluva lot more effective and a helluva lot more safe for our troops—Thank God!"

The Chinese controlled the other side of their Air Power. The NVA lost a lot of troops to our Marine Close Air which is our 'Bread and Butter' as far as ground support is considered. In Vietnam, it all began with the A-1 Sky Raider trade, the Spad or A D was the aircraft's nickname. It was a single radial engine attack aircraft initially employed by the Marines and Navy. Pre-Vietnam some Air Force higher-ups were mesmerized by the plane's ability to 'Carry its own weight in Bombs.' Unfortunately for the Air Force they traded their McDonnell F-4B contract to the Navy for all the Navy's A Ds which included the Marine's birds as well since we are part of the Navy. Our Generals readily complied and with glee I might add. The Air Force designated 'Air Commando' squadrons with much fanfare and sent them off to Vietnam. Unfortunately, drastically inferior to the F-4, the A D could not pull off safely above the enemy 37 millimeter AA guns and often, even their small arms fire.

The numerous 37s (Fonda Janes) we encountered were light, detachable, easily transportable, and highly effective against 'slow movers' such as the Spad and helicopters. As I said, the Spad with a full load of fuel and bombs would slow to 145 knots on pull up against gravity out of the enemy zone. (Not too difficult to figure out regarding CAS that the Air Force made a huge mistake.) Eventually, due to the high aircraft and pilot loss, the 'Carries its own weight in bombs' mesmerization had to be disbanded. The highly touted 'Warthog'—A-10, I mentioned would have gone a similar route had it made the Vietnam scene for it too had no afterburners to get it out, up and away rather swiftly as the Phantom could perform. Within seconds from tree top, we F-4 pilots already doing 500, were breaking 5, 6 thousand feet on up to ten thousand for our turn around and back in again out of small arms fire and the 37s. Worse, for the enemy, they never lead us enough when they were firing. Once in a while they did have tracers and you could see that they were not leading us enough. These tracers, always coming up and falling behind, were no doubt our captured weapons and ammunition. The Wart Hog coming in at 350 and no burners would be a sitting duck in comparison over jungle terrain.

The Phantom was near perfect for close air. It had the pilot in front within a fishbowl cockpit with the best visibility platform and not half blind on one side as in the A-6 Intruder that had the two pilots side by side. The A-4 had equal visibility but could not carry a Phantom's load nor stay on station nearly as long. Also, it could not get back as fast to re-load and re-fuel to return back to the battle area. Those beleaguered troops below want you back as soon as possible. That is why the Marines always want a land base so you can get turned around quickly. On a carrier, you go below after being trapped by your tail hook. The Navy did try to effect reloading and refueling topside carriers, but land bases were more practical and most often closer to combat operations involving ground troops. Marines practice CAS, although in my time we wasted more time with those RIOs (Radar Intercept Officers) and not dropping practice bombs while in training stateside. Our few remaining F-4s are now being wasted as target drones. D.O.D. stupidity.

The NVA realized the deadly effectiveness of the F-4 and obviously quite worried when the Air Force began receiving F-4s to replace their less effective single engine F-100s especially when it came to CAS. The Chinese figured out how to possibly save the war, however. They baited the Air Force with MIGs, some older models even. It was a too tantalizing bait for the Air Force to refuse. Squadrons of F-4s went airborne after MIGs, refueling several times; hence disregarding CAS against the NVA which was shelved. Grandeur Ego over common sense prevailed. The Focus of War became remote. It was MacArthur all over again—his failure to inspect the ill equipped 8th Army in Korea and disregard of the intelligence on the North Korean military buildup. The 'Shogun of Japan—Imperial Palace' grandeur was too overwhelming. Distraction! Not much difference than that Marine Commander Adams in Afghanistan texting that attractive 'Chick' 20 times a day instead of focusing on his troops getting blown away. In China—both would be hauled to Beijing and sent out to the rice paddies if the jury felt lenient.

I learn a lot from my vantage point at Crazy Horse Museum where a million tourists a summer pass by my book selling table there. Thousands of combat veterans stop by to chat and relive old memories. Recently an AF F-4 pilot who did two tours told me it was not uncommon to have 100 AF F-4s in the sky at one time coming from various bases outside of Hanoi and Haiphong for MIG Cap operations. The Marines were left to do effective CAS but there were not enough F-4 Marine squadrons to carry out the needed missions to subdue the NVA, especially when they became offensive with their operations. Who won the war?

1. Number one requirement in CAS is that you have to get away to return again and again. Your machine, fully loaded and fully fueled, has to accelerate against gravity. That first pass, you need to know exactly where your troops are before you drop. The Air Liaison below or spotter bird is talking to you to make sure you do.

2. Be big enough to carry enough fuel to stay on station to drop one at a time, preferably tree top level where you can see where your own troops are.

3. Get back to base after your last drop rather quickly and back again fully loaded and refueled. One thousand knots is rather quick.

4. Carry enough Ordinance. F-4 carried 12—500 pounders. F-100 only 4 and A-4—6. Both slowed on pull up fully loaded. A-6 carried 22 but blind on one side for the pilot and like the A-4, no after-burner for get away. Getting blown away on a velocity slowing pull up due to inadequate power does not do that combat infantryman below much of a favor, does it? He needs you and will tell you so in years to come as I often hear from them speaking from near-death experience as I autograph my books to this day. Everyone, so far is critical of Air Force technique and commend highly the 'Tree-Top' single bomb, down and dirty pattern the Marines use. The dead from inadequate CAS can't talk. The misuse of the majority of available F-4s in 'Nam' along with the politicians was a major reason why we lost that war; my opinion. Put me back on duty in the Corps. TAD me to the Air Force. Save our remaining F-4s. I have some experienced advice.

8 SAM MISSILES

Phantom jets in Vietnam

Combat

I wrote this memory not long after I had finished law school, which began immediately after I left Vietnam. Actually, I was only eight days out of a combat cockpit before I was sitting in law school. I had missed freshman week. The following is written in third person but is an accurate presentation of what happened after I had attended Fools Crow's *Yuwipi* at his reservation cabin before leaving for 'Nam'. More accurate than what I could recall now.

It was nearly noon when he left the debriefing room at the operations Quonset. A helicopter gun ship buzzed low across the distant row of tin-roofed huts sitting on a sand dune. There was little to do at Chu Lai but wait for the outdoor movie, wash clothes and clean the hut. The endless boredom of shifting sand and dreary shacks made him yearn to go home. He had resigned from the Marines to attend law school, but had first requested a combat assignment. His orders home were due. Any intention of remaining in the service had ended with this war. The Marines had allowed him to rise from enlisted rank, but a warrior's role in a war like this one had proved too frustrating.

His grandmother's advice echoed in his memory, "There will always be a war, Grandson. If they can make a business out of their religion, war can be a collection plate, too." But the war, despite the frustrations, had provided the way to reach for what he must. Even Fools Crow, a pacifist, never objected to his involvement and had helped his warrior's role with the coming of the *wotai*.

Later, he would learn to contend that the war was mostly political and economic, no different than most, where the poor were rallied for cannon fodder through a sense of patriotism and, especially in this war, the higher realm, those in control, the elected and economic leaders, strove to keep their warrior-age sons out of combat units, taking no share of the direct and deadliest exposure. In but a short time, he would set his course upon another path and would leave the warring to politicians.

Alone with his thoughts for the moment, he rested his head against the ejection seat. Before leaving Vietnam he would fly over one hundred missions. All that had been foretold in the ceremony held at Fools Crow's cabin had come true. This was the ceremony that a small stone came in, it had an eagle within its grain. A special stone entering into one's life is called a *wotai* (woe tye) stone. Chief Crazy Horse wore one attached to his ear when he went into battle. Crosses and crucifixes are all manmade. A stone with an image is put there by Creator. White Man doesn't want to admit this but Truth is Truth. Spirit people had entered, predicting that he would see the enemy many times. "Bullets would bounce from his airplane," they said. He took the Sun Dance vow. "I will dance the Sun Dance if the stone remains." At the end of the ceremony, there it was, wrapped in a leather pouch. He wore it around his neck on all his missions.

Spiritual Predictions

The high-finned Phantoms circled like a pair of tiger sharks above the South China Sea. Two electronic-laden Grumman A-6 Intruders orbiting off the coast of North Vietnam were contacted by the F-4s. The Grummans took their positions, holding a separated, lengthy, racetrack orbit, their missile surveillance scanners sweeping inland. The mission's target was located in SAM territory. He was getting close to his last mission. He was due for discharge and new pilots were checking into the squadron. The cruising fighter-bombers turned inbound. The thin beachhead giving way to beige landscape, looked little different than South Vietnam, except for monsoon-flooded rice paddies casting mirrored reflections of false tranquility. The late summer storms were saturating North Vietnam, Laos and Cambodia further inland. Meteorology predicted that Chu Lai would receive heavy rains by noon.

He glanced at his watch. His main gyroscope for instrument landing had turned faulty and he didn't want to make an instrument landing at Chu Lai in heavy rain. The pilots had noted the cloud buildups west of Chu Lai. All Laos and Cambodia missions had been canceled. He hoped to leave Vietnam before the monsoons; emergency missions were launched regardless of weather and more than one crew and their aircraft had disappeared in the torrential downpours.

He unzipped the top of his flight suit, adjusted his pistol shoulder harness and pulled the braided cord at his neck. He tugged to bring the small lump of buckskin from underneath his survival vest. He fondled the buckskin. His orders were overdue.

"Where are my orders?" he asked as he clutched the *wotai* pouch.

Square coastal rice fields thinned away to rising piedmont, the rice paddies climbing with the terrain, narrowing to stepped radial bands ending at mountainous, dark green, almost impenetrable jungle. Yet, fifty miles further, somewhere under the thick foliage, a North Vietnamese truck company was hidden and protected by surface-to-air missiles.

The first warning tone issued by the patrol planes crackled like scrambled eggs across his helmet's receivers. His muscles flexed like a prizefighter circling an opponent. The voiceless tones meant North Vietnamese, or more than likely their Russian advisers, had activated radar sets and were no doubt tracking the Phantoms. Both pilots tensed on their flight controls, their feet poised to jam down the rudder pedals in coordination with a sideways slam of the control stick to full aileron. On an earlier mission, at this stage, a rush of wind had rocked his aircraft. The radar intercept officer screamed out, "SAM, SAM!" It was like the turbulence of a Great White shark nearly brushing a surfer. The pilot quickly dove the aircraft but no other missile came up to destroy them.

Any further warning beginning with the spoken code word for the sector, in which they were flying, he would do an abrupt split "S" maneuver to his right, at the same time igniting both afterburners. Fritz, the section leader, would roll in the opposite direction.

The split "S" maneuver was the most expedient means of losing altitude and changing direction. The plane would roll over on its back like an upside-down turtle before it dropped its nose straight down in a dive. In theory, the launched missiles would be radar-locked to a computed destruction point out ahead where target and missile were calculated to converge if evasive action had not been taken. Below, the enemy controller would attempt to alter the missile's course into the targets. Fortunately, for the fighter pilots, the missiles' smaller steering surfaces made the projectiles awkward and clumsy in comparison to the fighters. Too much correction and the SAMs would tumble and cartwheel futilely. If the early warning surveillance aircraft detected the upward-bound missiles in time, the fighters usually had a high survival rate…if the fired missiles were detected in time.

Pilot error jeopardized the pair of fighter-bombers from Marine Fighter/Attack Squadron 115. The lead A-6 surveillance aircraft from a Navy squadron, having flown north longer than the uneasy pilot had wanted, suddenly banked seaward before signaling their counterpart. At this point, the surveillance radar was blind and it was now the mission of the second A-

6 patrol plane, trailing further south, to scan the enemy areas inland. Precisely at this moment, the experienced Russian missile technicians fired a salvo of three missiles.

Fortunately, an alert radar operator in the second A-6 had anticipated the lead aircraft's turn and was already sweeping his scope inland to locate the Phantoms, while three ascending blips were off the bottom of his screen for a few long seconds. When the three ascending dots appeared, the operator's eyes went wide. He punched the emergency warning indicator without a moment's hesitation.

"Q-B Seven, Q-B Seven!" The code word for fired missiles was shouted out across both pilots' helmets. Q-B was their sector by latitude, Seven by longitude. Both pilots reacted to the code word as instinctively as if their own names had been yelled in alarm. The lead plane rolled left, his wingman rolled right. The inverted pair hung suspended for a long, precarious moment before the black noses dropped, hurtling down, down to the green jungle, miles below.

A flash of gray, like a fat telephone pole, roared ahead and past the wingman's window. It was the second missile. The first missile had been directed at the section leader's plane and was now tumbling wildly out of control. Preoccupation with the lead missile caused the enemy controller to err, detonating the second missile too late. The shock waves reached out with a solid thump, but no damage was inflicted to his plane.

His inverted machine was just beginning to scream downward under full afterburner power when the last missile flashed from below like a giant spear, detonating much closer. The vacuum shock from this blast snuffed out his left engine, sending the machine spinning. Around and around the F-4 spiraled down, the dark jungle revealing a glistening silver streak bisecting the whirling circle, the peaks and valleys growing deathly sharper. The G-forces paralyzed his leg upon the rudder. He strained to release the pressure upon the rudder and pushed back on the control stick toward a neutral position. Down he whirled and he began to panic. Something told him he could not panic. It was the time to concentrate and believe in the Way. Believe in the prediction in Fools Crow's cabin.

The streak of silver transformed into a discernible river before the pilot managed to neutralize his controls, pushing the stick forward against the centrifugal force with all of his strength and pushing his foot with equal difficulty against the rudder pedal opposite from the spin. The stabilator, rudder and aileron surfaces responded, the spin ceased, the dive shallowed and, finally, the plane came under control. Smoke trailed from hot kerosene in the dead engine. He pressed the aileron and rudder controls to point the machine out to the safety of the South China Sea.

His adrenaline began to subside. He had been too excited to notice the loss of the engine. The power of just one afterburner, coupled with the supersonic speed accumulated from the dive over ten thousand feet, concealed the loss of the engine. Now, as he brought the throttles out of afterburner, the sudden deceleration warned him of his situation. He checked the dead engine's RPM gauge, relieved to find a wind milling turbine indicating that the port engine wasn't frozen, decreasing the chance of battle damage.

At that moment, Fritz called across the radio, "Chief, Where you at?"

"Feet wet," he replied.

"C'mon back, Chief," Fritz ordered, disregarding radio formality as he glared down through his canopy at the telltale smoke trails. "I got the bastards spotted." The vindication in his voice flooded through his transmission.

He scanned the left engine instruments, satisfied with their readings. He double-checked the fuel flow, pressing the quantity indicators, calculating his reserve fuel. The Phantom was a flying kerosene tank: fuselage cells, wing cells and two external tanks fed the thirsty machine. Abnormal fuel loss would indicate battle damage. It was against battle regulations to re-light an engine that had been taken out of action if one had adequate power to return to base.

He had adequate power to return to Chu Lai or Da Nang on one engine and could disregard the section leader's order. Another order, considerably higher, from Air Force Command, decreed that the destruction of SAM missile sites within the DMZ area, including the QB sector, required U.S. Air Force clearance. Even if missiles had been fired, a half-hour waiting period was required before attack. Fighter-bomber pilots were at a loss to understand this directive. Was it to allow the Russian crews time to escape? The telltale smoke trail left by the SAM missile did not last a half-hour.

The regulation made his decision for him. He recalled, with disgust, proclamations made by dove senators on college campuses. It was close to his last mission, unless emergency missions demanded his duties. What would they do? Ground him and send him back to the States? He laughed aloud.

"Let's get the bastards," he remarked and banked the Phantom hard; skyward and inland.

The silent engine lit without incident. Satisfied, he pointed the big machine back toward Finger Lakes. Fritz called out his altitude and position, boldly oblivious to enemy radio surveillance. He lit both afterburners to scream back to the section leader, homing on a black orbiting speck.

"Fritz. Are you in a left hand turn?" he called. Without answer the lead F-4 darted downward. He slowed his afterburner speed to take careful distance from the F-4's bombing run. The lead plane had spotted the black smoke contrails left by the fired surface-to-air missiles rising upward and leaving a black smoke trail back to their launch site. Fritz carried seven napalm bombs. Slowly, it seemed, the Phantom F-4 descended, flattening out its dive to approach at under 450 knots. Napalm fuses were touchy and often proved to become duds if flown at higher speeds. Fritz came in low, around five hundred feet off the jungle and lesser foliaged slopes. A flash of fire erupted from below the machine while the pilot bent his plane hard to the left to get a look at his drop. He immediately became swearing over the intercom.

"Goddamnit, Chief! I'm two hundred long." Which meant for the trailing pilot to drop his bombs two football fields (two hundred yards) short of the napalm fire. The dog bone bomb selection switch was clicked to six 500-pounders and armed (half the load of the fighter bomber). The right thumb rose over the 'bombs away' button while the fingers held the control stick. A slight tap or two adjusted the rudders at his feet while his left hand on the throttles controlled his now flat approach at close to five hundred feet, his speed over 450 knots as the bombs did not have the napalm's detonation problems. When the estimated two hundred yards approached, the bomb drop button was pressed while the pair of throttles were pushed forward to full afterburner; the control stick leaned to his left and the port rudder pedal pressed firmly by his foot. Almost immediately the ground seemed to erupt behind him as he turned the plane hard to get a view. A flaming secondary explosion erupted from the jungle when the first load of six bombs detonated. "Right on, Chief," Fritz yelled with exuberance across the radios. The section leader expended his remaining napalms close to the fiery jungle, sending a ricocheting fire streaking a half-mile, obviously igniting a missile, like an errant Fourth of July rocket or a Roman candle flaming through the jungle tops. The last of his bombs scattered the diminishing fireball below with resultant lesser explosions.

After several victory rolls, the section joined back in formation, departing south across the mountains north of Da Nang. Out ahead of the monsoon, scud clouds were lowering below the mountains to the coastline, moving toward Chu Lai and Da Nang. Within an hour, the rains would be drenching both bases. At a thousand feet, both Phantoms streaked above the landing end of Chu Lai runway, the lead plane peeling away, breaking sharply to arc smoothly back to the touchdown point. The wingman held his course for several seconds more above the runway then rolled ninety degrees to the horizon, following in a wider arc to increase the landing separation from the leader. The drag chutes deployed as each aircraft landed.

The pilots offered little at the debriefing. They reported possible secondary explosions, presumably a minor truck depot. Possible ground fire was alleged; anti-aircraft fire was reported to be negative. The aviators were thankful they were not career men and that they'd both be rotating back to the States soon. He walked across the sand dunes with his RIO and Fritz, their conversation oblivious to the mission. Instead they laughed and reminisced about two attractive schoolteachers the pilots had met in Okinawa. They stopped at his hut for a rum and coke, despite the time of day.

After Fritz and the RIO left, he sat on his locker beside his bunk and mixed one more rum and coke. It had been a good mission. He languished confidently, assured that there were fewer Russians to fire missiles at the fighter-bombers. He never finished the liquid in his canteen cup. The ever-present heat and the rum made him drowsy. He fell back on his air mattress and was soon asleep. Before he fell backwards, he managed to stand and hang his shoulder holster and pistol on a nail above his mosquito netting and then placed his *wotai* pouch across the pistol butt jutting from the holster. While he slept, the maintenance crews checked his aircraft to correct the gyroscope. Despite the engine squelching blast scorching the blast side intake, not a mark was to be found on the huge Phantom. "You will see the enemy over 100 times, and the bullets will bounce from your machine," Fools Crow had told him.

Now dear reader, you should well understand WHY I have returned to the Natural Way!

9 UNIVERSITY AND THE MISSIONARY

University

I returned from war. Eight days out of the cockpit I was in law school. I had a thirty-day leave coming to me and my discharge papers had been held up when we landed at El Toro Marine Base in California. Law School Freshman Week had already started. I took my leave time and told administrative G-1 that I would return once they got my papers sorted out. Within two days I was standing before the dean of the law school, Dean Scarlett. "Glad you're back." He rose to shake my hand. He had an unusual office. Instead of a normal, secluded room, his office opened to the main hallway. My back was to the opening to the hall. Unbeknownst, a figure had passed behind me. The dean motioned quickly for me to step back into the hall and look to my right. "Tell me what you see," he commanded.

I saw a small man in unusual attire, walking away. He was dressed in what was called a Nehru suit and a funny looking hat, at least to me, the kind that 'Red-Dot No-Meat' Indians wore. (That is our Sioux term for them to differentiate from we meat-eating type Indians.) They are smaller than us and speak a British form of English as well. "That is the Torts professor, Prakesh Sinha. He is the arch Peacenik on campus. He has sworn to flunk you!"

'Yipe', I thought. 'Haven't even started and now I get flunked?'

I was an activist to some degree back then but never imagined that I would be much more of one by the following fall and on through law school, and not for the issue I started out with—the war in Vietnam. I did write several lengthy articles to the *Sioux Falls Argus-Leader*—the state's largest newspaper while I was in Vietnam. I simply revealed how we were fighting the war…and losing. I described the many opportunities we allowed the enemy. A few examples were eight-day truces, and an open Haiphong harbor where even our NATO allies could unload their military industrial supplies to North Vietnam. On the ninth day following the truce the Viet Cong and NVA were now healthily re-supplied and we on the opposite side would get the hell shot out of us. This is not the way to fight a war and expect to win. We Sioux were well aware of how the White Man can foolishly fight a war. We defeated him quite handily for two decades. Had he trained his horses the way we trained ours, had he utilized the Winchester repeating rifle, which he made and we had, versus his single-shot, and had he rode with both hands free—Mongolian style for much more accurate aiming—he may have had a better outcome. Harvard and Yale eggheads are poor examples of War Department administrators.

How? Why did we have a superior repeating rifle, holding up to 15 rounds of the shorter pistol ammunition while the Cavalry had only a single shot? The Winchester was invented by a gun mechanic named Henry and the first versions in 1856 were named the Henry Rifle. It was as marvelous a firearm weapon as the Colt revolver. Winchester Arms bought Henry's patent, hired him and began turning out thousands of the lever action rifles— the cartridge cocked into the chamber from the storage magazine and cocked the firing pin hammer at the same time. It was so deadly that it could hold off ten men with single-shot Sharps 45.70s. Even moreso if the men were firing the much slower-loading black powder muskets.

Winchester believed the War Department would buy practically all they could make but their competitor, Springfield Arms, was entrenched in the War Department administration along with certain key politicians who were bribed and bought off akin to our former Vice President Dick Cheney who amassed millions while Secretary of Defense. A story was fabricated that the rifle would use up too much ammunition. No market for it existed in the Eastern States so in desperation, close to bankruptcy, the company sent their rifles west. Traders and trappers found a ready customer with the Sioux. Abundant gold could be hand-picked from Black Hills and some Colorado streams. *Lelah Ahtaah! Wahshichu–enah. Mazah zizi witkokolah.* (The yellow metal drives the White Man crazy.) From before the Civil War to the Treaty of 1868, Chief Red Cloud; later Crazy Horse, amassed an arsenal of Winchesters which in turn allowed a supplemental arsenal of Sharps 45.70 single-shot carbines captured from the repeatedly defeated cavalry along with their horses, pistols and ammunition. One Union commander hocked his farm to purchase Winchesters for his battalion which in turn defeated a Confederate Regiment (three battalions) yet the War department never purchased the far more efficient weapon.

The Haiphong Docks where ships came in to unload their war supporting cargoes were off limits to our fighter attack bombers. The higher ups in our Defense Department were overly concerned that merchant ships could or would be bombed. I offered that we could easily sever the docks from the unloading ships by utilizing a very accurate invention called the snake eye bomb. With that weapon, you come in low and parallel to the ship and the smaller size bomb could easily destroy the waiting dock with little damage to the ship. Mr. Christopherson, the editor, treated my letters as editorials and even had a nice picture of me in my captain's uniform. CAPTAIN MCGAA SPEAKS OUT, he captioned them. Professor Sinha obviously read the newspaper.

"You will be the first freshman in the history of law school not to take torts until your senior year," the dean called out to me. I returned to his office, his beautiful blonde secretary looking up at me, obviously a bit startled at seeing a Marine captain in uniform. Later I got to know her. She admitted to being quite impressed. On a list of five or ten, I have to admit that she was one of the most beautiful women I have known. After Shirley and I had stared at each other, the dean interrupted with a polite cough. "You will be taking torts from me in your senior year." I never thought of it at the time but that meant that the peacenik Sinha would no longer be at the law school. "Because of your past," he added. "You have a lighter load this semester." The beautiful secretary smiled up at me. I barely heard the encouraging dean. "You will be taking summer school to catch up." I thanked him and turned. Beautiful Shirley offered her hand and stood up from her desk. "Welcome back, Captain. Thanks for serving our country."

Cheryl Tiegs

I was walking to the Student Union at the university after a morning class for a cup of coffee. Such a new life I was enjoying. The war for me was a long ways away in more than one category. A pretty blonde stood beside a small two-seat Cessna 150 airplane that was oddly parked in the parking lot of the student union. From death's door to beautiful blondes was a welcome, appreciated change—and this one was a pilot, as well. She had flown it in close to the campus with the local police blocking off a certain avenue devoid of wires and tall cottonwood trees. (My favorite tree, incidentally. I recently had six mid-growth sized ones planted at my Black Hills home.) This one looked somewhat like Cheryl Tiegs', a popular model in those days. She had her abundant hair tied up with a red, white and blue scarf. It was Fall weather and she wore a top coat with high calf-covering leather old-style aviator looking boots. Underneath those boots were a gorgeous set of legs, I would later find out. Like the famous model, she was around 5' 7" or 8". She smiled at me as I approached and waved her hand. "Hi, Captain McGaa."

"How do you know me?" I walked toward her.

"Everyone knows you, Captain. The newspaper. Do you want to join our flying club?"

She eventually checked me out in the little airplane (so small compared to the Phantom). Gas was fairly cheap those days so I used the plane a few times to fly to places where I gave speeches. As slow as it was, it beat driving to a Dakota town several hundred miles away. I was a hawk for the war back then while one of our senators, Senator George McGovern, was on the opposite side, along with Morse, Fulbright, Gruening, Hatfield and Kennedy. A host of others as well. South Dakota is and was a strongly Republican state and very hawkish as far as war is concerned as many of the 'Red States' are nowadays. I had quite a few requests to go out into its hinterland and deliver speeches favoring their cause given my experience at fighting. The Doves, however, were proven right. They were right and I was wrong. Many years later, a month before George McGovern died, he stopped to visit me and I told him so.

Later, the university acquired a larger four-seat Cessna 180. It had a tail wheel and could land in a short distance. It was faster than the piddly 150 model, a perfect airplane for carrying professors in and off gravel or pavement airport runways or with reservation police blocking both ends of certain highways with their warning lights. Two reservations had convenient tie-down rings in cow pastures next to the highway. You simply call the reservation police department and give an estimate as to when you are coming out. You buzz the station a few times and a couple squad cars come speeding out with their lights flashing to block the road. They were always happy to oblige. It gave them something fun to do. Several times I brought Bill Eagle Feather down to the university this way. He spoke good English and gave valuable lectures on Sioux culture. He would be standing alongside the highway with his trademark metal suitcase.

The second semester my grades were good enough that the dean allowed me to have a part time job flying professors across the state. The demand was more than I could handle. Innocent and beautiful 'Cheryl Tiegs' had a commercial flying license. She became the other pilot of the Cessna 180. We also wound up using a Mooney 21. It was equivalent in speed to the 180, much faster than the pitiful little flying club 150. Both were perfect planes for interstate trips and paid for a considerable amount of both our education bills. I also flew for the Marine Corps Air Reserve located in Minneapolis. I would fly one of the two airplanes or the 150 once a month usually to the municipal airfield and fly Marine H-34 helicopters on weekends. That position also helped defray law school expenses. Believe it or not, I paid for my attractive wife's last two years of college at a nearby Catholic woman's college (Mt. Marty) and my law school without owing a dime come graduation. That would be impossible in this greedy, inflated world we live in nowadays where university presidents and their fleet of minions make millions at the high expense of student tuition. They most often retire after setting up some program as the University of Minnesota president did and drag along their buddies to keep them employed as well.

Father John Bryde, 'Doc' Bryde.

I carried Doctor Bryde often in both planes as did 'Cheryl T.'. What a wonderful opportunity for me. Here I have the 'Dr. Einstein' of Lakota Sioux history sitting next to me for an hour or two of flight out to some distant Dakota town or Indian reservation. I would listen to his lectures on Sioux history and be able to ask many questions on the way back. At the time I would never dream that I would be writing a very accurate Sioux History book, *Crazy Horse and Chief Red Cloud,* and sell it by the cases at Crazy Horse mountain museum as well as in a goodly number of Dakota bookstores.

I challenge any book regarding the accuracy of depicting the Big Horn battle. It lasted maybe a half hour. Major Reno's writings admit that he was stopped in about five minutes of withering fire at the opposite end of the camp, losing half his command, and saved by immediately retreating from the barrage and crossing back over the river into protective cottonwoods. On the other end, Custer, with equal forces as Reno's, had to travel several hundred yards before meeting Sioux, Cheyenne and Arapaho who unleashed the same withering barrage. As Custer retreated, the attacked forces from the south end hurriedly joined the action with their Winchester repeaters and single shot Sharps captured cavalry rifles. It was absolutely impossible for a single cavalry man to ride through two thousand armed and experienced warriors, yet even the last Custer Battle book has them doing so—and this book was written by an Indian. Writers falsifying John Wayne-flavored epics, copied mostly from Marie Sandoz's writings, carry Custer's attack all day into flanking movements and battle strategy. My information was supplied to Doc Bryde from the warriors who were there. "As long as it takes a man to eat a meal," is what they told him regarding the duration of the battle. Major Reno, who lived, certainly backs up their depiction. The Little Big Horn Battle Association lecturers now state the same since metal detectors and several documentaries have shortened the fantasized Sandoz length considerably.

Doc Bryde, had been a former Jesuit Priest on my parents' reservation, the Oglala's. He learned to master our language enough so that my mother who was very fluent, would exclaim, "Oh! That Father Bryde. He speaks good Indian." The old timers on the reservation heard about his ability and came pell mell to tell him about their far more accurate version of Sioux history: the famous battles and chiefs such as Spotted Tail (Sichangu Lakota), Crazy Horse and Chief Red Cloud, (Oglala) and Sitting Bull (Hunkpapa). The eastern based Dakotas were not involved in our famous battles, only the Lakota. Not only did he learn from the Oglala veterans, but he would be assigned to other reservations to fill in for sabbatical priests or those temporarily incapacitated due to some illness. Hence his Lakota Sioux warrior historical knowledge would be broadened considerably.

Beautiful Connie Bowen—University President's Wife

Doc Bryde was not the only important passenger that I would fly during those three years. I flew none other than the beautiful wife (yes, a blonde again) of the university president. Connie Bowen needed to be taken to several destinations to attend various functions. University yearbooks of the latter sixties should have pictures of how pretty she is. I was in my early thirties while in law school and she was, too. Her kids played with mine in school and she became a strong benefactor for our university Native American club. We would bring Chief Fools Crow, Chief Eagle Feather and Ben Black Elk for valuable speaking engagements. They were notable and knowledge producing events. Ben was the interpreter for the world famous book, *Black Elk Speaks*, between his father and the writer, John Neihardt. Connie could get fairly much anything we Indian students wanted for speakers and have them transported, boarded, fed and paid them needed honorariums. She attended most all of our meetings and planning sessions. She would even stop by my rented house and pick me up for some meetings. My wife would tease me when she would drive up or knock on the door. "Here comes your girlfriend."

Nothing romantic ever happened between us; not at the University. If the Roman Catholic Pope was her pilot, he couldn't help but to notice her attractive legs while she sat in the front of the cockpit. What? Me, an Indian law student and the university president's wife? That would have been as dumb as these high school coaches who fall in love with their players. She was beautiful, bright, and Spiritual far more than she was religious. She even came with her family to view my second Sun Dance. I remember being pierced for my first time. I went to the end of my tethering rope and leaned back, feeling the first pain before attempting to break free. I looked to the left and there close to the edge of the dance arena was Connie's beautiful face staring a hole right through me. I thought I was in a dream. A university president's wife at an early Sun Dance? Impossible. I concluded that I was having a vision! Later after we dancers had broken our bond and were lined up to receive the handshakes of the hundreds of devout spectators, mostly Lakota, my sisters came through the line and there, right behind them was Connie. I can't help liking blondes. They always seemed to like me and more attentive than others. Not my fault.

Years later, Connie had me do a very powerful Sweat Lodge for her. She was dying of cancer at an early age. I am no Holy Man, and never will be, but at that particular lodge, it was probably the most powerful (received positively by the Spirits or whatever Mystery that watches over such) ceremony I have ever been involved with. After my graduation, Connie got divorced and I was fortunate to date her for a period of time since I was divorced also. We both wondered what life would have been like had we married. We certainly got along well and our spiritual inclination was so alike. She came down with cancer and came to me. She was way too young to die: So beautiful in both looks and mind, and the mind the most important for selecting a mate. She said she wanted to go back to Sweden and see her relatives. She asked me to do a sweat lodge for her and beseech to the spirits. That previous weekend, I had done several for a summer conference at a college south of the Twin Cities, Carleton College. She called the president there as he knew her former husband. He responded to her plea and had the lodge quarantined off with those police-type yellow tapes. Everything we needed was provided. One of the college maintenance men was an Indian and he built the fire and heated the stones. Only Connie and I went into the lodge. She was fairly weak when we drove to Carleton. Inside the lodge she simply asked the Spirits to give her strength to go back to Sweden. She came out strong and was healthy for her whole trip overseas. She called me when she returned and I went to meet her and her sister. We kissed each other goodbye and she went home to die. Her wish had been granted. She told me to look at the setting sun and when it is turquoise to think of her, which I do. If I die tomorrow I will get to see her, is my belief. I am quite sure there is a Spirit World Beyond. When you get older, dying is not so bad. Think of all the close ones you get to be with again.

Politics and Airplanes

My letters to the editor had caused enough stir in my home state to generate political requests for Right Wing doings in the midst of numerous demonstrations from the Left side of the political specter. My phone would ring and a well-heeled rancher, farmer or businessman would request my presence at a political dinner or function, most often as a keynote or the only speaker. Some were held at local veteran's clubs and were well attended. My statement was to 'Fight to Win or Get the Hell Out.' We were handicapped considerably the way we were forced to fight in Vietnam.

The usual gist of their request would be, "Captain McGaa, one of our members heard you speak at such and such a town. We'd like for you to fly up to our town and say the same. We'll pay for your airplane and offer you an honorarium as well." I'd generally fly up on a Friday or Saturday event for an evening deliverance. At all veteran's clubs where an open bar would be available, I would most often stay overnight. If I did fly off at night, I would often have to ask for a pair of pickup trucks parked at each side of the runway end, which were usually gravel and a few were just plain grass. I would aim between the pickup lights at full power, leave it on into the climb and turn around and buzz the crowd below. They liked it!

My senior year was a political election year and the Republican Party wanted to oust Democrat Senator George McGovern who was so popular that he later was drafted as a presidential candidate. Governor Archie Gubbrud was chosen to run against him. I was visited by the House speaker, Senator Hirsch of Yankton, and asked if I would be a part of the governor's final speech to be aired on television just before the election. It was probably illegal but I wore my uniform with its decorations and gold wings and told why I believed we were not winning in Vietnam. Senator Hirsch spoke after me and was followed up by the Governor.

Fate

Possibly Fate, the Force, or what have you, wanted me to be back in my home state at a time when tremendous change was happening. Finally in America, citizens were speaking out and needed change had to come about. As a helicopter pilot before I started flying jets, my squadron had been dispatched to Mississippi University to stay at a football stadium with several companies of Army Airborne. Our H-34 choppers carried the Airborne into several key points at the University and the town to hold down any red neck intervention. Martin Luther King was making changes and students everywhere were protesting the war.

On my reservation, the traditional Oglala and Sichangu were rising up as well, challenging the missionary instigated government ban on our Sioux religion, our ceremonies especially, which are key projections of our Nature-based Spirituality. Our two tribes of the Lakota seven were always out in front, ready for change. We were the first to cross the Missouri almost fifty years before the other five. We were the first to enter the Black Hills and now were the forerunners to challenge the unconstitutional ban of our ceremonies. We utilize our ceremonies to beseech to our concept of the Ultimate Power, *Wakan Tanka*, Great Spirit and/or Great Mystery. And you know what happens? They do communicate with us! I don't like excuses that white men make for their preachers being exclusionary. White religious leaders do not have the focus that ours do. They are too distracted by power, control seeking and materialism. Their concept of real truth is not our version of real Nature-based, not Man-based Truth. We have contact. They don't. Maybe several centuries from now the intelligent ones among them will figure this out.

The annual Sun Dance ceremony was banned but my tribe conducted it anyway. The missionaries and the Bureau of Indian Affairs officials became a bit fearful to block our ongoing movement with the outside world making everyone aware of civil rights. For the most part, both left us alone except for one particular Jesuit priest who finally had to be confronted. If Fate is real, then I guess, that was the warrior's role I had to enact. It cost me a preferred career in the Marine Corps.

I had finished my first year of law school. I had to fulfill my vow taken in Chief Fools Crow's *Yuwipi* ceremony before I left for Vietnam. I would go through the four-day ordeal without water and without food. The second day of the Sun Dance was little different from the day before except that the pangs of hunger seemed to be more pronounced for me.

The Sun Dance is the annual thanksgiving to honor Great Spirit for all that it provides. A cottonwood tree is selected and brought into the arena the day before the official four days of thanksgiving will commence. A deep hole is dug and strong men raise the tree and implant it into the hole. Ropes hang down from the tree. On the fourth day, the Sun Dancers will be pierced through the skin of their chests (but not through the muscle). Their skin will be pulled out with a needle and a sharp awl will be tunneled into the skin and out the opposite side, maybe about an inch or so. A smooth peg about two inches or so and about 1/4th inch in diameter is tunneled through the pair of slits. The dancer will then be skewered and the end of the rope from the tree will be tied around the peg's ends and wrapped with a thong. The pledger will rise and take his place distant from the tree with the other pledgers. The ceremony will culminate when all pledgers are pierced and after a few minutes they will all lean back and break free. They are giving their pain so that the people may live and to give thanksgiving and appreciation to the Great Mystery. More elaborate description and explanation may be found in the many books I have written.

Pledgers take vows when an event in their lives occasions them to be especially thankful. I vowed that if I came back from war I would dance for four days. Another pledger lost a daughter, drowned in a river and her body went missing. He asked the Spirits in the Spirit World to help him find his daughter in a spirit calling ceremony. He pledged to do the Sun Dance. The Spirits told him she was snagged by an immersed old cottonwood by a certain turn of the river. She was found. The Sun Dancer usually asks for a certain favor and pledges to endure four days of fasting and no water. You ask. You give back through the Sun Dance. Some pledgers need not ask, they are simply appreciative of something good that happened. I had a nephew who had no problem with drugs or alcohol, but his son did. His son sweat lodged and endured the Sun Dance. He went clean and now runs a successful business. My nephew simply wanted to show God (Creator) his appreciation. He danced ten years in a row to show God his appreciation.

This harmless ceremony was banned by the U.S. government through the zealous lobbying of the missionaries. They always meddle and stick their noses in where they shouldn't. They have to continually prove to themselves that they alone know who or what Creator is and what Creator wants them to do, especially regarding us who do not believe exactly as they do. Many wars and deaths have resulted from this human idiocy.

The pipes of the six Sun Dance pledgers were offered on the second day, causing the ceremony to last a few hours while a small crowd looked on. I did not have a peace pipe and Chief Eagle Feather did not yet present his pipe although he danced along with us. After the morning ceremony, I took a long walk into the hills leading into the Badlands toward the northwest. It was late afternoon before I returned to the campgrounds. The afternoon was cool enough to allow the sighting of two rattlesnakes emerging from their holes to start off early on their evening hunt. The fasting made me tire easily. I headed for my sister's Airstream trailer parked not far from the Sun Dance arena.

My sister Mildred had been crippled up from a bad fall and suffered occasional pain. Ralph, her husband, became extremely nervous when she would go into a spasm. It was pretty hard on them both. I started powwow dancing at an early age, about the seventh grade. Mildred would come and watch me dance. Oddly, many Indians were ashamed back in those days. They were like the Mexicans nowadays who are ashamed to state that they are Indian. Look at my last book, *Spirituality for America*. You ask one, "Los Indios?" About 98% I have queried, respond, "No, No!"

I say, "Latino?" "Si, Si," they readily agree. "Chicano?" The same agreement usually with a tinge of pride. I then throw at them, "Mestizo?" That means, "Are you half Indios?" "No, No!" comes their emphatic denial. Hell most of them are darker than me!

My beautiful blonde wife spoke fluent Spanish and taught me to say, thumping my chest and pointing to myself, *"El Rojo Indios! Norte Americano!* (I am a Red Indian from North America.) *Aquí, estamos orgullosos de ser indio!* (Here, we are proud to be Indian.) *"Los mortuo. Oglala Sioux guerrero* (Warriors) *Gringos Federales—Ocho."* (With a cutting of my throat.) "Sioux *Guerrero— Uno."* (Trying to say in my broken Spanish.) "We killed eight soldiers for every warrior lost."

My words fell on deaf ears. Odd, how an entire nation that is by far, Indios, denies what they are. 98% of them never had a clue as to what I was saying to them. It all went over their heads, such has Organized Religion molded them to deny real truth.

Can you blame us North American Indians for being considerably disgusted with such an attitude? But, unfortunately, it will be but a matter of time before these Indios will eventually inherit this country due to their organized religion-promoted birth rate that has no regard for the dangers of overpopulation. Too bad they cannot accept our environmental respecting theology/cosmology/Spirituality.

At my high school which was almost all white with a smattering of Indians, just about all the Indian students wanted to be white. To dance Indian, they would have shuddered with embarrassment if told to do so by their parents. These better educated, ashamed Indians went on to become academics. Remember when I told you about the Jesuit-run gymnasium where Curtis and I cemented our friendship? Well, there were two good basketball players there older than me by several years. One had a car and carried his mother and my mother to their all Indian women's meetings at the Winona Club. Zonda Swallow and Laverne Yankton danced Indian and were beautiful dancers and looked handsomely - Old Time! Laverne was no movie star in ordinary clothes but when he got dressed up for Indian dancing he was breathtaking. Zonda was not far behind him. As a pair, the crowds went spellbound over them. In our small Indian world, they were local celebrities. At the gym, Curtis and I were becoming so good that the bigger boys welcomed us into their league and we pretty much held our own. Zonda became very protective of me and almost got in a fight over one guy trying to rough me up. Laverne also supported us. Zonda was extremely handsome with or without dance regalia. He looked a lot like that Madrid, Spain soccer star, Ronaldo Christiano. Well, it wasn't long before I grew enthralled with Indian dancing probably because those two were becoming my heroes. They had enough regalia spare parts to get me started and my sister made the rest. Poor Curtis wanted to dance, too, but I told him he couldn't because he was white. He got mad at me and I never saw him during the powwow months but once basketball started up, we became friends again.

Author Powwow Dancing

I enjoyed dancing so much that I didn't give a damn what the hell the white kids or sell-out Indian kids thought. I guess I was kinda' like a kid my hockey-playing son knew. They both played together and my son succeeded to Mites, Pee Wee and on up to A Bantams, but the friend got into Figure Skating and had to quit regular hockey. My son understood and squelched any criticism for his friend as he and another understanding friend were pretty tough defensemen. Indian dancing is such finesse and utter beauty. You just cannot help but fall in love with it no matter what the circumstances.

So as I was dancing my sister would come and watch me. She said the drums soothed her. She also helped me make my pitiful dance outfit more elaborate and made her husband buy a fancy eagle feather tail bustle for me. He didn't like it but always strove to please his wife. She gave me too much attention and I couldn't blame him for getting jealous. He thought she was the Queen of Sheba and was always reaching to hold her hand in the car when we would go fishing. I never thought my sister was any raving beauty but I guess many brothers are like that. He was one big tough guy and used to play at an adjoining card shop where I got my haircuts. You could sit in the barber chair and watch them play. One day I went into Bud's Barber Shop and Ralph was playing cards. I looked pretty much Indian as a kid as I was always outside a lot and picked up quite a tan. Some wise guy remarked about me being an Indian and the barber should clean his scissors. Ralph told him to shut his mouth and the man stupidly called Ralph a squaw man. I never saw him get so angry. The guy was equal in size but Ralph picked him up right out of his chair and drilled him, sending him flying into the wall. He picked him up and hit him again, yelling in rage. God! Ralph was mad. Several guys had to hold him back as he might have killed the idiot. No one ever mentioned the term again in that card shop or ever said anything about me getting my hair cut in there.

Anyway, my sister would sit in a wheelchair at the dances. One time she got up and hobbled around the dance circle. I was surprised to see her out in the arena. She had a pretty blue shawl and blossomed with a smile. She went back and sat down. Pretty soon she got up and made two rounds. Next week we had another dance and she danced quite a bit. Eventually she became normal and all that summer she and Ralph hit the powwow circuit, going far away to Crow country. The drums, the drums, they healed her. The Crows treated Ralph well and showed him some good trout fishing since he was married to an Indian. My sister always claimed it was the drum beat that cured her and, of course, the Spirits and Creator. Ralph forgot about his jealousy. He said to me one time, "Thanks for getting my wife back."

As I was walking toward the Airstream I spotted a new camper van turning from the highway to the campgrounds. Eventually, a priest stepped from the parked van, walking a straight line for the silver camper trailer. I slowed my pace and watched him knock on the screen door.

The following is written in third person and taken from my only novel, *Eagle Vision*, now out of print: written over two decades ago. Since that was a ways back my memory was much keener then. Although it is from my only fictional writing, it is a very accurate portrayal of what happened. It is much like an early chapter of this book, wherein Cross Dog suffered the consequences of the train. That too was written way back. For the sake of higher accuracy I have chosen to avoid first person writing in some portrayals. My mind back then was much closer for recall and I am glad I wrote so many events down despite their appearance in fiction form. It did not harm their accuracy in my opinion. Buchwald is the real life Jesuit zealot Paul Steinmetz, and Charging Shield is me. (Charging Shield was a great grandfather on my mother's side who was in the battle of the Little Big Horn). Mildred is my oldest sister who hovered over my mom and dad and lived next door about half a block away with her husband Ralph (a former All-State football fullback two years in a row). He was very devoted to my sister and they had no children between them. She also doted on my sister next to me and my friend Stan Curtis. In a way she resembled Audrey Meadows in the Jackie Gleason sit com. She even acted a bit like 'Alice.'

"Is your mother here?" Father Buchwald inquired anxiously to Mildred.

"She wanted to stay, but Brother Hobart made her go back to West River. Mom's not getting any younger, you know." The woman made a welcoming gesture. "Come in and have some coffee."

Buchwald took a seat on the couch while Mildred peered out the screen door at the new van. "My, that's a nice one," she exclaimed. Her tone was warm and laudatory.

"It's from a government grant. The mission is working on a study: the urban reservation relationship and alcoholism," added the priest.

"I think we've been studied enough," Mildred replied bluntly. She took several steps toward a coffeepot on the stove. "They ought to spend some of that money on the Indians."

"Now, Mildred. Indian secretaries will be employed," Buchwald chastised with a scolding air. "That bus is a research vehicle for field work. All in all, the grant will put money into the community."

At that moment, Charging Shield passed close to the trailer, stopping to listen through a side window.

"Field work? What you mean by that?"

"Well, ah... Extensive field work in the reservation and urban community. The van affords privacy for compiling research data. It's an encompassing project, Mildred, a feasibility study centering on reservation needs...and urban needs evolved from a culture still too rooted in the past." The priest's academic voice pretentiously lowered to a worried note. "And, of course, the devastating alcohol problem." A paternalistic smile lit his face.

"Well, you've lost me." Mildred's answer was blankly polite. "You always told us, Jesuits are the most educated ones. I hope you can do some good."

"We're the soldiers for the Holy Father." Buchwald puffed his chest, adding zealously, "The shock troops for the Lord."

"Your feasibility study is more money down the drain. After you're through, you'll milk another hundred grand to study us." Charging Shield sent a cold, commanding voice into the recreation trailer as he glared from the doorway.

Buchwald jumped at the first sound of his voice. Still somewhat startled, he stared in fascination at the Indian. So now he would confront this militant who had turned against the church. His hunched stance made him look as if he were about to leap forward off of a diving board, or out to catch a real, live devil. Some said he was hypnotized by Fools Crow or Eagle Feather...and the old Badlands witch, the Grandmother. Her devil's influence was still alive. This militant had no business on the reservation. Her poisoned babble had brought him back to carry on the heathenry. The priest studied the Indian's face intently. The cold-blooded look coming from Charging Shield's eyes unnerved him. There was nothing conciliatory in that look, why,...he was more vicious looking than his brother Lawrence. Buchwald's hand unconsciously rose up to rub his temple. Buchwald noted that Charging Shield lacked the mannerisms of a beaten, economically subjected people. Worse, he was outside of the priest's grasp, no longer a helpless boarding school child. On second thought, Buchwald decided to avoid a confrontation.

"Well, Mildred, ah, I'd better be going," Buchwald stammered, shrinking back from the low table.

"Finish your coffee. I want to talk to you," Charging Shield commanded.

"Now, Kyle, I'm not looking for trouble," Buchwald's voice quavered. "I've come in peace. I've been on this reservation longer than you, and I'm simply paying my respects to dear friends."

"Look, Buchwald, I know what you're up to. You want to pressure my relatives, especially my mother. You 'Soldiers of the Lord' are plenty worried about a lone, damn, swear-wording ex-Marine captain taking part in a Sun Dance. If I go back, then the others might get ideas...and you and your kind would have to make a living off our reservation." Charging Shield dipped his head over his shoulder toward the van, lowering his voice to a whisper and raising an eyebrow with an exaggerated half-smile. "And if we go back, we might solve our alcohol gift from you people, without another worthless study." His voice mocked Buchwald's pretentious tone.

"Kyle, I didn't come to hear militancy."

"You didn't hear a word I said, Buchwald. Not one damned word."

Buchwald was spellbound. He managed a weak nod. Never had he heard an Indian or anyone talk to a Jesuit in such a brazen manner, at least not on a reservation.

Charging Shield leaned forward to speak again almost in a whisper and with the same eyebrow raised, "Don't wait for a lightning bolt to strike me dead." He began by looking up to the ceiling. "You might have some of your brainwashed, boarding school products fooled, but not me."

"Kyle," Buchwald said with placation, "I've known you since you were a little boy. Why, your mother…"

"Hold it right there," Charging Shield interrupted. "I'll listen, only if you'll listen to me. Then maybe we can have some dialogue."

Buchwald's face flushed. His anger began to flare. "I'm not here to play silly games. Someday you'll beg to have the Blessed Sacrament, like your sister here and the Lord have mercy on your soul. The direction you're going is hopeless, son. You'd better return to the Lord our Savior."

"How about the Great Spirit?" Charging Shield countered as he pulled up a chair to sit facing the priest.

"The Great Spirit; *Wakan Tanka*; the Sun God; devil talk. They will all fall before the risen Son of God who was conceived by the Holy Ghost and born of the Virgin Mary." Buchwald stood up, his words recovering their aplomb; his customary, superior smile returned, covering his face like a mask.

The Indian stared at the floor and lowered his head. Buchwald stepped forward from the couch.

"Kyle, you can't fight the Lord. It's foolish to fight us. We Jesuits have a history of adversaries, but they all fell." He swept his arm like a flail across the room. "Kings, dictators, politicians… They've all fallen before us."

Charging Shield continued to sit silently in his chair thinking back to Cross Dog and his brother Lawrence and their strategy, planned before they entered Buchwald's office to be punished. "We'll go in acting scared," Lawrence had said. "It always throws them off guard."

Buchwald felt a sudden surge of power over Charging Shield who was beginning to slump in his chair. "It isn't your fault, son. Some of these old medicine men are the slickest fakers in the world. Why, they know sleight of hand, they have tricks and the power to hypnotize. You may have been hypnotized or drugged, you never know. We were shocked to hear your mother had gone to one of those *Yuwipis*. You could have been responsible for her soul, son, dragging her down to Fools Crow's, thinking you'd get protection for the war. If she'd died, her soul would have gone to the depths of hell." The priest pushed the flat of his hand out as if stopping some unseen force. "I had her come to confession and the sacrament of Penance, and the Blessed Sacrament of Communion removed the stain of mortal sin. Now should your mother depart, I'm sure the angels of the Lord and the Blessed Mother will welcome her with open arms." Buchwald pointed his finger at the slouching figure. "Your mother, Kyle, is no doubt our greatest missionary just through her example. Your parents worked hard, spent their money on their family and not on drinking. Your mother saw to it that her family followed the church's teachings."

Charging Shield's head hung lower. He brushed his eyes with the back of his hand. Mildred stood by the sink, staring in baffled astonishment at the sudden, subdued change displayed by her brother.

"Kyle, I know all about these medicine men." The man in black placed his thumbs in his front pockets while he slowly paced the tiny living room. "Why, you take Fools Crow there. The old faker does this thing simply for the money. You can't blame him, in a way. He feeds every Tom, Dick, and Harry that comes to his place. Yes, money, money is the root of all evil. That's why we in the Jesuit order have the vow of poverty." He grimaced, baring his stained teeth, as if the sermon was drawing to a close. "Now, nowhere have I ever heard Mr. Fools Crow take a vow of poverty like we Jesuits. Not only that vow but we also will not take up with a woman like he has. We truly can devote ourselves to the Lord's work without diversion."

Charging Shield put his head between his hands pretending to stare at the floor, masking the glint in his eyes. *I will hear you out, Buchwald... And then you'll listen to me*, he thought.

"Ah, yes, money..." Buchwald went on. "Money and Mr. Fools Crow. Kyle, as you get older you'll learn these old fakers are in this for the money game. Otherwise they'd be out doing an honest man's work digging ditches like your father did. Of course your father didn't attend church like your mother, but he was, nevertheless, a good man." A disturbed frown gave way to a benevolent smile. "That is why we allowed him the last sacraments and a Christian burial. Now, if your father were alive, he wouldn't approve of Fools Crow…or the Sun Dance. He'd ask that you listen to your mother."

Buchwald continued his sermon with calm relish. "We gave you the opportunity to gain eternal life. A confession is what you need. Now son…" He reached for the slumping figure's shoulder. "The true church can help in more ways than one. Many a BIA college scholarship has gone to intelligent young Indians due to our efforts. I know you're on your way back to school. The Lord will provide for those that beseech him." Buchwald was the epitome of confidence. "Don't feel bad, boy. If you want, I will tell Fools Crow that you have seen the light and he won't be able to harm you." The Jesuit's face was covered with an accomplished grin. It was obvious to him that Julie Charging Shield had dictated to her son that he wouldn't be taking part in the Sun Dance. The trips to West River and the sessions with Julie had borne fruit.

"Mildred, your brother here," he said, as he clutched Charging Shield's shoulder and turned slightly as if to cast a dramatic paternal pose for some invisible photographer, "I'm sure he's seen the light. I'd better leave the two of you to your thoughts."

He beamed down on Charging Shield's awestruck sister, holding forth an anointing hand. "Someday you're going to be right behind your mother when it comes to working for the church." Buchwald reinforced his declaration with a sanctimonious spreading of his hands. He thought about reminding her about living with Ralph, a divorced man, only as brother and sister, and she might get to receive the sacraments but thought this subject needed another time and probably total privacy. "You get led astray like your brother here, but then Mother always brings her sheep back to the fold. I'm sure Julie will rest easier now. Ahh, I have said enough. You must think of our Lord Jesus." His face looked serenely toward the sunlight. He puffed his chest and spread his hands pontifically. "Jesus, Our Lord…is speaking through me!"

Charging Shield rose from his chair to stand in front of the doorway as the priest spoke. "Just a minute," he interrupted. "I want to tell you something."

Flush from his unexpected victory, Buchwald failed to note the abrupt change in the Indian's voice. "What is it, my boy?" His eyes stared in disbelief at the vicious smile. "Why, why, Kyle. What's going on? What's the matter?"

"Priest, it's my turn now…"

Buchwald looked for a moment in disbelief, then remembered something unconsciously from the past. His hand went instinctively to his temple, massaging his head for a moment. The sharp elbow thrown by Lawrence, long ago. It all came back to him. His face began to get red as he flushed with anger. "No, I won't be intimidated. You won't speak to me that way." He attempted to push the Indian aside.

Charging Shield lost his balance and fell back against the wall. He managed to spring forward in time to lower his shoulder solidly into Buchwald's soft stomach, sending the Jesuit staggering toward the couch.

Mildred ran to the narrow hallway to stand frozen as she watched the Jesuit still standing but doubled over, trying to catch his breath.

The priest's pained gasping left Charging Shield unmoved. "Missionary, that's nothing compared to what you did to us in that boarding school. When you get your wind back, sit on that couch. It's my turn to talk."

"You hit me, you militant!" The priest gasped fearfully. "I never beat children. I never…"

Mildred ran forward to shake her fist at the Jesuit. "Don't you lie!" she screamed. "You were one of the worst. All of you beat us; you and your God…damned…leather…straps. Don't lie!" Her voice choked and she began sobbing.

Charging Shield's eyes reddened when he saw his sister crying. Tears welled up for a brief moment when he thought about the boarding schools. The memory of Cross Dog made him wipe his nose on his sleeve and put his arm around his sister, turning her toward the rear of the trailer house. He set his jaw, as he glared at the missionary. "I heard your story, preacher. Now we'll hear what an Indian has to say." His words were slow and deliberate despite the reddening of his eyes.

Buchwald retreated toward the couch but refused to sit. "No, Kyle, I won't be forced. I'll have you arrested for assault and battery." His eyes widened when he saw the Indian reach for a rolling pin beside the kitchen sink. The crass tone of his words gave way to panic. "And intent to kill," he hastily added.

Charging Shield stalked the missionary. "Priest, you're going to hear my side," he said with bitter malice, raising the rolling pin. When the priest shifted his balance to block the impending blow, Charging Shield caught his adversary's shoulder with his free hand, slamming him into the couch. He brought the rolling pin down hard on the coffee table.

"Priest, I see boarding school all over your goddamned, wicked fucking face," he yelled. "Don't interfere with me! Understand?" He screamed loudly.

The priest stared back in disbelief. His face was white, his mouth open.

Charging Shield slowly regained his composure, but was still hot with anger. "My turn to talk," he began with a menacing stare. He waved the rolling pin in front of the Jesuit then threw it into a corner.

"You are a deceiver, Charging Shield. You are nothing but deceit. A true devil you are. You're possessed with an evil spirit. You pretended to listen. The real Indians would never deceive like you."

"Deceit…evil…devil…" Charging Shield threw his head back with harsh laughter. "We had to learn those words from you to survive." He paused for a moment then continued in a vindictive tone. "I told you I'd listen, if you'd listen to me." He began slowly and softly then with a raised pitch. "Missionary, we're going back. We're going back to the Great Spirit our way. We don't need you, priest." He drove his finger to emphasize his point. "You're interfering with something way bigger than your church when you try to stop our Sun Dance. That ceremony is a teaching from a culture that honed it for thousands of years. A real proven earth stewardship." His voice lowered. "The Buffalo Calf Maiden was sent to us by the Great Spirit. She told us to use our pipe in the Sun Dance. The Six Powers showed Black Elk that our sacred tree would return. Those are pretty big forces to meddle with, priest. I wouldn't think of trying to stop you from saying Mass in your chapel. Why should you interfere with what is holy to us? Don't you realize that you are nothing but a pitiful human being like the rest of us here on our Mother Earth? You don't know any more about God than I do and that's not a helluva lot." Less harshly he added, "I have always left you alone, why don't you leave us alone?"

"You are bullying me; uttering filth and slime…to me…a Jesuit Priest. Is that leaving me alone?" Buchwald shot back. "You can't know about God, the way you swear, then mention your Buffalo Calf Maiden cock and bull in the next breath."

The Indian stepped backward. "Yeah, Priest, I swear. But I don't beat captive kids and I don't try and destroy another people's religion." He paused and added in a less defiant tone, "I'm sorry, but you wouldn't listen to me otherwise. Maybe I was too long in the Marines fighting your wars for you. Maybe you people exasperate the hell out of me."

"And I won't listen to any more of this witch talk. We brought God to you pagans, not this Buffalo Maiden cock and bull." The missionary shook his head at the floor. "And worse yet, so many of you heathens believe it." A wild glint sprang from his eyes. "It's the work of the devil. That peace pipe fairy tale…and you all run around a tree like possessed savages."

The manifest boldness of the priest's declarations left Charging Shield staring back at his adversary, unable to reply. The missionary closed his eyes with a supercilious smile. "I've heard you, Kyle. I don't believe you and never will. You can kill me, but I will not give up my faith in the risen Lord, the fulfiller of all religions. He is the fulfiller and the redeemer of even your sinful soul. Without him you are lost and a thousand buffalo women are worthless."

The priest stood up

Charging Shield slammed him back into the couch. "Sit down! You fucking anti-Mother. I haven't finished yet! No one's asking you or anyone else to give up a damned thing. All we're asking is that you leave us alone…just leave us alone!"

Foam flecked Buchwald's lips as he yelled back in a frenzy, "This is false imprisonment, Kyle. False imprisonment! I'll have you locked away for years, you militant devil."

196

"You stand up again, anti-Mother priest, and you just may go to your reward," Charging Shield replied calmly. "They'll blow Gabriel's horn for you."

The priest sat, a blank stare fixed on the coffee table. "Anti-Mother? Anti-Mother? Just what do you mean by that? What kind of a statement is that demented mind of yours trying to make?"

Charging Shield laughed long and with a wicked grimace. "You and all that you stand for have been letting our Earth Mother get thoroughly raped. The Negroes use the term *motherfucker*. You know, missionary, I think that term applies to a whole lot of you so-called organized people, but in an environmental sense of the word. Your theologians could always look the other way anytime there was some more of Mother Earth to dig up or forests or indigenous people to be cut down. I think that the beavers and the buffalo would agree with me. Whatever the wealthy wanted to do or the Kings and Barons, you were right there to tell them it was okay to do it." He paused for a moment to let his words weigh. "Your motto was, 'Go ahead and fuck Mother Earth!' That is anti-Mother in my book. I hope it catches on. It's a perfect term for you kid-beating, anti-Mothers."

From the dance arena, the announcer called out the social dancing agenda. The afternoon's activities repeated across the loudspeaker displaced the icy silence within the trailer house. A pious grin began to grow on the Jesuit as if he had not heard his adversary's remarks. His head came back; his half-closed eyes were directed at the ceiling. "I'm willing to die for the Lord. Yes, die for Him," he exclaimed with fervor. "Jesus, is my Savior, and I will live for his name… To the very end." He rose slowly. In contrast to a few minutes before, he was now devoid of fear. "My Lord, my God, my Savior. I will give my life to bring eternal light to my people, the Sioux…in His name."

"Why you hung up martyr." Charging Shield grimaced a pained scowl before he pointed at the doorway. "Get out, Buchwald. Get out," he said with an exasperated shake of his head. "You'd love to be a martyr, wouldn't you?"

The missionary's smile was triumphant. "And furthermore…" He held his words until he had safely reached the doorway, "And furthermore, you pagan devil, I'll stop your heathen Sun Dance," he remarked with a smart smirk as he threw open the screen door and leaped out of the silver trailer.

Charging Shield held a hopeless look for a long moment before he dashed from the trailer to yell at the figure walking with hurried strides to the research bus. "Leave our Sun Dance alone, you bloodsucker," he called out with venom. "You've sucked my people white."

This very same priest whom I have characterized, later came into my fifth Sun Dance, the one I call, 'The AIM Sun Dance,' because the American Indian Movement came purposely to protect our ceremony from mainly him and his followers. I will reveal greater detail in a later chapter. Russell Means (now deceased) wrote in his book about the priest jumping in (carrying an oversized peace pipe and clad in his mass vestments) between Russ and me during the beginning of the ceremony. Russ and I were both Sun Dance pledgers which was conducted by Chief Fools Crow in the early '70s. The priest took part in the processional after we entered the arena and presented our pipes. Afterwards, during the recess, as we sat under a shade-providing bower, the head of AIM and I confronted the priest and asked him to leave as he was disrupting the ceremony. Actually, we had to tell him to leave as his intentions were too disruptive. His actions were no different than if we were to wear our Sun Dance ceremonial attire and barge in on a Catholic High Midnight Christmas mass. I strongly believe the audience would soon be dialing 911. The priest foolishly got carried away with his zeal and took over the microphone and initially condemned Russ and I as not being 'real Indians' since neither of us lived on the reservation anymore and that he, a white man, "I am more Indian than those two because I have spent my life here for you people!" He added, demanding, "You must put Christ in your ceremony." In the old days he could have brazenly got away with his actions but it was the beginning of a new era, an era of freedom for us to choose to return to our old way and no longer be sent to the death needles of church-lobbied federally built, staffed and funded Canton Insane Asylum (121 graves, no doubt more). "Get him out of there!" I yelled. Clyde Bellecourt leaped over the announcers railing and took the microphone away. He stated, "There will be no more interruption in this ceremony." Lehman Brightman, a former star running back, grabbed the priest and physically threw him, vestments and all, out of the booth. Higher ups finally sent him away on a long sabbatical and now our Sun Dance ceremony has blossomed to over 50 events a summer according to Milo Yellow Hair who keeps a tally and tells me proudly the numbers at the end of the summer. I guess you can say, 'We Won!'

10 PATRIOTISM

The Sioux Tribes will never dishonor a warrior coming back from battle. During the heat of Vietnam they were all honored.

The third day, Saturday morning, the sweat lodge fire was tended by Eagle Feather. The evening before, I slept so soundly that I never heard the new arrivals coming into the campground, many from long distances. The following morning would find the camping area doubled in size. The Way was starting to grow.

At the first hint of day, I walked toward the bright blaze near the ceremonial lodge aware that the hunger pangs I had felt severely the night before were now no longer existent. Somehow, I felt as though I had been given a totally new and fresh body and this time one without an appetite. I huddled close to the fire covering my shoulders with my sister's navy blue shawl.

"Nephew, so far you have done well, but we still have two days to go," Eagle Feather said as I sat next to him. "I was the first to predict you would do the Sun Dance." The flames reflected traces of gray in the Rosebud holy man's close-cropped hair. "I predict you will see many adventures in but a short while." Eagle Feather continued in his matter-of-fact manner, "This Sun Dance and those airplanes behind you are only the beginning."

I was pleased with the holy man's words. His eyes rested on the thin bark of a limb bursting into flame. The comfortable fire and the large framed man sitting next to him gave him a secure feeling. I recalled the return of the Sun Dance when Eagle Feather boldly brought back the piercing. I had sat with my grandmother that day, more than a decade before. Since that time, the old woman had fulfilled her circle of life. My mind drifted below to the tall cottonwood tree guarding my grandmother's abandoned cabin and the shallow stream. I remembered her words as they watched Fools Crow pierce Eagle Feather in the center of the curious crowd numbering less than a hundred. "Put your head down and pray hard, Grandson. This is a pitiful ceremony compared to the old days. You pray hard that these old ways come back."

"Nephew, so far our ceremony is going well," Eagle Feather's lowered voice interrupted my thoughts. "The missionaries haven't made their move yet. We'll have to be on the lookout today."

"They already have, Uncle," I answered. I grimaced at the fire before explaining the incident at my sister's trailer house.

Eagle Feather shook his head slowly. His tone was fatherly. "Nephew, it is good to fight for the return of our way, but you want to be careful around those black robes. I've studied the white man all my life. I guess I got a right to, seeing as how he's always been studying us. I've discovered the white man doesn't make a move against someone unless there's money behind it." I crossed my legs and glanced in the direction of the mission boarding school, several miles from the dance grounds. "That mission's a business more than it's a church."

"Money?" I threw a perplexed frown.

Eagle Feather nodded with a blunt look. "That mission operates a big money getting pogram."

"A money getting 'pogram'? You mean program?"

"There's a fancier name for it. You know, when they have the Indian students write up those plastic tipi letters and send out little salt shakers covered with Indian signs through the mail asking for donations?"

I nodded, "You mean their solicitation program?"

Eagle Feather beamed and sounded out the word phonetically. "Yes, that's it. The so-lic-i-ta-tion pogram. They get all kinds of money that way, mostly from the East. Lotta whites got guilty consciences about Indians. That pogram supports more than the mission. It takes care of those priests' retirements, travelin' vacations and the head office down south. They own lots of land, too." A disgusted look came and went. "That grave yard above the mission, they know how to work on those old people, you can bet your boots on that. Those last sacraments to get you in the Spirit World has got them lots of land. And those Bureau superintendents are in cahoots with them, they take that last rites land and switch it for the tribe's land surrounding the mission. Donations and land, it's all a big business, more money than we can imagine. This ain't the only reservation, either. That one up in Crow country makes more money than any of them." He looked at me sternly. "Fight them, Nephew, but be careful. Be careful around those black robes," he repeated.

Business. The word left an indelible ring. I shot the holy man an appreciative glance.

"They'll try to stop you, Nephew. They don't want you in this ceremony. An old fool like me with little education, they can make fun of. You, that's a different story. You escaped boarding school out there before they could break you. Now you've gone out and traveled the white man's road, yet you come back to the old Way…on top of this you're going on to college. They're afraid sooner or later someone like you could blow the whistle on them."

After more sun dance pledgers and holy men gathered around the blaze, a man with a weak heart was brought to the sweat lodge. He barely crawled to the rear of the domed structure for a curing ritual conducted by Eagle Feather. An honoring song to Chief Gall was sung and the heat within the interior of the lodge seemed more bearable than the day before.

I was apprehensive about the condition of the coughing man who seemed to grow paler each time the flap was raised. The ceremony concluded. All filed out except for Eagle Feather and the weak-hearted man. Out of curiosity, I remained close to the entry flap while Eagle Feather chanted a dirge sounding like a buffalo lowing in a lonely wallow. A pipe was brought inside of the sweat lodge and the flap left open while Eagle Feather and his patient smoked slowly. Eagle Feather reached into his medicine bundle retrieving several silver gray sage stems. The odd species of sage puckered the man's face with the bitter taste. After a short while, a healthy color flushed the patient. Before the man left the sweat lodge with a spirited gait, he was cautioned by Eagle Feather to return for added treatment.

I followed the holy man to the ceremonial lodge with renewed awe to dress once again for the Sun Dance. After the dancers formed the processional line outside the tall lodge, Gap, the bearer of the buffalo skull was placed at the head of the procession followed by the holy men, Eagle Feather, Fools Crow, Catches and Lame Deer.

Red Bow, a young Oglala in his twenties, was to be pierced for his fourth time the following morning and was immediately behind the holy men. Several members from the Rosebud and Hunkpapa tribes were placed behind Red Bow. I followed his cousin, Sonny Larvee, with Fools Crow's adopted grandson, Black Top, the quiet, shy boy in his first years at the boarding school, at his side.

The barefoot dancers entered the arena from the east. Again the boy and I were placed with our backs to the tree to face the rising sun. The singers sang and the eagle bone whistles kept time to the beat of the drum. I blew on the small wooden whistle that I had found in my sister's trailer house. Its sound was pathetic compared to the shrill eagle bone whistles. During the first recess period, after the peace pipes were offered, the boy and I rested with the other dancers under the circular bower. The dancers sat at a special recess place cordoned off by ropes under the shading bower's western side.

I rested on a thick plank, a sturdy two by eight nailed to two sawed cottonwood logs. I sat pensively, appreciating the shade offered by the bower. Coming down the road and approaching the eastern gateway to the arena I noticed a procession marching in a military manner. The marchers carried the American flag and the tribal flag at the front of their column. Each flag was flanked by a rifle-bearer carrying World War One, bolt-action rifles. Behind the color guard, a tall, warbonnetted man walked proudly. He appeared to be a decade younger than Fools Crow. As they drew closer, I recognized the man as the tribal chairman. The man's name was Enos and was a close friend of my older brother. He had remarked several times that our family was blood related to the tribal chairman.

Fools Crow and Bill Eagle Feather walked across the arena to greet the procession. The two holy men joined the parade of marchers immediately behind the color guard, each flanking the handsome chairman. The whole procession entered the dance circle to parade in a complete circle around the arena, bringing the crowd of onlookers to their feet, including the sun dancers. As the two flags passed by, members of the crowd held cowboy hats and baseball caps over their hearts while women sang out tremolos.

When the procession stopped in front of the sun dancers, Fools Crow motioned for the audience to sit back down. He then walked toward me, indicating I should stand. Fools Crow then grasped the sage wreath tied around my wrist and led me to the announcer's booth near the south end of the arena. The tribal chairman followed close behind them. The announcer handed down a microphone to the holy man and the Sun Dance Chief began to speak in Lakota. Fools Crow paused and turned me around to face the audience, then began speaking again. Several times the audience murmured and applauded. A few women tremoloed.

As Fools Crow continued to talk, the chairman stood next to me. I greeted him with a handshake. "You understand Indian?" he asked while the microphone blared Fools Crow's voice.

"Only a little," I replied. "Not enough to understand what he is saying. It's something about Vietnam, isn't it?"

"Yes," Enos replied with a raised voice. "He is proud that the spirits have answered his ceremony that he held for you. He's telling them that he will have an appreciation ceremony for you—to thank them—probably after you get started back in school." Enos continued to interpret for the combat pilot. "Now he is telling them that this Old Way is coming back and it will be good for the people." Enos surveyed the crowd. "With this bunch here, they already know that." He made a head motion behind them toward the town to the south. "The ones not here are the ones who should hear what he is saying. I'm a traditionalist like you. I support these ways." A sour note crept into his voice. "But I'm outgunned right now. Too many of these church-Indians on the council and I get outvoted."

I felt surprised that he was considered a traditionalist. I assessed the chairman's words and reasoned that I probably could be called a traditionalist. At least I wasn't a church-going Indian and I was in the Sun Dance. I knew though, that I understood very little, especially the language. Maybe I wasn't exactly a real traditionalist but I was moving in that direction.

Enos seemed to read my thoughts. "Don't worry about the language, Kid. It is what you stand for, that is what counts. I ran around with your brother, back in my day. I can't run too much anymore because of these politics but we are still good friends." Enos managed a smile. "Oh, I still get together with him when I come up to Rapid." His voice dropped. "We're related, you know."

I nodded in agreement, "My Mom, and my sister, they all told me. They say it's on my father's side." I looked at Enos and noted his nod. In the background, Fools Crow's voice began to slow down.

"Sounds like you are going to have to say some words," Enos offered.

My eyes widened. "But I don't talk Indian."

Enos laughed. "They know that, Kid." He shook the eagle feathers of his majestic warbonnet. "Just get up there and tell them that you appreciate your life. And tell them that the Way is going to come back." The tribal chief puckered his lips for a moment. "You believe that, don't you?"

"Yes, yes, I do!" I answered awkwardly and began to clear my throat.

"Don't worry, Kid. Just tell the truth." Enos spoke assuredly. "Just remember. This crowd is on your side. Mostly older people are out there. Not many young ones, yet. We've got to get the young on our side. They're wandering around in the bars…or still brainwashed by that boarding school and these missionaries. This Way has got the power to get our young on the right road and out of those bars. Missionaries had their chance but their way ain't working. Tell it to 'em Kid."

Fools Crow stopped speaking and handed the microphone to me. As I grasped the microphone I felt nervous and apprehensive about speaking out in public.

Typical of Sioux culture, there was no rehearsal. No time to plan and go over what should be said and what should not be said. Custom dictated that an important speech should come from the heart. Without being warned, a man or a woman reached into their mind and brought out the highlights of one's experience and wisdom, if it was there in the first place; wisdom and understanding from the richest of the experiences. The rest would flow as long as the speaker was truthful.

I stammered with my own introduction but gathered force as I talked. I began with Fools Crow's *Yuwipi* ceremony, even my mother's reluctance to attend. I then told about wearing the stone in combat that came into Fools Crow's ceremony and my belief that the Spirits had watched out for me. The crowd applauded and again the women tremoloed. I ended by sweeping my hand in a semi-circle. "Look around us here. Look over at the sun dancers. How many of the young do we see?" I paused then yelled out, "It's time to go back! Go back to the old Way!" I heard a call coming from the tribal chief at that moment.

"*Hokahey! Hokahey!*" over and over, Enos repeated. The crowd picked up the acknowledging expression and chanted back.

"We must all return to the Way. The Missionaries have had us for too long. They have had our young for too long and have turned them into *wah shi chus* (White Men). I was lucky. I escaped their brain washing when we had to move out from the boarding schools." I pointed to the Sun Dance tree. "This Way proved to be my protection." I ended with a flourishing wave. "Go back. Go back, and get your young to go back. We have but one life to live, why not live it as a true Lakota?"

I handed the microphone to Enos while the crowd cheered and then I took my place beside Fools Crow. Enos removed an eagle feather that had been pinned near the chest pocket of his shirt. He signaled for one of the drum groups to begin a drum roll. At the sound of the drum he called me to step forward.

"Eagle Boy, my relative," he began, "you are to be honored for being a veteran and going across to fight an enemy in this war that is still going on." He looked around and held up the eagle feather in a pointing and fanning fashion. "All of you who are veterans out there and you who are related to veterans, all of you are also honored." He raised his commanding voice. "In the old days, a warrior was honored by his people. This is the backbone of our life as social people here upon our Mother Earth. When a warrior returned from a war party, or a defensive battle with the soldiers, so that our people may live, he was honored and respected. And appreciated." He paused with a long silence then began slowly, "Many of our relatives have never returned. The first Great War, when we were not even citizens, yet we went across anyhow. Then the second Great War, the one which most of you were in, including myself. The Korean War which our relative here, Eagle Boy was in. And then this Vietnam, our relative was in that one, too. And now he stands before us here and is truthful to proclaim that it was the power of the Way that allows him to be here."

Enos held up the eagle feather and presented it to me. "Wear this upon your Sun Dance rope, my relative, when you pierce." He turned and walked away.

Back to Chu Lai my thoughts traveled. The year before, Enos had taken a large American flag, the one that was now flying over the Sun Dance. The flag was sent to Headquarters Marine corps with a letter from the Tribal Chairman that this flag be flown over the enemy. Also that a Sioux Indian pilot (Me) be the one who should fly it. Unbeknownst to me, the flag was sent to my squadron commander. I was scheduled for a mission and it was tucked up folded under my ejection seat.

I carried napalm on that particular day and remembered dropping one at a time over a suspected truck park hidden in the jungle. One bomb would not release so I went out over the ocean and did some acrobatics, pulling some abrupt G-forces but it clung tight beneath me. I made sure my dog-bone bomb selector switch read inert before landing back at Chu Lai. I reported a hung bomb to the tower so that the morest crews at the runway approach were notified. They make sure that they stay clear of the area where you will be landing. If the bomb does come off, the pilots speed and the aircraft's wheels insure that you are safely away in case the bomb explodes. We had a 500-pounder explode one night and the next night as well. The pilot was safely down the runway and no one got hurt, just a big crater in the sand. He had unconsciously pressed his bomb release button on his control stick from the jolt you make when you practically crash your bird on landing. It comes down pretty hard and doesn't just float like in Hollywood movies. Carrier landings, you have to 'stick' it on a tiny place. A hung bomb can come off. This pilot left his dog bone on (the bomb activating switch). He was fatigued from too many back to back missions and had over a hundred missions, so no pilot error charged.

I taxied up to the revetments and noticed a flock of photographers waiting. "Looks like some big shot is coming in," I remarked to my RIO. A plane captain directed me to park the Phantom out in front of the revetments. I figured it was because of the hung nape. As I shut off the machine I saw the squadron commander approaching. "Ooh Ohh!" I remarked. "Wonder what the hell we did wrong now."

The colonel punched my ladder as I opened my canopy. He climbed half way up and yelled as my engines were still loudly unwinding. "Chief, reach under your seat," he ordered.

I did so and yelled back, "God damn, Skipper. There's a fucking flag under me."

He screwed up his face with a disparaging look. He put his index finger to his lips. "Goddamn it, Chief. Tone it down, we got a bunch of news people here. *Stars and Stripes, Leatherneck*, you name it."

"It's all folded up, Skipper."

"Yeah, I know, I put it there, this morning."

"What's going on, Skipper?"

"You are, Chief. Now unfold it and tell your RIO to grab the back end and spread it across the bird."

The picture made the rounds of the news world. You can see the lone napalm bomb at the bottom. Photographers never paid it any attention. Probably figured it was some kind of external baby fuel tank.

Sun Dance Flag and Hung Napalm- Phantom F-4

In a few minutes, the color guard passed out of the arena and the Sun Dance continued. As the morning drew on, I looked as close as I could to the sun without being blinded. The eagle feather was tied to my belt over the navy blue kilt. I blew the wooden whistle and danced steadily. The temperature rose quickly during the early morning. My neck ached and my mouth was dry. I wanted to sleep and felt as if I could while dancing in my place.

Looking through half-closed eyes, I watched a cloud slowly drifting. A woman seemed to rise from the top of the billowing cumuli. Then the cloud became a buffalo head and then a man's head, then it was both—a buffalo man. The woman reappeared as the cloud parted. Her shoulders stood out prominently above the cloud. It was evident there was power within the woman.

The final song for the morning was sung. Fools Crow tugged on my sage wrist gauntlet to lead me to the exiting procession. We dancers left the arena and filed to the ceremonial tent. Ben Black Elk joined us. He had his father's pipe. (Ben was the interpreter for the famous book, *Black Elk Speaks*. Every word went from his father through him and on to Neihardt, the author and note taker. Every question back from John Neihardt went back through Ben while the highly respected author's daughter, Enid, took short hand.) Huddled tones murmured from the foursome with occasional looks toward me. As I removed my kilt, and put on my jeans, Eagle Feather, Black Elk and Catches exchanged a low conversation with Fools Crow. "*Waste aloh*," I heard Fools Crow remark. (That's good.) Ben Black Elk handed his father's pipe to Eagle Feather.

Eagle Feather made the announcement: "Eagle Boy, tomorrow you will be allowed to pierce. You will not have to wait until next year." He coughed gently. "We have decided that you no longer have a child's name." He pointed to Ben. "He named you as a child. Now you have been a warrior. Maybe you have seen as much danger as any of our warriors including Crazy Horse." He rose from where he was sitting holding the pipe and puffed his large chest with pride. "Enos, our supporting chairman, Tribal Chief, has heard stories from the Marine Corps about you. They have no regrets that you were chosen by them to go into battle for them." Catches interrupted in Lakota. The large Sichangu holy man queried both Eagle Feather and Black Elk in Lakota. Eagle Feather reached over to his medicine bundle and touched it with the Black Elk pipe. Inside was a green jade pipe, highly unusual and different from all the other medicine men's pipes. Eagle Feather also sported a crew cut and not long hair. He was his own man. He walked toward me, pointing the mouth piece end at me. "You are now *Wanbli Wichasha*! (Eagle Man)"

It was a double barreled honor, but the fear of being pierced stifled any exuberance that may have accompanied such an award.

"Do you take the vow to be pierced?" Eagle Feather's raised voice filled the tent.

"Yes, Uncle, I vow," my answer lacked hesitation. "It is but a small sacrifice compared to what the Great Spirit through the *Yuwipi* has spared me. I am not dead nor am I a prisoner of war. I shall be honored to pierce."

"That is why we have made an exception." He handed me the pipe.

"Tomorrow you shall carry this pipe. We also wish to honor the request of our tribal chief, who is one of us and has a hard road with those others. You have been off to war, far across the ocean, and you spoke well today. You are not afraid to fight for the Way. You believed that the Way would protect you and for those reasons your people will honor you further by allowing you to pierce in your first dance. Do not forget what you saw far across the ocean. Wars have been too much a part of those who have taken over this land. The Earth will need help and two-legged cannot be fighting wars. We pray that only peace will come to this land. But, since you have faced death many times, it is proper that you pierce tomorrow to thank the Great Spirit for your life."

Chief Eagle Feather extended his hand to me. After the handshake, Eagle Feather removed his eagle bone whistle from around his neck and presented it.

I was so impressed I was momentarily speechless. First I have a new name and now an eagle bone whistle. I composed myself to decline the holy man's special gift. "I deeply appreciate your gift, Uncle, but what will you use for a whistle? I cannot take such a gift while you have yet to Sun Dance."

Eagle Feather threw his head back and laughed heartily. "I won't be using that little pencil pip squeak you've been blowing on." He walked back toward his pipe bag, reached in and brought out an eagle bone whistle. "We found a rancher that's been poisoning coyotes, but the eagles got to the poison. I've got all I need for a while." The holy man looked at his new whistle. "I don't like to see eagles get killed this way and we're trying to educate the rancher but at least he's listened to us and, of course, has given us the remains."

After I finished dressing, I proudly draped his eagle bone whistle around my neck and carried my shawl kilt and the sage wreaths toward my sister's trailer house. On the way I stopped to blow several shrill notes on the new whistle.

I entered and placed the eagle feather on a shelf above the couch. When I sat on the couch in the empty trailer, my thoughts dwelled on the tribal chairman. After a while my mind drifted to the holy men. I had seen firsthand how costly a war could be. As I started to doze I hoped their prayers could avoid more wars. The announcer's voice came over the microphone. "We have a new name. A Naming. Eagle Boy is now Eagle Man. Eagle Man, *Wanbli Wichasha*," he spoke in Lakota. Around the campground, people called out. Women tremoloed in praise. My legs were tired and as long as I slept, I wouldn't have to think about eating or thirst. I removed the eagle bone whistle from my neck and blew on it several times. The shrillness seemed to cause a moment of magical sound. I set the whistle on a folding chair and began to sleep, dreaming that my Phantom flew into the cloud which had appeared in the vision. The strong woman appeared in the cloud. A mist seemed to shroud the woman's features, yet I could see her black hair was braided, and she wore a buckskin dress. The buffalo man I could not find although I circled and looped the cumulus cloud. All this time the powerful woman looked on approvingly. I was afraid of her but as long as she appeared as an ally, I continued my search for the buffalo man. What I would do if I found the buffalo man, I didn't know. I wanted to see that vision again though. It had so much power. I circled once more before my Phantom hovered close beside the woman. The mist parted, revealing a face and posture like my grandmother must have had in her younger days. Her eyes were like a soft fire. The eyes became windows drawing me closer. I was no longer in the Phantom but was looking outward from the window of my Grandmother's cabin. In the sage-grown driveway an eagle pecked away at a lifeless jackrabbit while a meadowlark sang. I forgot about the buffalo man and the woman. Nothing else mattered anymore, except the two birds and the tiny part of the world around them.

11 LONE CLOUD SUN DANCE

You can see where Nature based ceremony has had a profound influence in my life. Religious rants and clamor on Sunday TV along with the rest of organized religion were becoming meaningless by the time I had reached my prime.

—*Author*

Three Medicine Men Lead a Sun Dance

New Age brought forth the impressive Harmonic Convergence; but not unlike Organized Religion, New Age could not or would not shed superstition. The Natural Way has no Superstition. Nature cannot have it unless devised, implemented and inserted by mythology-phobic Man.

It is time that we Indigenous speak up in this hemisphere and it is time that Dominant Society keeps quiet and listens for once, after all these centuries since first coming to America. The ongoing environmental catastrophe happening at this very moment tells you to introspect and listen to a people who have lived safely, harmoniously with Nature down through many more centuries on this continent than Dominant Society has. From my observation, the White Man is bent on the appearance of obtaining personal salvation. The North American Indian is more concerned with planetary salvation. He is not worried about reaching the possible life Beyond, as long as he follows and respects the True Rules of Nature over the attempts of Man. In obvious truth, it did not take Dominant Society long to undo the successful environmental pattern the Indigenous employed. We do not believe that we need to be 'saved' from our Benevolent and All-Providing Creator who made us. Such superstitions the white man has placed upon us, even banning our religion and language to force us to comply. Religious extremists built a federally built and staffed, all-Indian patients (mostly Sioux and Chippewa) insane asylum in Canton, South Dakota to primarily contain our religious leaders. Thanks to the Martin Luther King civil rights movement the federal (government) ban was finally lifted in 1978 through the Congressional Freedom of Religion Act. In the meantime, we faithfully served our country beginning in WWI and on into Vietnam, Iraq and now Afghanistan, and who knows what others will come. There are plenty of wars for U.S. citizens to enter into wherein the sons of the rich most often avoid the actual battle scenes.

Sun Dance and the Missionary

I went off to war having watched the priest say his holy mass at the base of the Sun Dance tree, thus curtailing the ceremony to only three days. After I returned from flying my combat missions the ceremony was held and this time the overly confident priest did not interfere.

The fourth day of the Sun Dance went on without incident. Paul Steinmetz had to be surprised to notice the increasing fervor the ceremony's return was stirring. After he had successfully curtailed the ceremony to three days only, he again did a repeat performance while I was in Vietnam. It looked like the annual ceremony was going to be shortened to three days, but Enos Poor Bear's tribal chairmanship was growing in popularity and Father Superior at the reservation mission had cautioned the zealot priest to lay back for at least a year and test which way the wind would below. An organization calling itself the American Indian Movement was starting to stir in the East, occupying the Bureau of Indian Affairs and supporting and being supported by the civil rights groups. Martin Luther King was raising needed issues. The Superior was political more than he was a proselytizer or an out-and-out zealot like Steinmetz. Actually, he was most concerned about his retirement. He didn't want the zealot priest to upset his exodus from the mission and have his governance tarnished. The wrong encounter with AIM, which was making national headlines, worried him.

I danced my fourth day with Fools Crow's adopted grandson beside me to fulfill the prophecy called out in the *Yuwipi* ceremony. After the ceremony was finished, I drove to Hot Springs, a Black Hills town that has a clear stream of naturally heated water coming from an underground volcano that runs into a large swimming pool just above town. It was a perfect place to go for a Sun Dancer after, of course, stopping at a drive-in and downing several oversized hamburgers, a couple of malts and French fries.

It was the next year that my second *wotai* stone would appear to me in that same stream. I have told about it in my other books. Eagle Feather told me that it would replace the stone I wore for Vietnam combat flying. (The *wotai* stone is now in my bank vault where I keep a large supply of turquoise for my necklace making. I don't want to take a chance on losing it or having someone steal it.)

I had vowed to participate in only one Sun Dance but the menacing Steinmetz put me on guard and I wanted the ceremony to flourish once again. I, at least, had to do my small bit according to my mentors Fool Crow and Bill Eagle Feather. I did travel with Eagle Feather to the Hunkpapa/Minnecoujou people where he held a powerful *Yuwipi* in an old abandoned Episcopal church basement. He also held several sweat lodges. I gathered rocks and firewood for the large lodge the reservation had built for him. It was a memorable time traveling with him. I drove my brother-in-law's pickup and we slept in an old cabin while we were up near the North and South Dakota border. I wound up doing six Sun Dances total.

The last Sun Dance for me was at Green Grass, on the Hunkpapa Lakota Reservation, several hundred miles northeast of Pine Ridge. Fools Crow and Bill Eagle Feather were there and officiated the ceremony. In just five years from my first Sun Dance, AIM had made remarkable progress with a growing membership led by Dennis Banks, Russell Means, and the two Bellecourt brothers, Vernon and Clyde. The year before the Green Grass ceremony, Steinmetz was stopped cold and sent away on some long term sabbatical, no doubt by the head of the Jesuit Order having become aware of the political ramifications of thwarting and attempted denial of Religious/Spiritual participation now that civil rights had finally opened people's eyes—and hearts.

Without further preaching, this is what happens for those that seek the Spiritual: At least for the Lakota Sioux.

Lone Cloud Sun Dance

On the final day of a Sun Dance in the late 1960s, a lone cloud appeared, in an otherwise clear blue sky, far to the south as eight dancers waited to be pierced.

Chief Eagle Feather and I were the first to be pierced.[2] I had returned safely from the hell of Vietnam as predicted. In that ceremony which took place before I left for Vietnam, I took the Sun Dance pledge. "If I can come back. I will dance the Sun Dance." All that was predicted by the entering Spirit for me regarding battle came true. There are various reasons why each sun dancer has taken his pledge and now we were at the height of that fulfillment.

The large Sichangu Sioux holy man stood next to me urging me to watch

---

[2] The sun dancer now is truly connected to Mother Earth. It is all volunteer; no one is forced to endure it. Woman never has to be pierced in the Sun Dance. She gives her pain 'so that the people may live' when she gives birth to a child. Women often die in childbirth thus facing far more danger. Therefore she is honored, and respected by never being pierced.

what was happening far away to the south. A distant growing puff of white cloud was the only image in the hot August sky. I was honestly too tired to offer it much attention. I was also thirsty and hungry, mostly thirsty from four long days of fasting and fulfilling my sun dance pledge along with the other seven pledgers. I have to be honest. At that particular moment in my life, I was simply counting off the final hour of the grueling sun dance. I imagined the relief I would soon be feeling when the ceremony and my four-day vow would be over.

The cloud seemed to be approaching. It was a vast western sky with no other clouds visible. The dry Badlands air was still, yet the cloud seemed to be moving toward us. I could feel a dull throb where I had been pierced in my chest. I held my rope's weight in one hand to ease off the pain. After a few minutes the pain changed to numbness. I eased my grip on the rope and let it hang freely while shuffling a slow dance step to the drum beat coming from the drummers at the edge of the sun dance arena. We watched each dancer lie on the bed of sage, face upward at the base of the sun dance tree and be pierced by the sun dance Intercessor, the Sun Dance Chief. Chief Fools Crow would push his sharp awl in and through the chest skin and back out again, then insert a smooth wooden peg into the first cut and tunneling under the skin he would push the tip back out. Onto this hardwood skewer he would tie the pledger's rope to the peg with a leather thong. The other end of the rope was attached high up on the tree implanted at the center of the sun dance arena.

Surrounding the arena was a pitiful crowd numbering maybe several hundred or so traditional believing Sioux. This was not a large number coming from the Oglala tribe that numbered at least 25,000 people back then. The neighboring Sichangu tribe of Sioux—representing some of the pledgers, including Chief Eagle Feather—were also sparsely represented, although they numbered approximately 20,000 in those days. Hiawatha Federal Insane Asylum (Canton, South Dakota) no longer existed but the fear of 'The Ban' by the government and instigated by the Christian missionaries lingered. (The last embarrassing brick of the asylum had been carefully removed almost overnight by the federal government several decades before.)

The number of traditional faithful was pitiful in those days. The reservation missionaries with the unconstitutional help of the federal government had done their job well—from their viewpoint. Little did we know or realize that the return of Native Spirituality would build like a tremendous storm. Thousands would return to the way of their ancestors and our lone Sun Dance would become numerous in but a few decades. Thousands of new pledgers would arrive. Nowadays, one Sun Dance would not be able to contain the many pledgers trying to fulfill their four day vows.

"It's coming closer." I remember Eagle Feather's awed tone. The cloud about the size of a football field approached slowly. I should have been in dead earnest awe but I was weak and tired from the four days of fasting.

Fools Crow came toward me after the last dancer was pierced. "*Hau*, Nephew." Bill Eagle Feather exclaimed. "That cloud is coming right at us!" The cloud was approaching the edge of the campground which was full of tipis, tents, and trailers surrounding the circular Sun Dance arena with its lone cottonwood tree at its center, decorated with colored prayer cloths. The drums were throbbing, seeming to speed their hypnotic crescendo; a pulsating, haunting tone which one hears only at a Sun Dance. As a Sun Dancer you will hear it for an eternity. It is so powerful; the pain in your chest seems to be carried away with its soothing, magical tone. Fools Crow took me by the sage gauntlet tied around my wrist and walked me inward toward the tree. All the dancers came inward, dancing a slow shuffling gait to the heavy rhythm of the drums, blowing their eagle bone whistles. We touched the tree and blew our shrill whistles. The tree shrilled back!

We danced backward to the end of our ropes. The ropes tightened and our thongs held firm. The drums throbbed as if we were standing before a gigantic, singing waterfall. Fools Crow signaled with a nod and we all danced back toward the tree, our eagle bones shrilly tweeting. Again the tree sang back! Four times in all we would dance inward. After the fourth touching of the tree we danced slowly outward, then leaned backward at the end of our ropes. The silent crowd would send up their prayers to *Wakan Tanka*, the Great Spirit whom we assumed was watching from somewhere.

The cloud was directly above as we touched the tree for the final time. It sent down soothing, light rain on the dancers and the praying crowd. We went back to the end of our ropes. Some sun dancers would have visions as they leaned back against their bond with Mother Earth. Eventually all would break free and the ceremony would be over.

Was Creator watching over that particular ceremony? Who controlled that cloud or rather, *What* controlled that moving billowing object of Nature which purposely made such a timely appearance on a windless day? Yes, a no-wind day! There was no fearsome, rolling thunder or terrifying lightning, no punishing hail stones, just pleasant, soothing, cooling, rewarding light rain. Is that a sign that whatever controlled that cloud, might be somewhat pleased?

What would be your reaction had you seen such a miraculous sight? Indeed, this was a very powerful experience. Would you deny what your own eyes had shown you? Would you be such a coward and never reveal what you had observed? The world is full of such cowards on their life journeys, oblivious to *why* they are here. Some folks would find it impossible to believe, would they not? How can some people be so indoctrinated by other humans that they would refuse to believe what their own God-gifted eyes reveal to them? They will actually be lying by denying before God, will they not? Such is the power of the indoctrination other humans hold over them! *Baahing* sheep are easily led.

We were beseeching, formally calling, formally acknowledging. Creator acknowledged back. But modern materialists of today are simply ignoring what they see with their own eyes. They actually do not want God or any power to interfere with their disastrous taking and couldn't care less about the generations unborn. Will Creator (God) intervene someday on our behalf, despite our foolish and irreverent course which has led us to this overpopulated, overheated, resource-depleted environmental situation we now presently face (and what we two-legged have created)? I hardly think a Creator will rush to our rescue unless we change our attitude. This ceremony was direct observation. It happened!

Nature forms of beseechment need to return or else we are all doomed. It is the only Spirituality/Religion that can convince the World's Population that Planetary Heating is the result of 'Too Many' (Over Population). Mathematical Exponential Multiplication spells Doom! Ceremony can offer tremendous impetus for mankind to finally open their eyes and minds to the power of Nature.

12 SPIRIT CEREMONY

What is knowledge? I believe knowledge mainly comes from what one experiences. The other part of knowledge can come from truthful associates who impart their knowledge. If it happened, then, why wouldn't some knowledge come from what one observed? Millions of books have been written on observations or what one 'thought' had happened. If what you are about to read is too much for you to comprehend from an Indian point of view then by all means simply state that it is all preposterous and could not have happened and we can both go on our way. I certainly am not going to insist that you can perceive and understand from my point of view. Maybe we come from just too extreme of differences in our backgrounds. I abhor arguments and do appreciate that you have come this far in this presentation. We can simply let it go at that and at least, by now, you do know much more about our Indian past and values. Together we can still go on and defend this great Mother Earth we are so fortunate to live in. I will not ridicule you and hopefully you will not ridicule me.

For the benefit of those readers who could or would appreciate its added value, I will go ahead and include the following—an actual Sioux Spirit Calling ceremony. This particular ceremony is so revealing that I have utilized its message in just about every one of my previous works. Yes, like the Lone Cloud Sun Dance, this too actually happened although before a smaller audience whom can verify its happening. I have often wondered, *For what inducing reason would the Sioux up and leave what appeared to be a lush paradise* (Carolinas) *and finally arrive at a much harsher Great Plains?* My answer would be the very same Spirit Ceremony that you are about to witness.

Although this powerful communicative happening is revealed in just about every one of my books, I must assume that those who choose to observe this work, have read none of my other works. I have to assume that a biography written by the author while still living will be one of the last to fade away. I primarily offer the following as an attempt to help those to understand more fully the mind of the two spiritual leaders, Fools Crow and Chief Eagle Feather, and their startling ability to conduct what very few in this whole wide world can do. It would be a great disservice to omit this Spiritual knowledge from the mass of humanity. I was called on to attempt my biography and hence set forth to attempt to offer the major highlights of my journey. These two events were certainly major highlights.

The experienced reader of my works will probably understand that this chapter is written for those who have very little knowledge regarding our Sioux/Lakota Spirituality and is a wide differentiation from Dominant Society's spiritual communication attempts. It definitely is an eye opener.

In America, this ceremony is probably considered an impossible ceremony by many, the majority actually, especially by the zealous and narrow minded and should even harvest more than a few accusations. Such is the mindset of modern society that maybe I should not object to such reaction. All that I can offer for verification is that many such ceremonies are held and have been held down through time by members of my tribe and other tribes with similar ceremonies. In one of my books, a similar such ceremony conducted by another tribe in the 18th century is narrated by Captain Jonathan Carver, an early American explorer. I cannot change history to satisfy what seems to be a growing multitude especially since the advent of Dr. Martin Luther King, the noted civil rights leader and the new freedoms he set into motion.

Dr. Wm. K. Powers, a noted anthropologist has written several books on the subject (*Yuwipi—The Indian's Spirit Calling*). I am not into convincing anyone, however, but I do not shy away from actual observation and real life experience. Doubters and skeptics are free to look me up in the Spirit World. By now, I think that most readers will be convinced that I actually think one exists. Again, I do not insist that you necessarily have to believe as I do. Like the 'Lone Cloud' which mysteriously came over our Sun Dance, this happening was another of my mystery-projecting experiences and was certainly observed with a host of other interested people. The participants in the following situation were all university related and some sported high academic degrees along with accomplished track records from an academic point of view. Unfortunately, Dr. Bryde whom I have depended a lot upon for much of my Sioux historical material, has recently passed away. He was present at this happening. Lula Red Cloud, who was but twenty years at the time, is the great-great-granddaughter of Chief Red Cloud and was also present. Lula can verify what took place back in 1970. Without further distraction let us continue.

University of South Dakota

At the request of the University Administration, Chief Eagle Feather came to the University of South Dakota to conduct a revealing *Yuwipi* (Spirit Calling) ceremony.

At this ceremony, in the late '60s, many so-called credible people from the white man's view attended. These were university professors with graduate degrees. (Therefore, I guess, a detractor would almost have to assume that they were maybe more credible than most ordinary folks.) This ceremony was for the benefit of non-Indian people and was held at the University of South Dakota to find five students and their pilot/professor who crashed a light, single-engine airplane somewhere in the cold, remote, snow covered region called the Nebraska Sand Hills whose terrain is akin to parts of Mongolia and Northern China. This area also receives a heavy winter snowfall. They were returning from Denver, Colorado to Sioux Falls, South Dakota, and encountered a blizzard. The pilot developed vertigo and it was presumed the plane had crashed on the windswept Nebraska Sand Hills and was covered by snow. An all-out search began—even the Nebraska National Guard was used—but after a while it was too expensive and futile to continue. The search was called off. At that point the University of South Dakota Indian Studies program, where I worked part-time since my major occupation was a law student, had connections with Sioux holy men and none other than the President of the school called upon them for help. At the ceremony, I sat next to his beautiful blonde wife, Connie Bowen.

Bill Eagle Feather asked for a map. He specified that he wanted "the airplane kind of map (WAC chart) and not the ordinary road map." A line was drawn from Denver to Sioux Falls, the light passenger plane's intended destination, and Eagle Feather proceeded to study it before the scheduled evening's ceremony in the basement of the school's museum. The aircraft held a maximum capacity of five passengers plus the pilot.

The ceremony began with Eagle Feather's ceremonial peace pipe being offered to the Ultimate Powers under one Benevolent and All Providing Creator. Lula Red Cloud, a university student, held the pipe after the opening. Chief Eagle Feather was bound and covered with a lightly wrapped blanket. We then lowered the huge man face first to the rug provided for some comfort over the hard floor. After the tobacco offerings were spread out and the lights turned off, the ceremony began in pitch black darkness.

The singer boomed out the calling song, an eerie loud, high pitched, staccato wail that sounded so ancient that one's genes knew that it was ancient and told you so. After a few minutes of this calling and drumming the Spirit People (or Spirit Forces) entered in the form of blue-green lights. Around and around before us, above us and in close to us at times they flourished seeming in tune to the mesmerizing drum beat. The calling song to the spirits finally finished as all who sat there were placed into a spiritual void totally separating them from all that was earthly. Such a power that was before us, that had one asked another what their own name was, maybe they would not have been able to answer or care to.

A brief discussion now seemed to occur between Eagle Feather's muffled voice and some other entity. This entity which was the called upon was simply Spirit (*Wahnahgi*). The conversation did not last long. A moment of silence between the two. A song was called for and once it began, the electrical appearing lights reappeared and seemed to exit through the wall. Eagle Feather called for the song of Chief Gall of the Hunkpapas. Whatever it was that had communicated to Eagle Feather, it had now left the room. The singer sang out, and at the conclusion of a special song, Grey Weasel, the entity, Eagle Feather's spirit helper, came back again.

A purring sound filled the room. The patter of small feet was accompanied by the excited chattering of a weasel. A weasel in America is very much like a ferret or an ermine or mink. Eagle Feather began to talk in Sioux to the animal, and the visitor chattered (spoke) back and purred as the holy man spoke. They continued to converse for a period until finally the animal no longer chattered but purred slowly.

Then Eagle Feather called for the same song. A woman sang. When her song finished, a loud crack came from the center of the floor and something slid toward the keeper of the pipe. I felt it impact into my feet with a sharp jab. I actually leaped sideways and into the lap of Connie Bowen. (Without her interest, support and belief in our Indian Way this event would never have taken place.) She was of Swedish descent as well. Many Europeans respect deeply our Nature-based Way and that is probably why her spiritual/religious concepts were not diluted or denigrated by religious America's negating propaganda against the beliefs and practices of others. Sheepishly, I remarked to her that something had hit me. You must remember that all of this was taking place in the darkened room within the basement of the university museum building.

Predictions

Once the song ended, Eagle Feather called out: "Ho, Grey Weasel has made seven predictions:

1. The airplane crashed in a storm not far from a town that has two creeks with almost the same name. We should send an airplane out to look for it. A man and woman will fly that airplane.
2. The animals will point to where we should go.
3. If we fly where the animals point and head past the town with two creeks, we will fly over the plane, but it is pretty well covered with snow.
4. The plane sent out will have to land but everyone will walk away from it. Do not worry, the pilots will be smiling as they look back.
5. In the next day or two some people who are not looking for the plane will be led to it by an animal.
6. Only five will be found. One of the six will be missing within the airplane. She landed away from the others, but she will not be too far away.
7. Her face will be upon an ice colored rock. She has a Chinese (pageboy) hairdo and wore big glasses.

"Those are the seven predictions. Now also, a rock that looks like ice has entered the room. It will have these signs I spoke of. Ho, Nephew (meaning me). Reach out in front of you and pick up the rock. Hold it until the final song. You are of the rock clan, and you should welcome your rock brother, not be afraid of it." Somewhat skeptical, or else still in a degree of remaining fear from the encounter, I readily handed the rock to Connie Bowen, who asked for it.

Before the final song and the lights turned on, Eagle Feather said, "the two who fly like the winged ones," meaning my companion (Carol D.) and I would hopefully find the crashed plane by flying and using the stone as a map.

The next morning, we flew a Cessna 180, single-engine plane from the university town's airport which was close to the Missouri River. As we lifted, I looked down and saw that the deer in the meadows were grazing, and they all were pointing downstream. We banked the airplane downstream. It must be noted that deer usually graze towards evening and seldom are seen in the morning hours. In a short while we came to another stream, a creek which emptied into the river. Deer were standing close to its mouth and all were pointing upstream. We followed the deer's indications which seemed to be foretold on the stone because deer images were inscribed on it. We came to the two creeks with the same name: One creek was named South Wolf Creek and the other was Middle Loup Creek. *Loup* means wolf in French. We flew on to see a town in the distance. We passed over the small town of Arnold, Nebraska, a very isolated and remote cattle town. The surrounding land and landscape was very vast with few or no fences and no planted agriculture— only vast grassland for cattle feeding and some stunted trees and tall cottonwoods at springs and dry creek collection points. We figured out that the cloudy, unclear sign on the opaque, ice gray crystal stone represented fog, as we were starting to notice the clouds getting lower to the ground. Across and away from the town we passed over a ranch where cattle were all standing on one side of a soybean/cracked corn cake feeding trough and pointing us toward some deer pulling hay from a haystack and who also pointed us onward in the same direction that the feeding cattle were indicating. Cattle, when feeding, always stand on each side of a trough, no different than when they are taking on water from an elongated container, but not these particular cattle at that given moment. We circled for a while over a spot as the fog was pushing us downward, visibility-wise we were beginning to get into flying trouble and soon we were homeward bound to avoid the descending fog. An eerie feeling came over both of us before we banked the airplane back to Vermillion, South Dakota and the university airfield as though those deceased down below us were telling us that we had arrived at their final destination.

Eventually, we landed back where we started, barely in time because the fog was settling on the runway as we put the airplane in its hangar. It could have been fatal for us had we not returned in time to find the runway because of the oncoming descending fog. Carol, the other pilot, held a commercial flying license as I did. She was very pretty, blonde and a good ten years younger than I. My flying skills had been honed by the military. She had flown many hours in civilian planes despite her youth, but she was a natural, gifted pilot and a welcome addition in the cockpit when adverse weather came in. In those days many pilots flying small aircraft met their doom due to weather conditions which could isolate you from direct visibility. We both were well aware of what we had escaped from. It was now dark and we promptly drove our two cars to Main Street and had several relaxing drinks as most typical pilots would have been prone to do. The modern instruments of today were not yet invented then. Even when I was flying the million dollar machine, the Phantom F4, navigational instrumentation was relatively crude when compared to the lifesaving (and aircraft saving) instruments now available to pilots. Cheryl Tiegs (my nickname for Carol) and I often flew together to take Dr. Bryde out to the Indian reservations. While we had to wait several hours or even a whole day or on into an evening, we visited many of the Indian people. The Indian ladies were quite in awe when I would tell them that Carol was a pilot just like I was and would embarrass her when I would tell them that she was equally as good as I thought I was. We became close friends and even more so after this demanding mission. Years have gone by now and I have often wondered where she had gone onto after college graduation. Maybe she became an airline pilot.

Several of Dr. Bryde's lectures would be held on the Rosebud Reservation (Sichangu Lakota). Those times, Carol and I would hail a ride to Chief Eagle Feather's dwelling. The jovial medicine man of the Sichangu welcomed us and we would spend a few hours with him. He liked Carol, no doubt respecting her for being a pilot. When he came down to the University, she wanted to attend his ceremony to find the 'Lost Six.' Naturally she was readily granted permission by Eagle Feather.

The next day, after our narrow escape, close to where we had reversed the plane's course, two hunters followed the tracks of a coyote. The animal's tracks led them to the wreckage of the Cherokee Six airplane. The tail of the doomed plane was exposed due to the rising temperature from the fog. They reported the position and soon rescue vehicles converged on the scene. All of Eagle Feather's (actually Grey Weasel's) predictions proved true.

Only five were within the plane. The girl was found out away from the others. It is speculated that her seat belt broke or came unsnapped and she shot through the fuselage or possibly the door from the extreme centrifugal force caused by the violent, fatal spin.

Summary

Well, there you have a ceremony that the preachers, popes, cardinals, and mullahs can never do. While other religions have their own ceremonies, there are a hundred clues as to the Beyond that lie within such a powerful ceremony. If prediction and spiritual communication are the standards, Nature's Path is truly the world's most powerful religion/spirituality. It is also the result of the sheer truth and dedication of the intercessor (the conducting medicine person) and, of course, the sincerity of the audience that allows or makes a pleasing atmosphere for the spirits to come in or whatever what you wish to call these information giving, knowledge probing forces who come in or want to come in. I suspect that various Chino/Mongol descended tribes that we Norte American Indios came from long ago, may have had this ceremony as well but called it different names. I imagine the preparation and sincerity of the old Celtic bards that were once in Spain produced similar ceremony. It is all an allowance of the Ultimate Power, however, our point of view. It is not possible unless the Intercessor—the Holy Man or Holy Woman conductor or beseecher—has extreme focus, yes an Ultimate Focus to cultivate an appearance; a bringing in of those Spirit Forces to come in to the ceremony. These men or women have cultivated themselves to arrive at what I call Pure, Pure God-Truth! Organized Religion does not have this ability and never will. They have too much distracting outer focus.

Without harmony and undiluted truth, however, nothing will happen. It is encouraging to believe that the Spirit World will truly be a truthful and sincere place where earthly lies and manipulation will not in the slightest be allowed or condoned. Nothing but pure truth will be the total mental (or thought-wise) atmosphere. Again, our observation of God's Nature readily displays, God's (Creator's) Nature is always truthful. Should not Creator's Spirit World be likewise? Makes one wonder why we long to stay here!

"Life is but a mere shadow on the wall compared to the complete reality that lies beyond," said Plato in his *Allegory of the Cave*. What we experience here, observe here, can and no doubt will be reflected to a related degree in the Beyond.

It is obvious that the spirit is able to go back into time and discern what took place. The girl who was thrown out of the plane had her seat belt come unsnapped by flying debris from a high G force, or possibly her extreme increased weight due to the spinning airplane's centrifugal force. Extreme centrifugal force ejected her through the plane, casting her out away from the others. This prediction would be impossible to conjure. The spirit guide obviously has the ability to revisit this happening back in time to be able to report specifically as to the findings. "One of the six will be missing. She landed out away from the others." I find that statement impossible to conjure and only come from an entity that had non-earthly help.

Pure, Pure God Truth

Pure Truth extends much deeper than simply not telling a lie. When a human being can develop themselves to shed all forms of untruthful habits, beliefs, false superstitions, exaggeration, irresponsibility, non-appreciation, disregard for thanksgiving, non-observance—especially of Nature's teachings immediately before you and all forms of disrespectful negativism— then that person is beginning to come into a position to extend oneself into a mode to communicate with those Spirits that surround us. When one does arrive at such a positive state in regard to Pure Truth there is no consecration, anointment or related recognition ceremony conducted by mere man who seems to love to insert various forms of hierarchy into his Organized Religions. Yes, mere Man, loves to elevate himself. Maybe he wants to be a mini-God. This attitude doesn't work if one seeks to call in the Spirits! Repeatedly, I will make the statement: Creator is All Truth and All Knowledge. It is all very simple. Many virtues must be practiced, developed and put into action for one's lifetime. Sharing, generosity, bravery, courage, observation, perception, and recognition. All will lead one toward a higher state and a definite preparation for a Spirit World which lies beyond whether or not one will ever or care to communicate directly as the indigenous medicine persons do. While one conducts oneself on such a positive Spiritual journey, one's body will harmonize with the surroundings of Nature and become a very helpful tool as well. Like a dancer at a powwow whose heartbeat synchronizes with the drumbeat and can dance effortlessly for hours, such is the body of a human which can harmonize spiritually with Nature. The animal brothers and sisters exhibit this trait, this connection, every day.

Carolina Influence

The Spirit Calling ceremony could quite possibly have influenced the Carolina Dakota and advised them about the danger about to cross over the Atlantic and the magnitude of the deadly danger (contagious disease) the Europeans had already brought. They up and left a lush existence rather suddenly. This would be highly unusual for an established society that was comfortably settled. Red Cloud, Crazy Horse, Sitting Bull and Black Elk undoubtedly knew of this ceremony and may possibly have depended upon it to some degree also when they so successfully fought the White Man's soldiers. I find that the *Yuwipi* ceremony has certainly influenced my journey.

Devil or Satan

What about the alleged power or manipulation of the white man's Devil or Satan? Well, first, the traditional Sioux do not believe in such things. They (man-conceived devils, Satans, spooky goblins, incubi, werewolves, etc.) do seem fairly preposterous.[3] Recently Pope John Paul II sanctioned classes on the clergy to perfect their means to exorcise the white man's devil. It was all on the internet news showing many young priests attending classes on the subject. For them, Satan abounds and must be dealt with. Traditional Sioux reasoning is that a Benevolent Creator has no need to allow such things nor would they (spooky devils included) be in the mind of such a powerful Force.

---

[3] *Malleus Maleficarum. The Witches Hammer*, authored by two traveling, torturing medieval Dominican monks was widely read in Europe for centuries. Within, Pope Innocent VIII, declares it heresy to deny the existence of werewolves.

Where in God-given Nature is there such evidence? We Sioux have never seen or observed such things and do not expect to. If you have such an entity, why is it we can never observe it?

Odd, that so many non-Indian readers (and some turncoat Indians as well) will sincerely believe that the above innocent beseechment, the *Yuwipi*, intended to bring closure for the bereaved families of the crash victims, which was a direct observation, and even generously intended to help their own kind (*Wahshichus*), will be considered preposterous and thus they will have to invoke some sort of evil conjuration to it. Not long ago, a few centuries, we would have all been drawn and quartered or burned at a stake for simply wanting to find the six victims. Thankfully, we Americans at least, now have the protection of the separation of Church and State and so far no police have showed up to punish me. Michele Bachmann, former Minnesota Sixth District Congresswoman, however, would like to change, even erase that protection. She stated that the Church/State separation clause should be abolished.

13 AIM - AMERICAN INDIAN MOVEMENT

Author with Fools Crow at the AIM Sun Dance

Fools Crow said: "Go get those AIMs."

The Tetons were one of the original Seven Council Fires of the Sioux. They increased significantly in population when they found the horse and the vast buffalo herds in the Dakotas and what now is part of Nebraska. They evolved into the seven sub-tribes or seven bands of the Teton Sioux. Chief

Sitting Bull, Chief Gall, Chief Red Cloud, Chief Crazy Horse, and Chief Spotted Tail would soon become their leaders; all would speak the L (Lakota) dialect. They were all members of the Teton Lakota Nation. Historically, three of these tribes stand out and are listed first below. If we refer to the Sioux as a Nation, then we can confer tribal status on the seven tribes. If one refers to the Sioux as a Tribe we would name each of the seven as bands. They are:

1. The Oglala (Red Cloud, Black Elk, Crazy Horse)
2. The Sichangu (Spotted Tail)
3. The Hunkpapa (Sitting Bull and Gall)
4. Minicoujou
5. Sihasapa (Blackfeet)
6. Oohenumpa (Two Kettles)
7. Itazipco (No Bows)

The last five representatives of the Tetons, including the Hunkpapa, would be referred to as the Saones. They populate two large reservations, the Cheyenne River Sioux and the Standing Rock Sioux which reach up from the northern half of South Dakota on into North Dakota. Once the Oglala and the Sichangu would cross over the Missouri back in 1775, the Tetons would soon be the most numerous of the Sioux, more numerous than the other two Dakota divisions further east put together.

My third Sun Dance proved to be the largest gathering of the people. The old Way was coming back. The once barely growing ember somehow kept alive by the stubborn, unrelenting full-bloods was now a healthy flame. Other bands of the Teton Lakota were now as deeply moved as the Sichangu and the Oglala. In early August they were coming down from their reservations to swell the Sun Dance campground circling the cottonwood tree-centered arena. From a pitiful crowd, the arena now was surrounded by several thousand, camping to watch the annual thanksgiving.

They were returning so suddenly that Steinmetz must have been giving his Mission Superior fits. My fourth Sun Dance, he was now set to combat everything contrary to Catholicism that Teton Spirituality represented—and believe me there was considerable difference! (One has to wonder, in light of all these present day bombings taking place and seemingly endless wars of various religious factions fighting each other, why the Sunnis and Shiites have been going at each other since the 1300s.) Creator is sheer Mystery. Why fight over a subject that no one knows for sure? It is utterly foolish. Is it man's ego? Does he want to totally control through his particular brand only? How can any sane person of reason attempt to claim he knows exactly who God/Creator exactly is? You have to be truly ignorant to so claim. You are definitely disregarding whatever inherent common sense you were allowed since birth. Somehow common sense gets erased due to man's influence and obviously false teachings. People tend to move toward ignorance. I feel so much more secure by our Sioux acceptance of Great Mystery.

I had come late to the Sun Dance, held up by an airplane I was flying in the south west where I had taken a job after law school graduation. I was doing more passenger flying than I was doing legal work for which I was hired and was planning on finding new employment. I danced on a Friday, the second day of the four-day ceremony. Fools Crow understood and was not loaded with specific rules. This morning of the third day I noticed everyone preparing for piercing. Ropes were being tied higher via a ladder before the ceremony officially started. There were a few more dancers and I was so tired that I didn't bother to ask any questions. When it came time to be pierced I finally discovered that Steinmetz had declared that he was going to say mass again the way he did in the past. A powerful feeling came over me. I wasn't going to do it. I told Fools Crow and he understood. The other dancers pierced. Afterwards my friend Sonny Larive asked me what I planned to do. He had known me since grade school. We sat beside the sun dancer's tent. We needed only one in those days. Now there are many huge spacious teepees. "I will pierce tomorrow, if I have to pierce myself," I stated. Sonny took me to Fools Crow. The wise old gifted holy man said, "I knew you would come. I will pierce you!" That was all we needed. The following morning Steinmetz appeared with his portable altar. We had a dramatic confrontation with Steinmetz and his supporters. The larger sun dance crowd overpowered them. Paul Steinmetz was told to put his altar back in his pickup. I won. That was all there was to it. I was a lone sun dancer on the fourth day and Fools Crow pierced me. I felt good about it. It was a much shorter ceremony.

"Go get those AIMs," Fools Crow commanded after the crowd had come through in a long line to shake my hand. We were sitting on folding chairs beside his spacious tipi. It was a 'Message to Garcia.' No questions asked. Just go do it.

Leamington Hotel—Minneapolis

The National Indian Education Association held a big conference. Skin speakers from everywhere. I was one of them. "Go Back. Go back to your Culture. Go back to your Spirituality," was my message and it was well received. AIM was there. Yes, AIM—the American Indian Movement.

There was also an ultra-beautiful woman there. At every speech or seminar I gave she was in the front row with a pair of the most beautiful legs I had seen in a long time. (My first wife had them, second one also.) What captivating scenery. She seemed to be following me, or at least that was my fantasized hopeful imagination. I had to seriously contemplate, concentrate as to what I was delivering which had never, absolutely never had happened before. But alas, I mistakenly thought she was a nun! What a lucky man Jesus was to have her for a bride. She was always with a reservation group of nuns and in those days of Martin Luther King they were also bringing out their liberal independence. No more stupid restrictive hoods and all the other b.s. - belts, beads, frocks and rosaries. This bunch looked like ordinary women complete with a modest showing of some leg, except for a very brief head scarf. But Beauty Sister had none so I figured she was some sort of older novice-type nun. I was never so damned mystically entranced by such a beautiful woman as I was her. She was utterly beautiful! She didn't have to be blonde. Fortunately, no one else seemed to think so and guys were not buzzing around her but then she was a nun or about to be one. Regardless, I could not help but approach her after the next to last day of the conference. I had just finished speaking and she was in the front row listening to me for probably the third time. We had just started exchanging pleasantries when a young Indian walked up wearing an AIM button and a headband. "Ed, they need a substitute speaker to talk to the AIM members. I looked at Sister Novice and was disappointed. "Can I go with you?" she volunteered. My heart skipped a beat. We went into a packed conference room and delivered. Afterwards the major leaders came up to me and shook my hand, completely oblivious to the Sister who was standing beside me. "I have to talk to you. I have a message from Fools Crow." I looked at Russell Means who was a top leader. He nodded. Another speaker walked in and the room was starting to fill with his followers. I pointed in the direction of the bar and suggested that we meet there. It had plenty of chairs and tables we could put together. I thought about Beauty Novice and asked her, "Sister, you don't mind do you? You can have a coke, if you want." She laughed, and squeezed my hand. "I am not a Sister."

Wow!

We all went in. Dennis Banks, Clyde and Vernon Bellecourt, Lehman Brightman and Russ Means sat across from non-Sister and me. I talked about how we were having trouble from the missionary followers, mainly Steinmetz. "Fools Crow wants you there next August." I looked at Russ. Clyde held up his hand. "I support you. But I cannot come, I'm a Chippewa." He paused. "That is Sioux country."

I nodded in agreement but said, "You have just taken on the BIA (Bureau of Indian Affairs). You were all together, mostly Sioux and Chippewa." (Now they call themselves Anishinabe.) Tribe didn't make any difference." I wanted to reassure Clyde. I looked at his brother. "You will be more than welcome. We are all fighting together to bring back our Old Way." Beauty reached over and squeezed my hand which was under the table. The tension at the table was relieved. I squeezed hers back and we wound up holding hidden hands. Dennis said, "We'll be there."

Clyde and Vernon became lifelong friends as did Dennis Banks. Clyde wound up conducting his own Sun Dance at Pipestone, Minnesota for years. Dennis Banks was one of the finest gentlemen, red, white, blue or black, I have ever known. Russ speaks well of me in his book. Dennis tells of me and the forthcoming confrontation with the missionary priest in his many speeches. After the meeting, Beauty-Novice-non-Sister snuck away with me and we went to a secluded dinner. I was dazzled. She charmed me. "Why did you bore yourself by listening to me speak about the same stuff over and over?" I queried politely. She countered, "You brought in new stuff every time. I learned a lot." I was mesmerized by her. "Your Way is so powerful!" She paused for a moment. Her teeth, her hair, her voice held me spellbound. "You don't rehearse or use notes, do you?" she added soberly.

I wasn't trying to be smart or smug but I answered abruptly, "Don't have too."

I wanted to add but didn't: If you know your subject especially through first-hand experience, you don't need notes or prompts.

I finally touched on the subject. My curiosity made me do so. "You are not a Sister but you are with the nun group?" I didn't know how else to describe her companions. "In your eyes," she put her head down and stammered. "I rode down from the reservation with them." She paused. "I'm worse." She looked over my head and avoided my eyes. "I'm a missionary's wife."

It was my fifth Sun Dance. AIM came. Russ tells about it in his book. Steinmetz arrived at the arena that first morning. Russ describes the priest's crashing our ceremony right at the beginning. He was adorned in his elaborate—hand beaded by devout Indian women—mass vestments and carrying a large peace pipe. The crowd was enormous. The sun was approaching mid-morning. A meadowlark sang. Russ was behind me. Several dancers were in front of us. Again Eagle Feather was absent but Pete Catches and John Fire stood abreast of Fools Crow waiting at the arena entrance. Eagle Feather, having tired of the missionary's disruptions, was conducting his own Sun Dance on the adjoining Rosebud Sichangu Reservation.

We were almost ready to enter. Steinmetz, walked up and of all places stepped in behind me and in front of Russ. A slight breeze had me upwind from Steinmetz. Russ's book tells of smelling strong body odor and sour wine. I couldn't blame Steinmetz if he did load up on altar wine for what he was going to attempt, especially with some real hellacious, tough AIM members with more than a few axes to grind. And then to brazenly step in between a lion and a tiger—Missionary-eaters both. Yes, it had to be okay to sip a lot of wine to be that foolish.

The ceremony began. Steinmetz awkwardly jabbed his pipe at the sky. It is a solemn time, the Sun Dance. Common sense dictated for us to focus on Creator and all its spirit helpers looking on. I could not allow myself to be distracted by Steinmetz. After about an hour to the Four Directions and presenting our pipes to the acceptors, we took a resting place beneath a shaded bower.

The priest looked tired. He had to have been up all night and probably fortifying himself with liquid resolve to carry through with what he was about to attempt. He was older than the rest of us. The ceremony is no short, fifty minute ordeal and we were also under a hot sun. We presented our peace pipes and were seated under a shade bower while a medicine man spoke. I sat next to the priest while Peter Catches gave his speech on the microphone sound system in the elevated announcer's booth. He began in Sioux.

"You are not wanted here," I spoke directly. I didn't get too close to him as the smell of body odor and booze breath was to repelling.

I could see the hatred in his eyes. I had beaten him the year before. I was no pushover Indian and he knew it. I stood up against so much of what he had gotten away with over the years. Now the people were showing their choice. "You're possessed," he hissed. "Fools Crow…Fools Crow…" he stammered. "He told me to pray with you people."

"He sure as hell didn't invite you into our Sun Dance," I argued back.

"I've said Holy Mass at this Sun Dance!"

"Yeah, I know priest, I was watching."

"I have dispensed holy communion." He pointed to the implanted cottonwood tree proudly with a smirk. "Right there." He held a meditating pose, shutting his eyes and then looking up to the white billowing clouds above us. "My Lord, My Jesus, My Savior. Oh risen Redeemer, our Savior. Guide me through these moments of trial. Make them see their salvation." Then he glared at me. "Ed McGaa, you are possessed by the devil. You are the tool of Satan."

"Then pray for me, priest. My God doesn't have one!"

I had been through too many of our ceremonies which held far more proof for me. It was just practical, plain common sense what I had observed. The protection for Vietnam, the SAM missiles, the miracle of stamina for the five hot pad missions back to back, my *Wotai* stone actually flashing at me in the stream, the one before that coming into Fools Crows ceremony and resultant Vietnam predictions. Over and over, the combat missions. It was too much for me to now ignore and listen to this White Man. Priest or not, they never again own me. Fools Crow and Bill, they had shown me too deep a connection into that mysterious Spirit World.

"You're not wanted here, priest, and you damn well know it," I repeated. At that moment Clyde Bellecourt and Lehman Brightman, both hulking strong men came up to us. Clyde pointed to the priest. "Is this the guy you were telling us about?"

I nodded.

"What do you want us to do with him?"

"Don't let him back out there." I watched Steinmetz's eyes widen.

A drum sounded. We were going to go back out for the second session. I stepped forward. The priest did the same. Clyde slammed him back down. "Keep him out of here." I pointed to the tree.

Steinmetz made another vain attempt and the priest went back down. Clyde held up his huge fist and told him he was going down if he tried again. Brightman held his fist up also. We went back out into the arena to the tone of the drums and to pray to Creator's universe and for the return of our Way.

A voice interrupted over the sound system. Steinmetz was in the announcer's booth commanding the microphone. "I have been on this reservation longer than Russ Means. I have been here longer than Ed McGaa. Both of them are not Indian anymore. I am more Indian than they are!" What an idiotic statement. "I have dedicated my life to the Indian people. They have not."

I yelled, "Get…him…out…of…there!"

Clyde vaulted the platform rail, Lehman right behind him. They jerked the microphone away. Lehman threw the priest over the railing, vestments and all. Clyde stood with the microphone, nervously holding it as if it were a poisonous snake. After a few moments he spoke into it. "There will be no more interruptions of the Sun Dance." He handed the microphone to the announcer, Paul Apple. Apple spoke excitedly, "No! No more interruption. My son…my son…he has vowed to do the Sun Dance next year."

The power of the missionaries was broken at that very moment.

The following year we were at the Hunkpapa/Minicoujou Reservation. Fools Crow had decided that we should go where the original pipe from the Buffalo Calf Maiden is kept. It is called Green Grass. His prediction was that the Sun Dance would grow under many medicine men. Different community medicine men and different tribes would have it spread. There was no longer a need for one Sun Dance. Far too many pledgers would make it impossible.

The Green Grass Sun Dance was more of a gathering than a bona fide four-day Sun Dance. No one argued with Fools Crow. Several medicine men from the Oglala tribe and Bill's Sichangu Sun Dance were available for those making their pledges. The Pipe Bundle held at Green Grass was to be opened for the first time in years. This was the main focus. A Sun Dance-like ceremony would be held on the first day, a Saturday, and the following day the Pipe Bundle would be opened and honored. I have a picture of that first day standing beside Fools Crow in a smaller arena than usual where a smaller cottonwood tree had been brought in.

Across a sloping meadow above the river two people, a man and woman, were struggling to drag a smaller than normal, younger cottonwood toward the slowly filling Green Grass Sun Dance Arena. We walked toward them. "Hi," I greeted.

"I'm Mabel...Mabel Mexican." She turned her head with a shy smile while beautiful blonde Mary stared at her from under her floppy cowboy hat which Fools Crow's wife had placed on her. She was the wonderful woman who bought my necklace on a Western Airlines flight and whom I would marry within a year after that last Sun Dance. Her hat looked more like a Marine Recon 'Nam hat then it did cowboy. "We'll give you a hand," I offered.

"John. John Mexican." The handsome, solidly built man a bit shorter than most Sioux nodded warmly while holding onto the tree's base. He was a decade older than me. Obviously he knew me, as by now, after five gradually growing Sun Dances I had acquired a reputation for raising hell with the missionaries, and now AIM had taken the helm. A lot of Sioux were still thinking that I was related to their imaginary Devil taught by the missionaries, but the Sun Dance stances I had behind me like battle missions were gradually eroding those missionary-instigated thoughts. The ember of the Way was now a steadily growing flame. At least there was one bigger battle cruiser, AIM, for the traditional folks' Fleet of Change who had been forlornly waiting down through the decades. I was still one of the adequately armed cruisers however.

He puffed his chest under the weight of the tree. "We're related," he added proudly. The tree they were dragging was more a symbol of the Sun Dance center than the usual tree brought in, which required many men to carry it. (Those trees, at the large gatherings we have now, never touch the ground after they are cut.) A little boy was following with an axe and a tree saw. I beckoned him over and took off several bottom branches to lighten the load. I gave the tools back and took hold where John was at and told him to take a break. I rested the tree butt on my shoulder and gave him about five minutes which he appreciated. I told Mary to take Mabel's place. She shrunk her shoulders and slunk down a bit. "Can I?" I frowned with a bit of anger, not at her, but the rule bound world. "God doesn't give a flat fuck what color you are, beautiful!"

"Yah but…"

"Yah, I know! But those are the rules dreamed up by the control seeking assholes of life." I knew what she was about to finish. I paused, and looked at Mabel. Mabel Mexican. I can still hear that innocent, bashful reply way the hell out beside the Little Moreau River. I caught her beaming with pride when John said, "We are related." I guess to them, I was sort of an English Knight coming in on a good horse to kick ass on the sons of bitches who were cutting off the fingers of their bowmen out 'illegally' supplementing their meager diet of stunting gruel with rich forest meat. That's why the Europeans were so damn small when they first came over except for the Vikings who didn't buy into that bullshit like the rest. They would slice your head off and hand it to you if you should come up with No hunting-No fishing rules. Siouxs are the same. Vikings didn't have Organized Religion either and lived a helluva lot better and ate what they wanted. They also kicked ass all the way down to Africa. We need some Viking or Sioux Knight or maybe the combination to come along and kick the one-percenter's ass. Too bad I am getting too damn old to do it. If I was younger I sure as hell would give it a try! Maybe it will get so bad as we keep going backwards within only these last three centuries. It could happen. Maybe the cowards will hurt so bad that they will finally develop some revolutionary balls and support the Knight.

We wouldn't find one beer can, not one coke bottle, nothing foreign where Mary and I would go swimming later to cool off. This is how remote and faraway from non-civilization we were. "Mexicans, Siouxs and Whites!" I laughed. "All we need is a Chinaman and a Black Guy. Red, White, Black and Yellow! Black Elk's colors!" A pleasant feeling seemed to sweep through as a gentle fanning breeze twittered the leaves of the cottonwood. I can still see her standing there. A beautiful, perplexed blonde airline stewardess in the middle of nowhere, on land resembling the Mongolian steppes where my ancestors came from.

Most of the AIM leaders were at the Sun Dance. All had now been thoroughly bitten by the Nature's Way bug.

A short time later, I would meet the same leaders at Wounded Knee. They had occupied a portion of the Pine Ridge reservation in protest against all that the Federal Government did not do according to the solemn dictates of the treaty of 1868 among other grievances. Dennis Banks, AIM leader, is one of the most impressive, genuine men I have ever met.

Just before the Occupation, Ben Black Elk died. He was an enormous factor in preserving our Spirituality by interpreting every word of *Black Elk Speaks*. This writing is a powerful basis for our Six Powers of the Universe concept, the Four Directions, *Tahteh Toepah*, Mother Earth, *Inah Mahkah* and Father Sky, *Mahkpiyah Ahteh* and of course *Wahkahn Tahnkah*—Great Spirit, Great Mystery above. (I am utilizing phonetic presentation the way the White Man does and not the academic spelling which is highly misleading.)

I was dating the future 'World's Greatest Step-Mother' then and flew an airplane down to the Rez, and hitchhiked to the wake where Black Elk lay. Russ Means was giving a speech when we walked in. Black Elk's relatives asked me to follow Russ. We did well, at least that is what Mary said and some of Ben's relatives said so, too. Steinmetz came and was supposed to say Mass afterwards but must have gotten so incensed upon seeing Russ and me that he took the microphone after me and wildly asserted that Ben was a follower of the Lord. He went over and over, almost shouting, about why Ben had to be a Christian. He believed that Russ and I were so powerfully misleading that the whole Reservation was about to go back to Native Spirituality, lock, stock and barrel. He wisely did not mention either Russ or me as we were never the politically correct types and would have hauled him outside and he knew it. Instead, that very night his Wounded Knee Church burned down. Maybe God did it…maybe not. People still wonder who did it. The Bishop must have thought, *enough is enough*. Steinmetz was sent off on a long permanent sabbatical and no more churches were burned down.

My phone rang in my office, one of many in the St. Paul City Attorney's office. It was the Mayor. "You have to go back to South Dakota. Your Congressman, Jim Abnor just called me. You are specifically needed out there."

I was puzzled. Technically I was a Minnesota citizen and didn't know or care who my real congressman was. Being a Sioux Indian, I guess some folks thought of us Sioux—Skins—as being a bit more than just, 'from South Dakota.' A former fellow law student classmate and now a congressional assistant had furnished my name as a mediator/negotiator regarding AIM who were now occupying Wounded Knee. I knew Jim Abnor from my many Republican-leaning speeches all over the state, mostly while I was in law school. Honorariums from the farmers and ranchers helped defray my education expenses. It wasn't difficult to figure out why I was being called out. I would become the congressman's on-scene direct representative and his negotiator. "You're booked on the 3:00 o'clock Western to Rapid City, Chief." I didn't even have time to go back to my apartment and get a warm coat. It was a mild day in St. Paul but fouler weather was approaching Rapid City, my destination. On landing I was met by the National Guard, a colonel whose last name was Wilson verbally gave me my orders. I would be met by the head U.S. Marshal at Pine Ridge, quartered and fed, billeted with four other lawyer negotiators, two of us were Indians. They were famous Bill Kuntsler, and Mark Lane, Ramon Roubideaux, a breed like myself (his Indian blood mostly from an Iowa tribe), and Ken Tilson, a lawyer from Minneapolis who knew AIM. We were the team to go in daily in a van and negotiate a truce to prevent bloodshed. We succeeded.

It was sort of James Bond-ish what later happened. I looked at the National Guard brass behind the colonel and asked where I could get a parka. The Colonel immediately slipped off his and handed it to me. It had a needed fur-fringed hood and Colonel Wilson's nametag. The tribal chairman AIM was fighting against, besides the federal government, was also named Wilson.

I was led to a waiting Huey helicopter and the pilot and I headed south. As we approached the vast Badlands, it got very black. No lights for reference, whatsoever, going through a vast stretch; it is about a hundred miles of separation and the pilot became pretty nervous. He started wandering, losing and gaining altitude. We were not much higher than the Badland buttes. I told him I had a couple thousand hours in Marine choppers and asked if I could take it over and spell him a bit. It was kind of fun. I think he was getting into vertigo because of the utter blackness and no land reference. There was no radio reference to guide in on at Pine Ridge and none at low altitude out of Rapid City. I noticed his abrupt heading changes. He was getting lost and we were spending too much time in the air. I spotted some dim, barely lighted haze way out on the edge of the horizon to the south, southeast, and plotted backward to the fading Rapid City FAA Omni (electronic direction responder) and guessed the dim haze had to be Pine Ridge. We were pretty low for adequate reception. I might have saved the U.S. government a helicopter by doing so. I told him to attempt to climb high in order to pick up on this particular faded vector to find his way back and stay on it. The Rapid City lights would be far brighter to catch their glow from farther out and he would be okay. He was nervous as a cat and had to be getting vertigo. Helicopters are notorious for inducing it as the whirling motion of the blades causes your inner ear fluid to swirl somewhat. He wasn't reluctant to let go of it. I made the approach toward Pine Ridge and knew where the gravel strip was as I had landed there quite a few times while flying for the university. He threw his lights on and got oriented. I gave it back to him and gathered up what little gear I managed to bring with me. It was pretty windy by the time we got down. He was worried about his fuel and I told him if he went wandering around he could be in big trouble. "Stay on that fucking beam and you'll see Rapid's glow way earlier," were my last words to him. I no more than stepped out then he leaped skyward and headed north. It was pretty dark out in the middle of that rudimentary airport.

I cursed myself for not having a flashlight as I heard a vehicle approaching without lights. Maybe they had early heat sensing gear. I heard people jump out. It sounded like a jeep. Odd how jeeps have their own sounds. I heard enough of them in the Corps. "Put your hands up." Then, "Lie Down! Prone!" a voice barked from the darkness. Next I was being manhandled by several U.S. Marshals. One was exceedingly rough, jerking my arms behind me painfully high to attach handcuffs, then rolling me over and jerking me to my feet. Next I was thrown into the back seat of an open jeep and whisked off toward the lights of Pine Ridge. Rough sat next to me once I sat up in the seat and threw me out of the jeep when we stopped before a cluster of men, all in grayish looking uniforms akin to the flight suits we pilots wore in 'Nam. All were heavily armed, mostly big knives and pistols. Rough jerked me forward. I had had enough from him and I turned on him and said, "Hey, motherfucker, after you find out who in the hell I am, your ass is going to pay!"

He shoved me forward to what turned out to be the head marshal on the scene. "Captain Ed McGaa, USMC, 081193, direct representative of Congressman Jim Abnor." I turned to 'Rough' and pointed with my lips. "This guy is an asshole, and if you take these handcuffs off me, I am going to beat the shit out of him."

They all looked at me dumbfounded. I had to add, "That was a fucking South Dakota National Guard Helicopter. Met me at the airport. You think I fucking stole it?" I pointed to my parka and looked down at the nametag with puckered lips. "Call Colonel Wilson of the National Guard. This is his parka." As an afterthought, I added. "I didn't kill him to be wearing it." They mulled about. Head Marshal nodded to make a call. Within a few minutes he was kissing my ass and released my handcuffs. I promptly went after Rough, but they restrained me. Head Marshal yelled at him, telling him to get back to quarters. He assured me that he wouldn't look good in his next fitness report.

I was satisfied. I have a penchant for wanting the assholes of life to get their comeuppance.

The ride in on that jeep reminds me of the scene in *Dances With Wolves* when Lt. Dunbar is captured and is tied and in the back of the army wagon. Corporal Spivey is agitating him. They also shoot the pet wolf. (Two Socks?) Rough jabbed me several times with his elbow, whispering laughingly, "Injun, Injun." Years later, a Vine Deloria aficionado, Elizabeth Cooke-Lynn (part Dakota Sioux) wrote a story eulogizing the hero academic (at least to the Indian Academics). Vine Deloria, disdainer and no supporter of AIM and the rest of us who tried to bring back our Indian Spiritual way revival. She was my age group, Deloria was, too, and no way was that bunch going to stand for our doings. They couldn't risk their plush academic thrones. Most all of them had their higher education paid for by Bureau of Indian Affairs scholarships or by the Church. Those two, the main culprits, were off limits from any criticism or exposure, especially about the boarding schools. Where does Deloria or his sidekick expose them? She stated that her hero was one of the negotiators braving Wounded Knee. He wasn't on our bus and I didn't see him at the negotiation table.

Bill Kuntsler had been a captain in the Philippines under MacArthur—he saw considerable combat. He and I kept the negotiator group enthralled with our combat stories while riding in the van. He had quite a sense of humor. Later, when the Wounded Knee trials moved to the Twin Cities I sat in his lecture to an elite clientele of some sort of Junior League, I think they called themselves, composed of well to-do younger future executive wives from the western suburbs of Minneapolis. My kid played hockey in one of them. Kuntsler said, "Well ladies, I am pleasured to see such a fine turnout of Native American interested fellow Americans. I have to congratulate you Suburban Brood Mares." Surprisingly, they just sat there and beamed due mainly that Bill was such a nationally known figure.

There was a brief truce celebration. Chief Fools Crow, Russ Means and I were photographed smoking a peace pipe. Somehow that picture wound up in my FBI file. Yes, a goddamned FBI file! This on a patriotic Marine who had put off his law school for a year to volunteer for combat missions and was a congressman's appointed, direct negotiator at Wounded Knee! Damn well disgusting is all I can say. I was shocked when I read my FBI file. Life as an Indian!

Oklahoma University- Indian Week

I was asked by the Oklahoma University Indian Students Association to come speak at their annual 'Indian Days'. Two non-Indian professors met me at the airport and exhibited an obvious nervousness as they took me to dinner before my opening speech in the school's auditorium.

"You know that this area is the heart of Bible country," they opened as we sat in a restaurant. "So, I heard." I replied nonchalantly. They didn't wait to get to their intentions. "Eagle Man. We know that you are very forceful in your speaking on Indian Religion." "Just telling what is happening." I replied. "At least my tribe is going back pell-mell'. Lotta' Sun Dances springing up now that AIM came to help us out from under the missionaries. Siouxs are happy that the religious Ban imposed on us has finally been lifted. Got to congratulate MLK ."

"But this is the heart of Bible country. You might offend many in the audience." "So, what you think I should speak about?" My reply in an obsequious, 'Iktomi' voice. (Iktomi is a fictitious trickster in Sioux story telling.)

"Ahhh. Ahhh." They stammered in unison. "Our Culture…. instead?" I volunteered. "Yes, Yes." They replied in relieved unison. "Maybe tipi life, bows and arrows….maybe leaving out killing Custer even?" I suggested in a conciliatory tone. Two happy, accomplished professors went on to eat our meal.

The auditorium was crowded. Indians are Indians deep within, especially the youth. Quite a few non-Indians as well attended. I figured those were curious faculty. One big Indian sat in the front row throwing not overly polite stares at me sitting peacefully while the two professors introduced me. The over-sized Indian and I locked stares as I made my way to the podium.

"Well, I hear that this is the heart of Bible country and that I might offend some of you in the audience if I speak on our Indian Religion that is blossoming strongly up in our Sioux country." My tone was academic and superior-istic. I pointed to the two professors who nodded back gleefully. I looked down at 'Big Indian. He threw back a growly frown. "We prefer to call 'Our Way' Spirituality and not Religion. Religion comes from Man in our way of thinking and Spirituality comes directly from Creator, mostly from what we observe from Its Creation- Nature. I agreed to speak only about our culture. But there is a glitch in my agreement." I glanced at Big I. A hopeful glimmer transgressed his face. "Well, folks." I paused against the deathly hush across the large crowd. "I was asked by Indians to come here to their celebration and they well know my reputation. If you asked Martin Luther King to come speak, you damn well can figure out what he will talk about." Big Indian gave me a broad, supporting smile.

I leaned forward on the podium. "Our Culture IS our Spirituality and I will speak about our Indian 'Religion' and how and why we, from up North, have gone back, at least a goodly many of us and if you don't like it, you can go to your own man-created Hell. We Sioux don't have one, nor a Devil either." Big Indian stood up and clapped. Later we went out that evening, He gave me his Seiko watch in appreciation. Gift giving in Indian is reciprocal. I had nothing of equivalency so took out my beaded bill fold made by my mother, emptied it and reciprocated. They are a bit slippery compared to leather ones, anyhow. I went on to speak, figuring Big Indian would be standing beside me if any altercation would occur. I received a standing ovation. Needless to say, I was never invited back.

14 CRAZY HORSE MONUMENT

Corporations

A White Man and an Indian see life from two differing sets of eyes. Culture plays more of an influence than we give credit for. In the White Man's world, there are corporations, institutions and even families that operate their holdings from a financial/economic influencing base. The Nobility Party, the Republicans, have even elevated the corporation to a full-fledged 'personage' concept. Being Indian, I find that philosophy hard to swallow. We are now paying $4 gas and Exxon's CEO retires with $500 million, thus the high salaries and bonuses reaped by the top oil executives raises the fuel prices higher and higher, and suffering among the masses increases exponentially. If Traditional influenced American Indians were at the helm in this country, and if they kept the old traditional values, (that is—IF) this legalized robbery would never happen.

Great Britain Sweat Lodge

I conducted an unusual sweat lodge in England. A smooth fluid lavender background immersed us in that sapling-framed lodge, sprinkled by a variety of 'cake decorating' lights—many colors. Yes, in the beginning it was a pitch-black lodge. Hard, almost impossible to believe, right? But a painful hand—was it nettles or a spider bite? An allergic reaction? Enough to make me delusional? Use that for an excuse if you must refuse believing such supernatural. The Brit islanders within that lodge will never change their startling-experience memory, however. The land of Stonehenge, the Tor at

Glastonbury and Solstice abounds within the Celtic Spirit, of which we Eastern coastal tribes just may well be connected.

Mentors

I was on my way back to another summer at Crazy Horse Mountain. I had missed the month of May, having to go to England again to promote a new book being published there. I would be selling my books for the tenth year—or eleventh or twelfth year. Indians don't keep exact track of what is not important. Normally reclusive during the winters I would now be immersed in many questions from those million tourists that walk by all summer from May to early October.

I do know my history, in contrast to so many Eurocentric-influenced historical-attempting authors—simply take a look at their works regarding our Sioux battles in case one wants to condemn my vanity. The errant penning by *wahshichu* writers (and now even a couple Sioux writers) claiming the Custer battle lasting a full day is enough proof—which the Big Horn Memorial Association is finally debunking thanks to metal detectors and several television documentaries. The astute and aware Crazy Horse Museum staff realizes it. At this point I must acknowledge my mentors: Dr. John Bryde, for his priceless interviewing of the aging warriors in their own language; and Hilda Neihardt who was present during the summer-long creation of *Black Elk Speaks*. Her father interviewed Black Elk about his recollection of the Great Vision via the translations of Black Elk's son, an excellent linguist. What better mentors could a man have? I must add my parents as well. They were born in the 1800s, (1880s—my father) and could reach way back; also excellent linguists as well. When I was growing up we had constant visitors as we had an extra summer house that drew many full bloods coming up from the reservation to shop at Rapid City, all of whom retained their language and preferred speaking it. Lakota (Sioux) was spoken at our home practically every day.

Crazy Horse Museum

The Crazy Horse Museum staff greets the million visitors every summer to view this gigantic mountain carving of Chief Crazy Horse. The colossal undertaking was started by Korczak Ziolkowski who has passed on now as has his wife Ruth and daughter Anne who was my boss as Curator of the best

Indian museum in the country. She used to have several of my necklaces behind her office desk. When particular Indian related questions arise, down to my table the visitors are escorted, bringing many a curious, concerned individual to my comfortable table. I am not a linguist but I can find my way around the many, "How do you say, Eagle, Buffalo, Deer, Wolf, rain, fire, water, West Power, North Power, Creator, Mother Earth, etc." I know some songs in Lakota as well.

Historical curiosity about the Indian's point of view abound. Many non-Indians declare that they bear some degree of Indian blood, mostly of Cherokee lineage. 1/8th, 1/16th, 1/32nd and are assuming subjective names and saying them in Lakota. Go on Facebook and take a look. It is not my doing and I am just responding. It is an enjoyable task and rewarding for both sides. I also pose for many pictures. The talented Indian dancers are photographed the most. The crowds are moved when they enter this great museum. It surpasses the Smithsonian, my opinion. Our ability to provide for not only the national but the international public as well, and our truthful cultural information, is of a much higher caliber than what the Smithsonian offers (or rather, neglects to offer). The Smithsonian is handicapped in that respect. They have to cater to all American tribes. Realistically, centering on one particular historically famous tribe, the one that has preserved their culture and Spirituality is a supreme advantage for Crazy Horse Mountain Museum.

Korczak

The beginning of the Crazy Horse Mountain carving was ultra-challenging to say the least. A dedicated man simply wanted and succeeded in following his dream. Korczak Ziolkowski was not just a giant among artisans but he was indeed a generous man as well. My older sister, nicknamed 'Chick' (she hated her name Eileen which reminded her of the Boarding School) befriended Korczak one evening at an early meeting regarding his quest to carve a huge effigy of an Indian, a Sioux warrior chief, out of a Black Hills mountain. It would become the largest sculpture in the world and would not be completed until well beyond his lifetime (it is still under construction and will be so for decades to come).

Korczak was explaining his intentions before an audience that also held a group of recalcitrant Sioux claiming the project would defile the sacred

Black Hills. They never mentioned the famed Mt. Rushmore Monument that was but a few miles away. At the end of Korczak's presentation, my forceful sister lit in to the Indians, claiming it was about time that one of our leaders also be so honored. The opposition retreated under her withering barrage. Afterwards, Korczak thanked her and invited her to come out to his work site. She and her boyfriend, who was the son of a well-to-do businessman that had strongly supported the Mt. Rushmore project, went out to Crazy Horse Mountain, as it would now be called. After a few cocktails, the three set out to climb the towering wooden scaffold that ended close to the top of the mountain. Near the top they stood out upon the place where Crazy Horse's arm would be carved. His head is now finished. Korczak told my sister that she was the first Indian woman to stand there.

The Mountain Postlude:

Crazy Horse Mountain portrays a great man who shunned publicity and the camera's eye. He was a man who avoided the limelight. He was a warrior, a superbly courageous one and he was deeply spiritual. He wore the *wotai* stone, as we have read, a special stone behind his ear when he entered battle. For who made the stone? For who makes all stones especially the protective *wotawe* (woe tah way), one's powerful stone which comes to one in a powerful way? Upon these stones are special images or maybe just one significant image placed there whenever they were formed by you know who. The image alone proves the power, the closeness of man to the stone's Creator and the required respect the warrior must carry, if he is to live. The stone is millions of years old; how old are we? The warrior who wears a *wotai* or a *wotawe* is indeed dependent upon the Spirits when he is in the midst of combat. It is Sioux culture, belief, the Way. One almost needs to wear such a stone and experience the utter ecstasy, confidence, sureness, yes even an occasional sereneness when in the heat of battle for one to truly understand. I do know this: one cannot convey its inner essence to another without having been there. Confidence before battle was just as important as the event, for one needed to plan one's move with a clear head devoid of panic, even in those last mini-seconds when ballistics, shells, arrows, lance heads, axes, tomahawks were on their way. It is indeed a special gift the Spirit World can grant a warrior and, in my opinion, Chief Crazy Horse had it. Red Cloud and Sitting Bull too, among so many Sioux warriors.

Ohhuzhea Wichastah (Oh hoo zhey we chah stah) is a Mystic Warrior.

One who follows the Way. They most generally carry a special stone or else an ingredient of Creator's Created Nature such as an eagle's or a hawk's claw, which also are directly made by the Ultimate. Even an eagle feather can have special images. Take a long deep look at one, especially the tail feathers. Every image will be dissimilar. I wore a special *wotai* in repeated combat. I can only speak from my own observation. It can even slow down time, the rising fire, coming up to dissolve you; these can be seen, and this can all be bent away by your calm, steady action for the moment. My combat stone had but one significant image. My next wotai stone, which came to me after my first Sun Dance piercing, has many images. I respectfully request all of those who have never worn a *wotai* and have never experienced combat, sheer direct combat, to hold their tongues until they have reached the Spirit World and then they can question such a belief, for indeed it is a profound mystery. If you have ever possessed such a gift it is difficult not to be moved deeply when you speak of it.

The great chief wore a stone and now he is cast in a huge stone—the Mountain.

Accomplishment & Errant Authors

My historical books, especially the battles, are far more accurate than the White Man's attempts simply because mine are based upon Jesuit Father Bryde's interviews with the Sioux warriors themselves who were there. A myriad of White authors and two Indian ones never based their historic attempts on linguistic interviews with Sioux warriors. Those authors could not speak our language yet they went on to dupe the public for over a century. Simply look at my book, *Crazy Horse and Chief Red Cloud,* and Larry McMurtry's works which are based on verified Indians. Larry severely criticizes and names certain authors who "are long on imagination and short on facts." Marie Sandoz is the greatest culprit. She errantly vilifies Chief Red Cloud and bases her fiction on only one unverified Indian and, according to McMurtry, the interview lasted less than a half hour. Dr. Bryde spent a decade interviewing in their language and said that not one warrior would speak without a verifier present to ensure accuracy.

"Eagle Man: What do you consider your greatest accomplishment?" I have been asked several times. "Raising my kids," is a natural answer. Aside from that obvious fact, I add: "Doing what I could to preserve and promote truthfully, Black Elk's Vision and, as well, the truthful and experienced knowledge of the Sioux battles, lifestyle, spirituality and culture." "Historically, utilizing Dr. Bryde's interview notes." *Mother Earth Spirituality* is at 48th reprinting. Not bad. I guess I could add, "And exonerating Chief Red Cloud." If any race needs a real genuine hero, or several heroes, it is the Sioux people whose youth have one of the highest suicide rates in the country. We Sioux would have been shipped to Oklahoma were it not for Red Cloud going to Washington successfully appealing to Senators and thwarting Grant's policy to do so. There would be no Crazy Horse Monument had he failed. We would have lost our culture in Oklahoma.

Red Cloud

Chief Red Cloud was twenty or more years senior to Crazy Horse. The actual date of Crazy Horse's birth is unknown. The older chief started fighting the Army back in 1856, when Crazy Horse was not yet a teenager, purportedly killing Lt. Grattan and all of his detachment who killed a Sioux chief. Red Cloud must be credited for procuring the Winchester repeater and having our warriors ride Mongolian-style—both hands free in the manner of the highly successful Genghis Khan whose armies defeated China, Islam and the eastern Europeans due mainly to his mounted archers. He declared Western Europe as not worth invading. Likewise, the Sioux cavalry decimated the U.S. Cavalry with similar strategy, tallying up an eight-to-one kill ratio and winning the treaty of 1868. Red Cloud demanded that the Army forts on the Bozeman Trail be burned down before he would sign. One billion dollars collecting interest sits in a bank today as a result of Chief Red Cloud's and Spotted Tail's warriors winning the Treaty of 1868.

Mary Ray McGaa (deceased). World's Greatest Step-Mother.

A Non-Deadbeat Dad

I guess I can qualify for this title. I can have myself verified through my kids and my first wife if I had to. My second wife, too, if she was alive. Throw in quite a few of my son's best friends and my daughters' too. I had a lot of help from second wife, I have to admit. She was always out there with the kids playing with them. We had airline passes, so that helped considerably. Ask them how many times they been to Hawaii and they will honestly tell you, "We don't know."

My second marriage started out pretty heavy with canoeing in the North Woods. Then my wife got us all into tennis. Then a golden retriever joined us. I now am looking down on Rex V at my feet. Sadly, they only live to be about ten or twelve years and oh such mournful passing. That led to pheasant hunting (and even a book) which my sons and their friends loved. I even had a daughter that liked it. She composed a funny poem. Bibles, (duck) blinds, bowling and badminton = Boring. Compared to tennis or pheasants, she's right. She thought duck hunting was boring compared to pheasants, and was not a church fan. The other two are obvious. Oh yes, I cannot forget skiing which my grandchildren are strongly into along with their parents. My youngest son was into hockey, which almost became our religion, and now I have a promising grandson who is playing on A teams too, plus a granddaughter who recently picked it up as well. We were active, no question about it.

I would make a couple of Rites of Passage sojourns every summer out to the reservation, mainly with stops along the Missouri to plink at rough fish, carp and gar on the Cheyenne River reservation. I knew some Indian ranchers on this huge reservation where you could go way back in and get lost in solitude. One particular outing we had several of my youngest son's buddies along, all hockey players. My 2nd son Mark was also with us. I love to pheasant hunt with him because he is such a dead shot. When his 24-inch Benelli comes up, usually a pheasant is going down. We went way back into some treeless prairie toward an old broken down corral where the owner said there was plenty of old corral firewood to camp for the night. We had a couple of illegal pheasants and two cottontails in our cooler and one rattlesnake. I stepped out of our van and stepped right on a young rattler, fortunately the head, and he was thrashing back and forth, his tail a buzzing. My son Mark was behind me with his Benelli 12-gauge. We went gathering firewood where decaying posts were stacked and *Wham!* I felt a breeze go past my leg and the loud shot gun blast. It was a large female rattlesnake just starting her evening hunt and all coiled up about to nail me. That evening we ate the rattlesnake and other fare with baked beans and baked potatoes wrapped in tinfoil.

We would do these 'rites' about every year. I still get quite a reception from these now grown men when I come back for one of their weddings. I very recently was out walleye fishing with two of them. They now take me and I don't have to provide anything and they are extremely attentive, seeming to worry a bit too much that I am going to trip and fall or overexert myself. They take me into their young clientele bars afterwards where my flight jacket is quite an attraction for the bar crowd.

15 EXPLOITED INDIANS

Everyone should be an Author or an Indian!

You can at least reveal those who wrongfully, cruelly, viciously or even unconsciously oppressed you. Some unknowingly harmed you without a care, of course, like the retiring Exxon $500 million CEO and all the rest of the oil barons. Those guys harm all of us. This big North Dakota oil boom hasn't changed the prices a bit, has it? No way will my mere words bring fuel prices down. The people have to experience a high degree of suffering before that happens. It will happen, however and Mother Nature will bring it. It will simply be a reaction to the way the atmospheric 'chemical soup' is beginning to react right now. Fracking and oil spills will damage more than just the economy. Water-borne diseases will take their toll. Maybe wars will end and the profiteering will come to an abrupt halt because we won't be able to afford them. Pray all you want but you may as well ask to change gravity. *Uncle Tom's Cabin* didn't do a helluva lot for civil rights until a century later when a brave man (Dr. Martin Luther King) came along. Some claim it started the Civil War to free the slaves, however.

An Author can expose certain oppressive people he or she comes across, which allows some satisfaction, but most find futility who long for justice to fall upon their oppressors. Few if any wish or want them to go scot-free. The Indian, however, can wait for them in the Spirit World. We get to administer satisfying Truth for an Eternity! If that is too much for you because the way you were programmed, then don't die an Indian.

Some folks are programmed to decry any and all moments of revenge. They state that one cannot release such anguish or memory other than to forgive. As a child they don't start out that way. They get programmed. Forgive? In all Truth, isn't forgiveness a declaration that the incident or perpetual degrading offense never happened? What happened, happened! My Nature-influenced mind states to me that the past, the actual happening, cannot and will not be changed in one's memory. What seems to work for others, simply does not work for me and I believe my culture is a major reason why I do not fall in line with so many who tout this word— Forgiveness. Its absence was probably the most single powerful force that deeply motivated the old Indian's conduct while on his Life's Journey. He didn't know about *forgiveness!* He didn't believe he would be forgiven and hence, he feared being condemned in the Spirit World by those he would wrongfully oppress, and thought twice, many times actually, which helped prevent wrongful acts. The dread of pragmatic, obvious condemnation from those he had wrongfully harmed was a powerful force within. The North American tribes viewed an extreme difference emanating from the first arrivals from Europe. Yes, we Indians are truly different in so many ways from the White Man. Genes, DNA—they do have an effect. I have observed it all my life.

Man's mere words cannot change what he did not do through lack of courage, perception or cowardly fear when he needed to help another, an animal or the Earth. What he did do maliciously, cruelly or cunningly to deprive or hurt also is recorded in his victim's memory. The oppressor who believes in forgiveness manages to salve his conscience about that happening or worse, continue with numerous reoccurrences. Eventually the perpetrator becomes immune, but not the victim. Should the bombers that blew the limbs off innocent Boston Massacre civilians be forgiven? Should Emile Castro be forgiven: now a household word due to his extreme atrocity of capturing and imprisoning young girls to satisfy his rape lust? Ask a victim. You know my answer.

I was teaching a class on Sioux culture and values. An English lady was sitting up front. I had gone to a coffee break with her and she confided that she was a victim of rape as a young girl by a pair of uncles—repeated rape! She had gone through a couple of divorces, been to numerous psychologists and even wondered if she should become institutionalized after thinking about suicide. Worse, her parents would not support her and even made excuses for the uncles (who employed her father). "Forgiveness, forgiveness," she spoke in lowered breath and angered glaring. "That's all the buggered shrinks could come up with. Forgiveness…and it will go away in bleary smoke." She had a heavy British accent. "Course they always liked to bite my dowry and call me back for blimey sessions." "They liked your money," I confirmed. Angrily she chirped, "Bloody well. The buggers." She hushed her lips with an index finger as if she had just spoken a major swear word. In my many trips to the British Isles, the Brits rarely swear, actually never, at least in my experience. I guess the word *bloody* is their limit. Everyone there advised me, "Chap, you just never was with the right crowd for bloody swear words." Just as in the statement I often make about their pubs, "I never saw a fight or even an argument. They are always so cheerful." Some of our western bars even have a layer of sawdust on the floors to ease the fall. Likewise, I am told that I was always in the wrong British pubs as far as fighting goes. "You can get knocked about, in some pubs, Yank. Ahh don't worry. We like you bloody Yanks. World War Two, you know. Keepin' those wily Huns off our backs!"

We returned to class and she sat in the front row. I thought I would center on this word: Forgiveness. I stated that revenge was an important trait among my tribe. It went so far to explain that an attack upon one group would be avenged. The Cheyenne cemented their friendship to my tribe historically by passing to us a war pipe to avenge a Crow attack upon one of their villages. The Crows did likewise to avenge an attack on their village and so on, with the Snakes and Utes coming to their aid.

Violators of moral and ethical social standards were quickly dealt with. Outright capital punishment was enacted or lesser sentences, such as banishment from the encampment for a period of time or even permanently if one was an extreme troublemaker. Often banishment would result in fatal results as now the criminal perpetrator would be fair game for lurking enemies. The rare pedophile would be buried with only his head exposed while the bereaved family of the victim would trample over him. Rape was also exceedingly rare. Usually the same fate would befall the rapist, although the exceptionally large butcher knives that all Sioux women carried would efficiently thwart most would-be rapists. According to campfire tales, some notable women went on to emasculate any attempter. The perpetrator has to sleep eventually. Thus over the years most Sioux women were more safe from sexual predators than women of today. If I was an attractive woman of today, there would be a .38 pistol in my purse, under my pillow or at least an exposed butcher knife attached to my belt. All of this I related to the class.

"Forgiveness. Forgiveness," I concluded. "We did not have such a concept. We severely punished violators and the victims at least felt some assurance that the tribe had looked after them." I waved my hand. "Now what about the victim. A rape victim, for example. What could help salve her memory?" I paused. "Now we do believe in a Spirit World Beyond." I had already related several *Yuwipi* experiences and believed that I had fairly much convinced most that a Spirit World quite possibly did exist. "In that Spirit World where we all most likely go—the good and the bad—there, hopefully, is a place of All Truth. The Ultimate Maker is All Truth. Would it not be Natural that Its Spirit World would have to be the same as IT is? If so, then would our intuitive Mind, now our Spirit or, as you White Folks say, your soul: Would not this Mind/Spirit deduce that one can call out or bring out what truthfully happened back here on our Earth? Back to your journey while here." My class was following me quite seriously. "I know what I intend to do to those who have victimized me in other ways. I was never sexually victimized, but I did suffer wrongfully from the acts of others. I intend to chastise or expose those characters for an eternal lifetime, if I so desire." I looked at the class and then at the English lady. "I will make them pay with the real truth for their heinous acts against me as long as I was innocent and they were definitely guilty." The British lady had her arms down and doubled her fists as if she was about to fight some delusion. "And," I added with unhidden relish, "I think I will feel damn good about it!"

"You mean I can get those, those sons bitches!" she screamed. She even jumped up and down with her arms raised in the air and violently smiling with sheer joy. She settled down and said calmly to the floor, tears in her eyes, "Yes, I can finally get those bastards." This coming from a woman who admittedly stated that she had never uttered a swear word in her life. "I am relieved…relieved!" she went on with boundless joy.

I guess I had one-upped the psychologists.

Memory—A Gift from God

We all have met those who stand out in our memories. It all started with our parents. Yes, far more memory, there in the Mind, where all thought is mysteriously recorded. Hmmm? Why did God do this? Why give us Memory? Seems we will be able to accurately judge our benefactors or oppressors – honor or chastise as we shall be judged in like manner. Seems quite practical and quite a load off Creator having to do it. Creator has galaxies to look after. Why trouble with each and every one of us 'held in the 'palm of 'His' right hand' – so claimed. Hmmm! Memory takes care of that time consuming chore.

Friend Stan and Love

My friend Stan is now deceased. I told you about his mother. No birthdays, no Christmas- apparently no love from his mother. Fortunately, he had a father who indicated he cared but the father was somehow hopelessly afraid of the mother and for his own sake stayed away from the home as a traveling salesman. "You are the reason I had to get married," she told Stan with disdain. Typical. Blame it on someone, other than yourself. I think his father cared for Stan and seemed quite relieved when Stan took an interest in basketball even though it started out with Indians in a supposedly all-Indian gym. Better they be Indians, than the crowd that had helped put him one step from the reform school. He had a bad car wreck involving two cars loaded with teenagers; it was his fault and he lost his driver's license for a year.

He was a couple years older than the rest of the kids in our grade. Stan's father would drop him off when he was in town, mostly fall and winters, or wait for me and take us both to the gym. He was always cordial and even came into our house to visit my parents. Stan at least had a Dad. I was driving by the time I had finished ninth grade. The older boys had cheap cars and since Stan was such a good player and taller than most, they were happy to give us rides until we purchased our own transportation. I remember Stan being hugged by my mother. He didn't know how to react. He just put his head down and stood there like a zombie. He did the same when my sister hugged him. Eventually he warmed up but you could tell he had very little love or none at all. My dad was not the hugging type but always good naturedly joked with the big white kid and showed a special interest in him.

Stan was especially proud of the nickname he received: *Oh mah nee cha!* (Beans). Stan was so proud of that name and would beam saying it in Sioux. All his friends eventually called him Beans. Dad said he grew like a bean stalk, hence the name. Love is pretty powerful and my family brought it into Stan's life. Once we were riding around and he came out with, "I think your folks love me more than they do you." It didn't bother me and I wasn't going to refute him. I had had so much affection when I was sickly and younger that I would push Mom's advances away as I grew older, independent and stronger. "Yeah, they probably do," I answered unconcerned and self-confident. He went on and became a successful citizen.

Be kind to Black Folk

I probably come across as hard-hearted, which is quite untrue, my opinion. What do on-looking Spirits think of when one acts just the opposite regarding humanity? Here is an example that actually happened. Once I was fishing with my 'Good Ol' Boy' friends in South Carolina. We had caught some nice stripers (ocean going, extremely delicious sea bass) in the twenty to twenty-five inch legal range and pulled into a Lake Moultrie Marina for refuel. My good friend Gerald Hayes has his lakeshore home and dock for his powerful fishing boat at a nearby marina. Several older black people were fishing not far away on the shore line.

When Gerry went into the marina I reached into the fish well and pulled out one of the stripers and indicated to one of the fisherman to pick one out and follow me as I stepped onto the dock. He pulled out a smaller one and I told him to grab a bigger one instead. We had fished the day before and had put plenty in the freezer. I walked toward an elderly lady wearing a large brimmed straw hat, fishing away with her long cane pole. My South Carolina companion was a bit perplexed as to what I was doing. "Hello, ma'am," I began. She turned and said, "My, dat a big fish you have der." "Yes, ma'am," I held it up closer to her. "Can I give you this here fish?" "Oh, No!" She surprised me. "Look at dat fish I has in my bucket. (A five gallon one.) If you gives me dat fish, den I'se has to give you mine." "Oh, no, ma'am. We has plenty." I looked in her bucket and saw a sizable catfish and a couple of brim. We stood there palaverin' for a bit before I finally talked her into taking the striper. "Ma'am, I *has* to give you this fish!" I spoke with emphasis and a sneaky wink. Her eyes widened. "Oh, I sees," she answered with a knowing smile thinking I meant we were over our limit, which we weren't, but I was not about to correct her. "Welllll," she drawled, "put dat fish in my bucket den." Was a good thing her bucket held water and the other fish as the striper's tail draped over the bucket edge. I looked downshore and saw an old black man fishing. I pointed to him. "Ma'am, you think he would like a fish?" She called to him, "Ol John." Her voice raised louder, "Ol John!" Finally after several calls he responded, "Yesssss?" in a slow drawl. These folks were in no hurry with their communication. "Ol John. Dis here man, he want to give you his fish." After no response she urged him with, "He give me a fish. He give you one, too." Finally, Ol John responded, "Welllll, I guess so." I motioned for my companion to deliver his fish.

Well, we went back out and I hooked into the biggest fish, at least one of the biggest for our group, enough so for good friend Gerry to hang on his wall. "Ed, we never see them down here," one of the Carolinians said. "You taught us a lesson—a damn good lesson." My friends there might be good ol' boys but they have been severely bitten by the Nature's Way bug after fishing with me for years. "The Spirits rewarded you with that fish."

Marine Boot Camp

The first day of boot camp, we were quite fascinated by about ten Negroes bunked out at one end of the Quonset billet and Texans at the other end. Never having seen any Negroes; that was the word back then, except some Harlem Globe Trotters and some friendly Pullman train attendants that invited us aboard for some free cookies and milk, we were naturally curious about them. We were on our way crossing the railroad tracks to watch Saturday matinee movies. First time I had ever eaten off a white table cloth. We were awed by the size of the Pullman attendants and their gold-capped front teeth. One even had a heart shape on one front tooth. We, of course, all stated that when we grew up, we were going to have gold-capped teeth.

Curtis and Jimmie Aho and some other South Dakotans were in my platoon. Curtis and I bunked next to the Negroes, as we thought they were funny as hell to put it bluntly. They liked us, too, and would always eat beside us in the mess hall. Curtis and a big black guy named Huff, just their presence kept the Texans from meddling with us. One guy named Tate liked desserts more than I did. After he had eaten about half his meat he'd reach over and spear my pie or cake with one bite taken from it, and I'd spear the half of Tate's meat. One Texan stupidly chastised me and got the hell beaten out of him that night by a black boxer named T.J. Wright. No more complaints from the Texans for eating off a 'nigger's plate'- as they would word it. Didn't change the taste one bit.

Duty in Korea was one big adventure. No one shot at me and I was happily busy working mostly on heavy equipment. I was thrilled once, when called on to go up to the front lines and weld some changes on some tanks still in their battle positions with their guns pointing north. No shell was allowed in the chamber, I was told, in case some nut accidentally or intentionally pulled the trigger. The North Koreans were watching me in their telescopes, and their Chinese advisers were, too. Probably taking notes about some 'secret weapon' I was attaching to each tank. I got to watch back.

Sister Mouse

I may have or may sound like I am complaining when I stated that my Mom was always down at the Mission when I was in high school. She was! Truth is truth, but I apparently had significant love back in those early, early years when and where I can't remember that it truly did not bother me that our dad was doing most of the raising of my sister and me. I didn't have a blueprint spelling things out and didn't undergo some goofy psychology exam to assure myself that my life was so-called designated normal, or at least harmless.

"I never thought about it, Eddie," she replied calmly. (I hate that name—Eddie—which she has used since we were kids.) I always called my sister Mouse, which I still do.

I queried my sister, Mouse (she was two years older than me), "Mom was always doing things for the good. She sure helped out the Indians. You know that. She just didn't have time for us two. Dad took good care of us. We were all right. I never thought about it. We'd get to be with her on Sundays, making us go to that boring mass with her. She and Dad would always cook up a nice Sunday dinner as long as nothing came up. Mom had the biggest funeral in Rapid City. You know that." There was not a hint of complaint or disappointment in her vocabulary as she rambled, simply stating how our life pleasantly rolled on. I commented, "Well, Mouse, I guess Martin Luther King's kids or that other Martin Luther, he had a brave courageous task to take on also. I guess their kids probably did not condemn them for what both tried for the sake of humanity. We have to be proud of both Mom and Dad!" I am fortunate to at least have a family member to talk to every once in a while. My other brothers and sisters are all gone. It happens—wait and see.

On the other hand, we (at least most of us) do not have entirely all pleasant (Hollywood-ish) memories do we? The fewer of these encumbrances locked away in our memory bank, we prefer to keep locked up don't we? Occasionally some nationally recognized psychologist will come along and suggest this or that regarding our not-so-fond memories, but most of us do not reach for the unlocking key do we?

Brother Russ

He was the first in my family that I knew to die. An older sister had died in Indian boarding school before I was born. Of my many sisters and brothers, all are gone except for Mouse and me. So many of my old girlfriends are gone, too. Five, at least. At least at one time they were a girlfriend and all very nice, too. Not one bit of animosity did we have for each other, before or after. Including my great second wife, five women I knew died of cancer. I guess any prospective girlfriend nowadays should think twice regarding my record soured by fate.

I came back from Korea and was out of the Marines. My ironworker bosses kept me employed with higher than usual pay checks—more than most college students cashed. That I could climb and weld when I got up high was their only concern. My brother Russ got killed my second year of ironworking. He backed off a B-52 bomber hangar during a conversion job from B-36s to B-52s. I was hired at the funeral to take his place since it was an Air Force contract and union rules demanded that a union certified welder had to replace him. That summer we were fairly scarce. I started the decking job right where Russ's arcing marks left the decking when he fell.

I got the word while I was down in Colorado Springs working for the same company that had won the ironworking bid for the Air Force Academy ironwork. All that morning when Russ died from the fall, my mind was heavy with him. I was in the railroad yards where the big building beams came in from Colorado Fuel and Iron. I would cut them loose from holding rods that prevented them from shifting during transit. Some of those beams placed a lot of tautness on the restraining long bolts. *Twang* they would often go, sounding like M-1 rifle shells, as I cut them loose with a cutting acetylene/oxygen torch. One guy was almost killed in the yards before I came in. We did pop a few holes in some parked cars, such was the stress on the beams. You could easily lose a finger or a hand from the shifting beams if you were not careful. The big American-brand crane stood by and we would lift out the beam and park it in a coded spot.

Mr. Rogers, the superintendent, came down and talked to my boss. He gave me my check, which was extra generous, per diem and all and paid up to the end of the week. He liked me from my work the year before with my older brother up in Montana. He said I might have to stay up in Rapid City on their job there. He was right.

I drove through the night and was at the church the following morning. I looked down on Brother Russ in his coffin. He was the one who had rescued Dad and Mom from the tented Indian camps. He had gotten government money equivalent to a quarter or half section of reservation land called allotment money and placed it down on a house in North Rapid City. About a half block went with it, maybe more. It seemed like a pretty good sized half block. Anyway we had a much better home than most folks, with a large lawn and trees, and an orchard even. I thought of all this when I looked down on him. He was more of a Dad than he was a brother to me. My dad was so much older that Russ could identify more with me and vice versa: Baseball gloves, fly fishing poles, transportation to fishing holes, or with my dad out getting cottontails or a needed meat-providing deer, plus all kinds of projects fixing up our home.

"You are better off. Dead!"

Russ was a lonely guy however. He fell in love with a neighborhood married woman and she loved him. She sent a telegram from California to my mom for the funeral. Later she called my mom, crying. Her husband found out about their affair, even their kids loved my brother. He promptly moved away to save his marriage. Russ dated various women but they were no match for the married one. What I saw of him within the bars of Glasgow, Montana the year before made me shrug. I was just getting used to college girls by then and the bar women the ironworkers hung out with were definitely not for me. Russ was lonely and did his share of drinking with the ironworkers. Me, I went fishing with an ironworker who had a big camper pickup and we caught our share of mostly walleyes and catfish on the weekends, and I saved money for college.

No one else was around. I looked down at Russ and said, "Russ, you are better off dead!" He was only thirty-nine, but at the time, I thought he was old.

Another Close Call

I had a few close calls as an ironworker, probably the worst one was I was carrying some long rebar rods, maybe an inch in diameter. They stretched out in front of and behind me, springing up and down slowly as I walked. Scaffolds are made in sections linked together. I was up about fifty feet, welding on a bank vault. The rods were to reinforce the bank vault. My helper was called away so I took the two rebar to my area. As I stepped on the next platform section, which held tons of large bar joists, my added weight was just enough to have that whole middle section collapse into a pile of jumbled iron down below. Dust billowed up as I went down with the bar joists, which could have easily amputated my legs, but instead I stopped and went springing back upwards from the two rods that had hooked onto the front standing section and the one behind me. I bounced up and down in the middle like on a watch spring. I settled down and began to hand walk toward the nearest scaffold. Two carpenters ran over to me more scared than I was. It had to be my youth because I exclaimed in a laughing manner, "Boy! That was a close one." I must have been destined to be a fighter pilot at that moment. I had a couple other close calls but nothing as close as this one so will consider them not worth mentioning. I did almost kill a plumber down below. I dropped a forty pound canister of welding rod and narrowly missed the plumber.

One incident was funny enough to mention. I was impacting high tension bolts in a dogleg section on a wooden float. Plenty of bolts to tighten down; the air hose blew off the Thor impact wrench and hit me in the mouth, knocking my partial out and on down fifty feet below. Two ironworkers fearfully stared at me when I opened my mouth and my front teeth were missing. They waited for the blood to start flowing but it never did. They must have stared at me for a minute or so. Finally I said, "I got to go down and get my partial."

Marine Officer Candidate School—OCS

Yah, I know, for the sake of orderliness I suppose I should place my ironworker close calls in the previous "Close Calls" chapter, but while I am on the ironworker subject, I may as well cover it here. From ironworking I went on into the Marine Corps to OCS at Quantico. Since I was a veteran, I had an agreement that if I did not pass Officer Candidate School training I could get out back into civilian life. About 50% would not make it (according to statistics). Veterans, however, had a higher retention rate. My estimate was that if you played sports, had a set of legs, worked construction and had half a brain, you should make it. Vietnam had not started yet—it was 1960—so therefore the Corps could afford to pick and choose who they wanted.

The third day of OCS the senior D I called we three vets into his office and threw an M-14 rifle book at me. "Chief, you are going to teach this next Wednesday." I replied, "But, sir, I only know the M-1." (I have one to this day and occasionally go down to the Rez to fire it just for nostalgia's sake. Cost a lot more than back in Korea.)

"Same action," he replied. "Wednesday you teach."

He looked at Nate and Jerry. "You two are going to teach drill." He paused. "Now you three are wondering what the hell do we get for this." Silence. "We are short of D I's. This don't make D I's outta you but you get weekends off from after Saturday chow to Sunday eve." He let it sink in. "Which of you has a car?" Nate raised his hand. The D I called the Provost Marshal's office. "Yeah, we got three OCs that will be checking out their car on Saturday and back Sunday eve." He gave names and dismissed us. Just about every weekend we went to Washington D.C. and chased girls. Nate married one after graduation.

I made it through OCS, and flight school at Pensacola went well. I was a second lieutenant and started drawing flight pay after waiting three long, anxious months in ground school. The Vietnam War had not started yet so 50% of flight candidates never made it. All in all you had one out of four chances to wear Marine pilot wings and worse odds yet to get jets out of flight school, which I did not. I went to helicopters and enjoyed them, especially the pilot camaraderie. Jet drivers, a lot of them were prima donnas.

It was quite an honor and a thrill when my wife pinned gold wings on me in a graduation ceremony, July of 1962.

Metropolitan Airport Commission

After my Wounded Knee assignment, I went on to a better paying job that allowed me to fly. About two hundred or so had applied for it. I began an enjoyable position taking care of three airports within the Metropolitan Airport Commission system that was a joint organization between Minneapolis and St. Paul. Besides revising legal regulations for tenants I flew different models of light planes from airport to airport to check out certain flight aspects. I even showed a Citation Jet pilot how to roll his airplane—we did it right over the main terminal then took it up and looped it. We would rent from different fixed base operators so as to not show favoritism. I don't know how many different models I have flown and the FBOs showed me enough respect flying without an unneeded check out. My flight jacket with its many patches, including a 110 mission patch, was my credentials.

One aviation hazard was a big cottonwood at the end of a smaller field runway. Several planes had hit it but upper administration would always fight me over its removal for some odd reason or another. It was tall enough to have been there for many years. I tried to get it removed but caught hell for not filing an Environmental Impact Statement from my boss. Can you imagine? A tall cottonwood right off the end of a runway? Hell I even grazed it one night after takeoff and a left turn out. Picked up cottonwood leaves in the cowling. About a year ago I talked to the mechanic that had cleaned them out. My boss, Claude Schmidt, had a kid nowhere near my qualifications that he wanted to take my place. I think his name was Gary. Gary has moved way on up toward the top of the MAC ladder. Nepotism it used to be called. He had one kid, I heard, that ran to Canada during Vietnam. I don't know if this was the same one or not. Ray Glumack was the head MAC nut and Nut he proved to be.

Nepotism Extreme

All of a sudden I had nine brand new pickups to dispense. I also had a new employee, an assistant airport lead man at our smallest light plane field where we had only one employee for mostly snow plowing and grass cutting. His name was Jerry Smith and he was Glumack's son-in-law. He wasn't there long until he was brought in to the main office for a position he was totally unqualified for, Assistant Superintendent, and neither did he deserve his big raise. The Airport Superintendent told me so in exacerbated disgust every time I paid him a visit. He was the main reason why we had the nine new pickups. Union Seniority required that other employees got one if the new hire got one and the assistant lead men on up could drive them back and forth to work. I realized then and there that I was now working in the wrong outfit especially since a plane hit the cottonwood at night and crashed and burned after falling into a house. Two people dead, and it was all covered up. Glumack and Schmidt never allowed me to talk to the FAA investigators who received a dazzling dog and pony show. I was muzzled big time, and sent to some conference. Later Glumack had his daughter open up a shop in the main airport without the mandatory bidding. He did anything he wanted do and got whatever he wanted. We had a highly oblivious, gullible, naive and basically stupid bunch of enthralled politically appointed Airport Commissioners that believed whatever he told them.

The Wild Dream

Fritz Mondale, from Minnesota, was Vice President then and for some reason I was told I was going to Washington D.C. to visit the vice president along with the lesser nut of the Airport so-called let-Glumack-do-what-he-wants-Airport Commission-supposed-Regulating Authority. Frank Beffra was the Head Commissioner, a big time television media honcho and Mondale supporter. Such plush hotel quarters we all had. Glumack did his best to get me intoxicated that evening, but I wisely paid the bartender extra to make his drinks twice as strong and mine weaker. Glumack was stumbling and I had to practically carry him to his room. Next day my meeting was supposedly canceled and Glumack came up with this wild, wild dream story that I was planning to ambush him during his morning walk by a golf course, load him up and take him out to my reservation land and bury him face out, like I must have told a story, one time or the other about Sioux punishment for severe criminals. A dream is a dream, I innocently thought. But upon our return, Glumack called a meeting with the commission and told them that it was no dream, but that I confided in him what I was planning. Why in the hell they didn't at least bring criminal charges and let me refute them is proof of the cunning of a power seeking mind. He must have scared them into believing that I was going to somehow kill or capture them, too! This is all so preposterous that I know that I must be the one who appears deranged and not goofy Glumack.

Dangerous Indian

I know, by now, Dear Reader, that if you have not had contact with some of these weirdoes that are actually out there in this goofy at times world, this is damn hard to believe. That is why I have never brought this out. Who in the hell would believe me? What format would I approach? Newspapers? No way! Not the *Minneapolis Tribune* or the *St. Paul Pioneer Press*. The *Tribune* wouldn't even review my books and damn well will not review this one. They are the chiselers of life. Glad to see them having economic troubles; the electronic world is coming down on those cowards hard.

Glumack knew I was too honest and had to go. He bragged that neither newspaper would touch him. Someone told me the Airport Authority had valuable extra land that made convenient warehouses and that was why the papers would never touch him. I never bothered to check that rumor out. Six outlying airports take up plenty of room. Plenty of space to dispense favors and Glumack jumped on it. He often bragged as to how immune he was. "I have all the aces." He was immune despite the blatant corruption he pulled. He had a fat open account at Eddie Webster's a popular bar/restaurant dive that he took me to several times. It was all hush, hush like I was such a dangerous Indian that I might try and kill them all. They paid me a fat, release fee and even lobbied for me a similar job at the Las Vegas Airport. You can't fight city hall, especially with all the stereotypes Whites have of us Indians. Besides, I knew that I could get these creeps later in the Spirit World which I will—for an Eternity. Was time to get the hell out of there!

The Holy Eucharist

Until my release I did my job as usual. Glumack believed that I was now a "safe" Indian because I could walk into his head office and see him about airport matters. Figures. He made it all up, in the first place. He was what I term, zealot crazy, like a few others I have met. I could even spar with him. Airport employees must have found that highly unusual as he was a paranoid controller so everyone was afraid of him, except for me. His secretary who typed up all his wild charges was a bit leery of me, however. Can't blame her! He would always tell her to shut the door when I would come into his office, and she'd get wide-eyed as though she expected a big bang from one of the two of us. He had told me (before his wild dream) that he and Claude Schmidt were armed and even showed me his Airport police badge. "You know I'm badged," he boasted so pompously. He never mentioned that the nuttier nut, Steve Collins, a Noise Abatement assistant, had a gun in his desk. I found that out from one of my airport police friends—the Assistant Chief who verified they were all nuts. Once Glumack was discussing the Church with me. He puckered up his lips oh so dramatically. He lifted his head up to heaven, squinting his eyes, and stuck his tongue out, not pouty but to receive Jesus. "I…I pray for you, Ed McGaa." His tongue went back out, this time he flattened his hands dramatically, prayer-like. "Every time I receive the Holy Eucharist!" Goddamn. Talk about a disoriented, hypocritical nut. These types have no conscience whatsoever. Another time I told him directly how nepotism in a public organization like the MAC was downright immoral let alone unethical. I didn't say illegal because Minnesota is such a nepotism-wracked state, that I figured it must be legally condoned. "Ed McGaa, you are trying to take the bread out of my children's mouths."

I thought, "Yah, you son of a bitch, you're goddamned unprepared for life adult children's mouths who are now forcing me out of my job for being honest." I think he liked to spar with me on occasion, because he never chased me out and always attempted to console me that they were planning on finding me another job—far away from the MAC. Those two burnt bodies, if an honest newspaper would have been in town, would have hung him. When I would come out of his office, I'd always wink at his secretary and point to her typewriter. "The typewriter that lies!" I'd laugh mischievously and walk on. I do have a sense of humor even at some morbid times.

A friend who also worked for the MAC at the time can verify what I am telling you. He was the main mechanic for the outlying airports mostly for fixing snow plows. I was a damn good airport manager. I would even do welding on those big plows in his maintenance shop despite wearing a suit and having to put on coveralls. Glenn 'Duke' Smith is my loyal friend, now retired down around Tyler, Minnesota. They tried to get him to sign a list of other hellacious false charges and he wouldn't do it. My secretary balked also and they made an office for her and got her out of MAC Headquarters. She wasn't a cover-up player. Oh, the other gun-toting employee, Steve, who was scared of his own shadow, was a Jesus freak loaded with goofy stereotypes regarding us Indians. From South Dakota naturally. They let him have a loaded pistol in his desk and probably hoped he would blow me away if I ever walked into his office since Glumack warned him I was planning to kill him, too. Got him to fear being the first one, of course. He may have had a nervous breakdown later which I suspicion our airport attorney did. He put a paper in front of me from cunning Glumack stating I would see an airport psychologist or psychiatrist. He said that he had to sign one, too, so I should. I told him to stick it up his ass and he was owned by Glumack and all the vilifying cooperation going on. Tom Anderson (or Andersen) was his name. The shit that goes on requiring innocent people to hold their jobs. Someday, in the interest of True Justice, a serious revolt is needed. Thank God, I am a Sioux and we have a truthful, just Spirit World. (I hope.) Back Elk's vision predicted that a 'Blue Man' of corruption and greed, untruth and deceit would roam freely among us. Glumack was definitely an example.

Pistol Range

Glenn Slack, the Assistant Airport Chief of Police knew a lot about what was going on and just shook his head in despair at it. He called me once to tell me not to come to work that day. I could always go to one of the three outlying airports in the mornings, which I often did. Glenn was worried that Glumack and Schmidt were priming Steve for shooting me, as they had him at the police firing range shooting away. "They got that nut, Collins, out at the pistol firing range." I guess they figured he was loony enough to blow me away in case I would drop into his office. Crazy ass crazy! I would stop by Glenn's place at times or he would meet me at Applebee's for a beer. He was retiring and safe and so was an airport detective named Chuck who didn't like what was going on.

Glumack knew that the burnt-to-death woman in the airplane, a singer named Olivia, (or was it Claudia?) were his fault and Schmidt's, too. They were in absolute error, Dereliction of duty and could not pin it on me. I had copies of the tree's removal papers request to both of them revealing its obvious danger and listed the aircraft incidents related to it. I was criticized for not making an environmental study! Hell, I even hit it once myself. That was plenty of personal evidence to convince me. Glumack had to get me out of the airport system.

Faegre/Benson Law Firm

I had a wealthy friend that had a hangar at one of my airports. He was a bit spooky during instrument flying (Flying blind in fog. You can get vertigo real easy in that stuff and crash.) So at times he would twist my arm and get me to fly him or pick him up with one of the four planes in his hangar. I always got to see the big air show at Oshkosh, Wisconsin that way. He was also nervous about doing the fly in so I'd get the yoke. "Red Baron, land long over the Cessna 180 on final and expedite turnoff. B-25 right behind you." That was thrilling stuff at an Oshkosh fly in. Taking off in formation with another Phantom on almost a daily basis with bombs aboard back in 'Nam made Oshkosh kid's stuff. I could always use one of his planes for myself, too, back in Minneapolis. He recommended a law firm, Faegre, Benson in Minneapolis. I told them my story about the MAC. They collected all kinds of information from me and seemed to be sympathetic, even telling me I had a case. Then one day, my lawyer told me they couldn't represent me anymore. MAC had hired them to look after some special case even though I was there first. Pretty sneaky, corrupt, unethical, dishonest, unjust, untruthful—you name it. MAC just had too big of pockets. Faegre sent me a bill. I returned it telling them to stick it up their ass, too. I never heard from them. I wish I can be a dictator in the Spirit World. These corrupt creeps would all be in cells and on bread and water for centuries. I should be around that long. Marines call it "piss and punk."

Aviation Practicality for America

One last item on Glumack, a practical, pragmatic one. The airport's commission named the street in front of the terminal Glumack Avenue. Too many major airports stupidly name the major roadway in front of their terminals to revere some politician. I suggest that all such located roadways, entryways across America simply be named Airport Way. This is the Age of Electronics and millions of travelers are trying to find their way back or to the airports on their locators. Simply plug in Airport Way and the name of the airport. You can be hundreds of miles out and your locator will lead you right there. Yup! Plain common damn super common sense! Too hell with a murderer's or politician's Avenue. The whole world will be helped. Many flights will no longer be missed. Step up, FAA, make up for those bought, botched investigators of yours. Require it. Forget that the suggestion comes from an Indian, one that has flown one hundred and ten combat missions.

Just good common sense. It would be a practical name change, and at least an attempt by the Metropolitan Airport Commission to wake up and take their political airport commissioner appointments seriously.

I have left out several other disparaging, extremely untruthful creeps that pulled their games. Even a couple close relatives! Thankfully I have met so many more very supportive Truthful folk that well overshadow these of a certain ilk on life's journey. They are also named in this writing. Spirit World! I might be busy for a while.

South Dakota's Humanities Council

My last battle, and it is still ongoing, is the State of South Dakota's Humanities Council. For some odd reason their director just does not like me. Plain and simple.

There was no way that I could have endangered this Sherri De Boer's director's job. It is too much trouble to attempt to find out. Not worth my time, but I can tell that I am South Dakota's leading living nonfiction author, or at least close to it, and have to wonder what the hell is going on. After the Glumack ordeal, one can get quickly weary of further injustice.

They have a yearly South Dakota Books Conference in which authors are honored. Lately they have been featuring certain Indian authors. Not one of them knows their culture or accurate history. When Vine Deloria was alive he was featured repeatedly. He was De Boer's hero; Custer Author Joseph Marshall too. My Crazy Horse book has the battle lasting – "As long as it takes a man to eat a meal" (30 to 45 minutes). Big Horn Battle Association now says the same in their daily lectures thanks to the recent, numerous television network's accurate documentaries (Utilizing modern metal detectors.). Finally, after years of outright lies led by the notorious fantasizer followed by a host of other copying authors neglecting the accurate warrior sources, Marie Sandoz who wrongfully, errantly vilified Chief Red Cloud has the battle lasting all day with 'flanking movements'. Ian McConnell, 'A shower of arrows.' Custer was down to about 300 men against 2,000 Winchester armed Sioux. Larry McMurtry (*Lonesome Dove*) chastises her and others as 'Long on imagination and short on fact.' All Day Battle, flanking movement fantasy authors – "Eat Crow and wipe the egg off your faces." Custer came within firing range and promptly was blown back by a hail of firepower as was Major Reno who wisely, immediately retreated…and lived! I was overlooked along with several other accurate authors for DeBoers show, but in my case I was too busy at Crazy Horse Mountain selling my books and jewelry to worry or fret over the slight. I was selling occasionally, a case a day of my *Crazy Horse and Chief Red Cloud* book and just couldn't be bothered with traipsing across the state and being gone for five or six days, losing at least one thousand dollars in daily sales at that time of the year, often more. Just to sit with and preen before a bunch of wannabe authors? My necklaces were a goodly part of that amount as well. A case at $15 a book is $480, go figure. *Mother Earth Spirituality* and others were selling besides. MES has been reprinted at one shy of fifty times by now if the Book-of-the-Month Club printing is counted and Harper/Collins published. I have three Harpers. In the publishing world that is equivalent as 'Pitching for the Yankees.' That's lots and lots of books. Not good enough for South Dakota's Humanities Book Fair, however. The western South Dakota book distributor Dakota West Books also sells heavily during the tourist season. Dave Strain can verify. He helped me out big time due to his tenacity, courage and support for well over a decade. He donated a huge Indian art collection to Crazy Horse Mountain. I paid $3,300 for my original book cover of MES and 15 inner drawings and donated all to CH Mt. Museum.

A Humanities Based Book

Ironically one of my books was used by a Edina High School Humanities class taught by Judy Layzell. My hockey playing son went there. I watched him rise from C-level hockey to A-hockey after just one season. He was good, had natural skills. My reflex genes and his Mom's athletic abilities were in him. The A coach came up to Pee Wee C's and watched him. They saw he was good. He was rightfully in C's as he had skipped Squirts for Karate, where he shined also. Hit, fast and could take a hit: same as hockey defensemen. He kept his hockey skills honed at the outdoor rinks with bigger, faster kids. Coach said to camp him and he had a chance for 'A' Bantam coming up. He made it after about five grand's worth of summer camps. University of North Dakota (Fighting Sioux) will hockey camp your kid for a couple of weeks. Hockey is expensive, a major reason why Edina has such a great Minnesota State Tournament record. I watched a lot of games. Ever wonder why Black kids don't shine too much in hockey? Costs too much when they are little. Check the Pro rosters.

The Edina Humanities teacher invited me to come to her class and speak on Native American Spirituality. Many speakers would come to her class and speak from various faiths and backgrounds including atheists, homosexuals, Buddhists, Islamics, rabbis and various Christian sects. A sheet of one hundred questions would be issued to each speaker several weeks before their speaking dates. *These are the most popular questions that are being asked by the students,* was printed at the top. *Who is God? What role do women play in your religion? What restrictions? How often do you gather? What are your major taboos or restrictions? Do you prefer certain foods? Do you forbid certain foods? Do you have a particular dress code? Do you believe in an afterlife?*

I was amazed at how professionally and encompassing the teacher had designed her course. I spoke several times to her class and told her that her accumulated questions from her senior students should be made into a book. I categorized them into ten chapters and it was printed: *Native Wisdom.* She got the first copy. Seems quite odd that a State Humanities Director would reject the author of such a book, doesn't it? Actually it is comical how far some people can take their racial hate? Or is it just plain Ignorance?

Here is the Table of Contents for *Native Wisdom.*

Chapter 1 Who is God?
Chapter 2 How did you become involved?
Chapter 3 Worldview Philosophy
Chapter 4 Good, Evil and Afterlife
Chapter 5 Beseechment
Chapter 6 Miracles
Chapter 7 Rules, Restrictions and Conflict
Chapter 8 Hierarchy, Matriarchy and Patriarchy
Chapter 9 Government and Social Issues
Chapter 10 Followers of the Natural Way
Appendix A. Humanities Class Questions

Doesn't look like I am advocating overthrowing the government, spreading racial hate, advocating moving all Indians to Oklahoma, or bringing back the boarding schools does it?

Crazy Horse Mountain Museum Book Table

By this time, I was conditioned to the fact, that, *Hey, you're an Indian. This ain't the Marines. You are just going to have to face a lot of ass Injustice.* Laughing all the way to the bank helped me accept this. I had a good looking blonde girlfriend working my table for me. She was about to go through nursing school and become an RN. I helped her. Told her to not worry about money problems. She took out student loans but I insisted on free board and room at least and more if she needed it. We even had a joint checking account. She was absolutely the cleanest, most self-reliant beautiful woman I had ever met. She even had a toolbox which she knew how to use, and had no baggage— no kids ever and no-stalking, make-trouble ex-husband. She was loyal, too. Never looked at another guy. Why should I worry one damn bit about the SoDak Humanities Council and their silly book fair packed with wannabe authors and their simpleminded Director?

De Boer has some sidekick Indians on her Board of Directors. Yup, all academics. One is Doris Brewer Giago, the Head Journalism Professor at South Dakota State University. What a treasure for cover up South Dakota. Ever hear of the Canton, federally built and staffed, All Indian Insane Asylum? Well, it is South Dakota's lowest secret. Doris, despite being Oglala like me, isn't going to tell you about it, nor make much hay over the boarding schools or protest the recent legislative bill shorting the Statue of Limitations against the poor pedophilia, boarding school victims at the hands of the missionaries and the then Governor's (Governor Rounds) signature placing their claims out of judicial reach after a meeting with lobbying bishops. The writer, Deloria wouldn't either. No one knows about Canton. A Canton resident guarded himself in a note sent to me: "Don't mention my name but here is a postcard of it."

Canton Indian Insane Asylum- Canton, South Dakota

Very recently there is a new watered down monument sign attempting to explain the Federal All Indian Insane Asylum and of course to take the onus off the zealous missionaries of that time, no different than the government-backed studies and church denial and cover up in Canada. It differs considerably from an Indian named Iron Shield who did a lifetime search, studying its history, and especially figuring out who was incarcerated. He states reasonably that it was primarily Sioux and Chippewa traditional spiritual-leaning inmates. One explanation, not Iron Shield's, claims that sixty-two different tribes were represented. If one hundred and twenty-one graves are revealed, that would average out to be only two Sioux and two Chippewa. Many more of these two tribes died there.

Indians were brought in, mostly innocent medicine folk. They are the least apt to go crazy, looney, mentally incapacitated, violent, troublesome, dangerous—you name it. My take on insanity is that a bad background, usually parental neglect or a shock on the head can bring on insanity. Excessive quest for materialism can also be a factor, at least in this modern era. Superstition, believing in the Devil or Satan, plays its role as well. A true

Sioux Traditional just cannot fathom Benevolent Creator allowing such a monstrosity. Humor is an important antidote as well. Siouxs are loaded with humor. If you don't have it, I suggest that you start developing it—might keep you out of the squirrel house. What a tragedy to lack this important ingredient in one's development. Nowadays its drugs or booze, but few if any Indians back then had such mental afflictions. In the old days, I guess it was the sea of grass, the early isolation that got to the white folks, especially the women. The State Yankton Insane Asylum was built for them. Indians back then, however, were rarely mentally deranged. The Sea of Gras' never bothered them! Materialism meant nothing to them and they had no Devils or Satans to terrorize them. They were not fanatically religious either, which can get just as bad. Take a look at the Muslims.

If the missionaries and the Feds are honest they will have to admit that Hiawatha Asylum (Canton) was built to hold back and eradicate Indian Religion and it was more than semi-effective. One hundred and twenty-one graves at least, probably more, just off the fourth fairway of a golf course are drastic proof. (I have heard there are actually one hundred and forty graves.) How did so many die? Why were they mostly Medicine, Native Spirituality advocating innocents? What did they die of? Because they would not give in to forced religious assimilation! Am I wrong to uncover such evidence? Why should I bring it up? Does it have any bearing on humanity? By bringing it out, does that have any bearing on attempting to erase or diminish racism, prejudice, and overzealous ignorance? Why the hell do De Boer and Giago oppose me if that is my stance?

Odd about Brewer-Giago. She asked her brother DeWayne why I don't like her. "Hey, Doris, obviously you have never stood up for me against that Humanities bunch located on the same campus you are." Actually it is my exposing Boarding School and Canton that should generate some form of support from her, my opinion. Her former husband, Tim Giago, wrote an Indian Boarding School book about the Boarding School atrocities. He is the only 'NDN' Academic I know who had the guts to write such an expose but I don't think she had any input on it. My mother took it upon herself to help Doris' hard working and dedicated parents who raised their kids in Rapid City. Since Mom ran the Jesuit rummage sales at the Rapid City Mission Center she knew every size of those many kids and made sure the Brewer kids got good clothing. I too wore rummage sale fare. One rich kid's parents who was my perfect size had his name sewn in hidden places into all his clothes and must have been sent off to one of those wealthy boarding schools back East. Likewise for food. A lot of our big garden went to them. Buffalo roundup meat came from culled buffalos, which my Mom helped butcher and then gave out the meat to Indians; Brewers got their fair share. Our freezer had a special 'Brewer' section for the deer meat my brothers got, or butchered steer meat we had. After Giago got married and had kids of her own, my crippled sister spent lots of her time helping the now divorcee raise her two kids. Beats the hell outta me what she has against me. She has a short memory that is for sure. I sent a letter to the head of the Humanities Commission Board regarding Director Sherri De Boer but never received an answer. Maybe some of you readers should send them a query. SDSU Humanities Dept. 1215 Trail Ridge Rd. Suite A. Brookings, SD 57006. Attn: Head Commissioner Michelle Deya-Amende. I sent a letter to Amende explaining my concerns through De Boers office. No reply. Recently I left a message to Amende regarding the same. No answer. Under fear of a harassment claim I have discontinued communicating. I offered to send my concerns prior to the publishing of this book and their rebuttal. They do not seem interested. If you readers are concerned about 'True Humanities' you might query them.

The early breed missionary families had to have approved of Canton and were probably in on its creation: The Ross and Deloria families and others. Deloria tells of these families in his book, *Shaking out the Spirit*. He glorifies his great-grandfather whom God told him to go out and kill four Indians, which he did. The book is dedicated to this grandfather. I doubt if there is money in the Spirit world but if there is, I will bet it on that family being in on the Canton Insane Asylum lobbying. Deloria's Aunt Ella condemned Sioux Spirituality because of her Devil/Satan beliefs and of course, we, who knew nothing about such manmade concoctions. According to her, we were allegedly loaded with them. She will be an interesting visit in the Spirit world. Most all of the Indian academics I know, never supported AIM or those of us in the '60s Trenches of Change. Deloria and his sidekick, Elizabeth Cooke Lynn, certainly were not supporters. Few Indian academics dance at our powwows and few support our Spirituality. I never see them at our sun dances and rarely, if any, are out there as a pledger, in the hot sun fasting for four days. Warriors? No Way!

What the hell kind of God tells you to go out and kill four Indians? Deloria callously dedicates the book to this guy. One Indian was innocently sitting on a hill. Innocent as can be and Deloria's great-grandfather rode up and fatally shoots the Indian filling out 'God's Will'.

One day I called De Boer and asked her why I was never invited to speak at her book fair, since numerically I was a leading South Dakota author—White or Red. (48th reprinting now (*Mother Earth Spirituality*) plus the separate Book-of-the-month-club print). My forthcoming 50th Harper/Collins reprint; remind me to send a copy to De Boer.

Author Receiving an Eagle Feather – Rosebud Sichangu Fair. Thousands cheered, women tremeloed and cried happily. Hundreds of strong men shook my hand in appreciation as I circled the arena. "You are not liked by the Indians" - Sheryl De Boer (State Humanities Director).

She answered, "You are not liked by the Indians." Apparently she might have been influenced by self-conscious academics who were overcome with jealousy since my big seller *Mother Earth Spirituality* was well received by then; *Crazy Horse and Chief Red Cloud* too, among others. She was obviously unaware of the Oglala Sun Dance or the recent large Rosebud (Sichangu) Powwow

Fair where I was significantly honored by thousands of Sioux for taking my stand against the missionaries who tried to stop our Sun Dance Revival. No less than the most well-known of the living medicine men - Crow Dog, gave two powerful speeches that day on my behalf, revealing the bold fight we early Sun Dancers waged from our 'Trenches of Change' back in the '50s through '70s. Zealous, fanatic missionaries and their brainwashed sheep do not go down easily. My strong suspicion regarding De Boer is her Right Wing Jesus-ism which does not blend well with a neutral humanities stance, especially when thousands of Sioux are forsaking her religion and heading back to our own thanks to Fools Crow, Ben Black Elk, Bill Eagle Feather…and Martin Luther King!

"That Damned Ed McGaa, I'll stop him!"

They sure as hell are not going to get too cozy with a guy like me who even had a picture of the Canton Insane Asylum in my books. Remember this is the South Dakota State Humanities Council. Let's keep this thing as hidden as can be! Yup! Keep pretending it didn't exist De Boer. A Spirit World exists and those victims are in there! Hiding truth just might bring an unpleasant afterlife and this goes for the rest of the Humanities Council who let her continue. What outcry did the Humanities bunch make when the Republican controlled legislature shortened the Statue of Limitations unlike Washington State and Minnesota where justice was allowed to go after the Church pedophiles?

An American Gulag (written in 1991 in partnership with Harold Iron Shield, journalist and editor).

The perverse history of governmental-Lakota/Dakota relations took a more sinister turn when in 1900 (ten years after Wounded Knee), the Hiawatha Insane Asylum was built. It operated for over thirty years, then was torn down. The bodies of those native people who died there are buried under what is now a golf course in Canton, South Dakota.

After the wars against native people, the battle for their hearts and minds moved relentlessly forward. Even in death, the 121 buried on the former grounds are mocked as golf balls whiz over their heads and the president of the Canton Area Historical Society Don Pottranz refers to their bizarre grave as, "It's something that people are aware of but its ancient history now."

With no knowledge whatsoever of native cultures, languages, customs, and spiritual life, South Dakota Senator R.F. Pettigrew introduced Congressional legislation in 1899 to create the nation's first native insane asylum. Congress appropriated $45,000.

In 1900 construction began after U.S. Representative Oscar Gifford (former Canton mayor) arranged for the purchase of 100 acres of land two miles east of Canton.

In 1902 the first patient was received and in 1908 Gifford was forced out when a physician charged that the superintendent refused to allow him to remove gallstones from a patient, who later died. Gifford was replaced by Harry Hummel, a psychiatrist. That same year, Hummel was charged by thirteen employees with mistreating patients.

In 1926, the matrons who had staffed the asylum were replaced by professional nurses. In 1929 Hummel was finally ordered to be removed. U.S. Representative Louis Cramton intervened and Hummel stayed. In 1933, patients were transferred to St. Elizabeth's Hospital in Washington, D.C., and in April, 1934, Commissioner of Indian Affairs John Collier closed the asylum.

In the interim, Canton and South Dakota congressional delegates fought to keep it open. Hummel had been charged with malfeasance and misfeasance in 1933. He was subsequently dismissed.

Averaging four deaths a month over the thirty some years of its existence, the asylum did not seem able to maintain the patients' physical health very well. Dr. Hummel, famed for his hair-trigger temper, ruled the institution for 25 years.

Now, freelance investigative reporter Harold Iron Shield has been researching the former asylum and the inmates whose known names are listed as buried at the site. Iron Shield is requesting native publications to list the names in the hopes that living family members will recognize them and come forward. He would like to know what the families might want to do about the grave and whether the remains should be moved. He also wants more information on the history of the asylum published, particularly the explanations of what was supposed to constitute insanity and why the individuals were selected for incarceration. From the reports of those who remember the asylum, according to Iron Shield, the reasons had to do with not following government rules, and not behaving in school. He suggests that the asylum was more gulag than governmental response to the mental health of natives.

Native people from all over the country were placed in the asylum. The records show that the physical conditions were horrific. Besides being shackled to beds and pipes, the patients were made to wallow in their own body wastes and clean sheets were not regularly issued. In Dr. Hummel's opinion, insanity was increasing among natives, and he was perhaps right in the sense that the well documented starvation on reservations during that historical period was causing pain and suffering, and people torn from their cultures were being pushed down narrower and narrower corridors of forced "civilization" and "assimilation."

The full truth about this chamber of horrors may never be fully known, but it was clearly a case of medicine and politics making a most poisonous mix.

-Laura Waterman Wittstock, Facebook entry, Canton Insane Asylum. May 5, 2013

(The Indian 'Grape Vine' holds that it was mostly Sioux and Chippewa medicine people incarcerated. Their victimization would have had to be instigated by overzealous missionaries in collusion with the reservation controlling government agents of like mind. —Author.)

Black Elk Speaks, John Neihardt (1934 to present)

I can't help but add one more culprit although they never have harmed me directly. I don't like what they omitted for several families of Indian people. Real Exploitation! The Neihardt Trust has never given a dime to the Black Elk descendants after several million copies printed of the book *Black Elk Speaks*. It was their Great Grandfather that started it all by telling his powerful vision to John Neihardt, Poet Laureate of Nebraska.

I was a good friend of Hilda Neihardt, the daughter of John Neihardt who wrote the book after camping at Ben Black Elk's father's place in Manderson, South Dakota way back in the 1930s. Nicholas Black Elk was the old visionary's name and he had a powerful vision. So much so, that it is a healthy ingredient of our Sioux Spirituality. Spirituality is fairly free of superstition. It is based heavily on our observations of Nature, Creator's Creation. Nature harbors no superstition. Man's religions, however, are loaded with it. Black Elk observed a powerful discussion of the Six Powers of the Universe that quite accurately explains for us Sioux, at least, the 'Spiritual Imagery' of our Spiritual beliefs. It would behoove all of those readers who are open minded, especially the spiritually minded, to read this book and also my *Mother Earth Spirituality* book which has an entire chapter explaining Black Elk's vision.

Black Elk Speaks has been re-printed countless times by the University of Nebraska Press and has been translated into many foreign languages. Obviously it has brought in hundreds of thousands in royalties. My *MES* had a significant first printing, (That earned me considerably. Can you imagine what *BES* has done?) And not one dime to the Black Elk descendants…at least that is what they told me. Like Crazy Horse Mountain, the ancestors of these descendants are the people responsible for the initial conception. Without the Indians, neither would have happened. Crazy Horse Foundation is planning a huge Indian University to pay back, but they have to finish the mountain first which makes sense. An Indian, Chuck Trimble worked for or was associated with the Neihardt Foundation but doesn't shed much light on it, and apparently had no access to financial records.

I never asked Hilda about where the money went or how much. I never thought about it, to be honest, and back then, I thought it would be none of my business anyway. Black Elk descendants came to me only recently. Hilda and I were good friends. I stayed at her place several times, did a sweat lodge on her lawn and later had the only séance I ever attempted at her urging and it was indeed powerful. I haven't done one since and never will again but that one certainly *worked*, for lack of a more poetic description. Neihardt and Black Elk both came in. I could go on and tell a few more revelations but I would probably be branded as some kook if I did. There is enough questionable activity in this work as it is.

Hilda passed on. Her daughter Coralie inherited the helm of the Neihardt Trust. Coralie removed the publishing rights from loyal and efficient Nebraska Press. Hilda has given me the rights to reproduce any and all *BES* material in my books. Why not? I am a Sioux writing about our Spirituality. I was very close to the interpreter between Black Elk (his father) and John Neihardt. Ben has told me over and over the whole book and then some. Coralie had the book moved to a New York press. Raymond DeMallie, Indiana professor, another meddling Paul Steinmetz, my opinion, came into the picture. He had to be in contact with Coralie all along. Now how important, how dear to the Sioux, the spiritually leaning ones, how do they feel about *BES*? I have finished my version of Black Elk Speaks and titled it as Black Elk Speaks IV since I strongly question the 2nd and 3rd versions especially most of the outsider commentaries and DeMallie's meddling with the original version from Black Elk himself as told to John Neihardt and interpreter Ben Black Elk whom I knew as a child and on up through my adulthood. I must point out that the original is devoid of outsider commentary and of which I have no quarrel.

Spiritual Exploitation

In 1902, Black Elk had an experience with a Jesuit missionary. Black Elk was innocently doing a healing ceremony, and Father Aloysius Bosch, an angry priest from Holy Rosary Mission, promptly set upon him. The then young visionary and practicing medicine man had his altar dismantled and sacred objects (peace pipe) thrown on the ground. The burly priest yelled at the Indians in attendance and told them to go back to their camps. This account is partially recorded by Raymond DeMallie in his book, *The Sixth Grandfather,* and the negative portions (from an Indian's point of view) have been excluded or not told according to Neihardt's notes. Hilda Neihardt told me personally she was quite set against DeMallie to whom she had given permission to see her father's notes. She was extremely disappointed that he omitted key materials in the so-called conversion controversy that modern academics are constantly bringing up regarding Black Elk. This professor also referred to Black Elk as a 'conjuror'. That word is usually reserved for fakers or one who plays with the so-called dark side of the supernatural. Traditional Sioux recognize no Dark Side in the Ultimate Creator.

What was omitted was that the Jesuit intruder, Aloysius Bosch, returned to the mission, and under a clear blue sky, lightning hit the priest's horse and he was thrown from it and his leg was broken. One account holds that he died. The Indians naturally believed that the priest should not have been so disrespectful to the Native Way and went on happily with their healing ceremonies. Within a few years, along came Father Lindebner and he did the same thing. Black Elk was grasped by the neck and yelled at: "Satan get out!" Black Elk was a slight man, not a typical Sioux warrior a priest would have a hard time subduing. He was also in the throes of despair at the time. His wife had died. After being thrown physically into a wagon by the overreacting Lindebner, S.J. in the dark of night and hauled to the Holy Rosary Mission to be exorcized by one Father Joseph Zimmerman, S.J., Black Elk was converted. DeMallie states that Black Elk was 'politely invited' to go to the mission. His exorcism was 'comfortable.' Both of these statements are blatant lies. Black Elk was issued a pass for his compliance and now could travel freely upon the reservation. In time, as long as he did the bidding of the missionaries, he could travel to other reservations as well, which he did.

Let us suppose that you have just come forth from a particular church service and feel quite satisfied as you chit chat on the entry steps waiting for Sunday school to let out. Your children are quite satisfied, as well, having done a bit of 'shopping' around. You like the open-minded, female minister and especially the social events your children are quite pleased with.

Suddenly some thugs come up, rush into the church and throw things about, they grab you and roughly haul you off to be exorcised into their belief system only. It is a long, dark terrifying night. Somehow you manage to call 911 and are rescued. What are you going to describe to your rescuers?

It would be most unfortunate, would it not, if you were told that the thugs were immune from prosecution and even insinuated to you that they were somehow 'polite' about it! Worse, what if you were warned that you could be sent away from your family? This is what happens when a Democracy does not fully adhere to the full application of Separation of Church and State. Overly religious zeal can be extremely dangerous to basic human freedoms. Unfortunately it is happening to the extreme in many countries throughout the world.

The Indian grape vine surely got the word to Black Elk about the ongoing incarceration of Sioux Medicine Men at Canton Indian Insane Asylum and that they never came back. Black Elk had to be on the edge of incarceration since his healing power was no secret. DeMallie never mentioned that the Canton Insane Asylum was in full operation at the time. Like many Jews in Germany had to, it was a lifesaving move by Black Elk to become converted. He played their game but slowly drifted back to his Manderson cabin, gradually unnoticed. The overbearing ego of the white men had been satisfied. Eventually, in his Spirit Power, he knew a man would come for his vision. Several writers came but he did not feel *washteay* (good) about them. When Neihardt drove up to his cabin, he prophetically announced, "What took you so long? You should have been here earlier." Neihardt had planned to arrive that spring or early summer, unannounced. It was now fall. Black Elk said, "I have much to tell you but you will have to come back when the grass is this high." He held his hand down to indicate early summer grass.

Black Elk never said a word to the missionaries about his next year's plans while his few close friends who would help verify his material for Neihardt never let it be known to the meddling missionaries. The reservation held few secrets due to the power of the confessional and controlling superstitious fear utilized by the Jesuits. The story was close to manuscript form before the bullying Jesuits showed up and demanded from Neihardt, who was far from being a Catholic, a copy of the manuscript. Neihardt boldly laughed at them. "What right do you have, to demand?" Black Elk obviously did not support the Jesuits. Doesn't seem like much of a convert does it? Ben told me, "When my Father was dying he asked for his pipe. 'This is the religion that I was all along,' he said as he held his pipe."

DeMallie coerced Coralie into having him narrate and comment for the world the text of *Black Elk's Speaks.* Yup! You who buy it are being duped. Your money is not going to go to any Black Elk descendant families either. That is akin to having me narrate and comment on the borders of Bible passages or Koran passages of which I know nothing about and don't care to know. I also, for obvious reasons, do not respect the Catholic Church and a few others. Especially those who lobbied Congress to ban our own Spiritual Ways to innocently beseech to Creator—Our Way and not that of our captors. DeMallie knows nothing about our deep Spiritual culture. He first has to Sun Dance, be exposed to powerful *Yuwipi*, vision quest, sweat lodge and respect our beseechment our way, plus historically learn to know us. He doesn't. He needs to expose the atrocities of Boarding Schools and Canton as well if he is to honestly portray us. He foolishly, brazenly attempts to be Wahshichu Wakan (White Man's God, not unlike the Jesuits.) when he blatantly declares the Earth Power, the Earth Spirit, the Sixth Power of the Vision is Black Elk himself and hence the title of his book- *The Sixth Grandfather.* Typical egomania.

Black Elk's introduction to the Six Powers in the Spirit World; each Power made their spiritual knowledge presentations to the young boy pointing out the Blue Man of corruption, greed, environmental destruction and deceit below the great spiritual plain and whom is spreading destruction to the flora and fauna where three rivers gather. Fish are floundering in polluted waters, trees dying, grazing animals gaunt, the winged falling from the sky and trees and plant life withering. The Six powers attempt to kill this sinister, man appearing symbol but fail. They turn to call on Black Elk whose bow turns to a spear as he looks down from his rearing horse. I would supposition that vast Creator wants us to know what tremendous destruction is coming. If Creator could communicate (via non-human form, interestingly) to tribal leader Moses then why not an innocent tribal member such as Black Elk?

The core of *Black Elk Speaks* is the revealing danger of the human formed, dangerous symbology emanating from the Blue man's power of destruction. The attempt by the Six Powers to destroy it is certainly worthy of commentary. Commentary and DeMallie's notations within versions Two and Three ignore the powerful social, civic and environmental message no doubt designed for these critical times. White Man's blatant ego again overlook and avoid what is placed before him. Moses did not forsake the Ten Commandments but the care takers of the vision have forsaken their duty except collect their royalties along with promoting DeMallie and junior Deloria.

I was hoping this work before you would be my last book but as mentioned I have had to write about Black Elk's Vision. It will be narrated by a Traditional Sioux, one who knew Ben first hand, and not by some meddling academic professor who has never sun danced and considers Black Elk a conjurer. A Deloria will not be invited to do the Introduction either nor DeMallie's *Sixth Grandfather* book pictured as Deloria's son has done in his Introduction of *Black Elk Speaks* (III version) obviously condoning the meddling anthro's mind set. Arabs do not narrate Jewish Bibles and Jews do not monkey with the Koran. Christians should stay the hell out of our *Black Elk Speaks* other than to learn Earth saving wisdom from it. They have done enough damage already with their boarding schools and pedophilia.

16 BOARDING SCHOOL AGAIN

Hearings before a Subcommittee on Indian Affairs
Physical Abuse of Children, Pine Ridge, South Dakota
Senate, on S.R. 79, 71st Cong., 2nd sess., 1930, pp 2833-2835.
Examination by United States Senator Frazier

Q. What is your name?

A. Mrs. Rose Ecoffey.

Q. Were you ever employed in the Indian Service?

A. Yes. I was matron in the school, boys' matron temporarily; I was there in August, September and part of October. Mr. Jermark asked me to go up there and take the matron's place.

Q. And when they got a regular matron you went home?

A. Yes.

Q. Is that the only time you ever worked at the school?

A. I worked as a nurse in the hospital.

Q. What about the conditions at the school? How were the boys treated?

A. Not good I would call it; runaway boys were whipped and a ball and chain was put on them and they were shaved close to their head; that is the way they punished them for running away.

Q. Why did they do that?

A. Because they run away and played hooky because they did not like the school.

Q. Do you know of any specific instances where they done that?

A. Yes; there was one little one 12 and another one 10, and they put a ball and chain on them and put them to bed and locked the door on them, and when I went in there I wanted to change their bed and the disciplinarian refused to let me; and it was not fit for anyone to see. They kept them locked up there for three or four weeks or a month. I asked Mr. Wilson, the disciplinarian about them—he was not here very long-and he said to leave them there.

When I look in the mirror, I see an Indian

My sister, Chick and her best friend Rosemon stopped in one morning for coffee. My sister Chick was the first Indian woman on the Mountain or at least one of the very first. I was just getting started on my writing. I had an old Macintosh that you had to put a disk into. They sat me down and Rosemon told most of this story.

We had read in the paper about another government research program. After Rosemon lit her cigarette, she sat back in her chair to blow a smoke ring at the ceiling. She waited for the smoke to dissipate before she spoke, "I'd like to see some of that grant money come up with a study on the boarding schools. I say a lot of Indians are alcoholics because they were taught to be ashamed of themselves. These studies and grants are always theorizin' about the Indian problem but they never take a look at the damage the boarding schools and missionaries did."

"Those two have always been off limits for research," I remarked.

"I remember when I was six, a bus picked us up in the fall," she continued, "We wouldn't see our folks for nine months. Can you imagine white kids in suburbia being sent off for nine months? And now they're bitching about busing. Hell, we had busing a long time ago, only it was a one-way trip. If you were lucky, you could go home Christmas vacation, providing your parents had money enough to come and get you or a round-trip bus ticket was sent in the mail. A one-way ticket, and they wouldn't let you go home."

"Most research grants come from the government, through the BIA or the Education Department. The grants are controlled by non-Indians mostly, or Indians like that creepy Rosalie Carlson. She's been at this University longer than I can remember and she's attended every Indian conference in the country. If she ever graduates, she'll step into one of the BIA positions and continue to do nothing except take care of her crony friends who are just as phony as she is. Rosalie wouldn't know what to do with a shawl at a powwow, let alone know what a powwow is. You'll never see her at the Sun Dance either. The sociologists, anthros and Indian experts work hand in hand with Rosalie's kind on the government grants. They aren't going to let the truth be told; hell no, because if you want to expose the truth, you don't receive the grant." She pursed a hard frown. "It's as simple as that. Telling the truth would put an end to their summer vacations."

I sat quietly, nodding my head to indicate agreement. I sure as hell would never receive a government grant except the GI. Bill, which I earned.

"Then there are the do-gooders that will give money to the church for research. That church won't tell what really happened. Hell, they're so damn blind and bigoted, they can't believe their boarding schools did any damage. How could it be detrimental they say, as long as the people received Jesus? What more could the Indians want? Give 'em Geesus, even if we take their kids from them. But you know something? When you're six, seven or eight years old, lonely as hell, lying in your bed in a spooky dormitory with a bunch of black hooded nuns floatin' up and down the aisle stringin' their rosaries, you cry. Goddamn, you cry. Even animals have a family. God made families but they stole us from ours and they gave us…Jesus."

"I cried for a couple weeks when I first got there," Chick chimed in. "But, what the hell good did it do?" She shrugged. "You had to toughen up to get through."

Chick reached for a cigarette. "The damned loneliness, especially the first nights away from home." She posed a sarcastic look. "They always offer that excuse—but they meant well."

Rosemon's reply was coldly emphatic. "Meant well! Hell, Hitler meant well for the Germans, they say. What the hell good was that for the Jews in the ovens and the concentration camps?" She continued with fervor, "A paper Jesus and 'meant well' can't replace human love, not when you're six or eight or eighteen, and lonely as hell in a cold goddamn institution." She paused to glance across the room. "You was lucky you didn't do much time in the boarding school. You went to school with the white kids. You came home every night to a mom and dad."

The remark evoked my response, "Some of the Rapid City kids at the public school made fun of us but I was fortunate. I played sports and had some baseball and basketball friends that stuck up for me." After a quiet moment of reflection, "Had big, tough, white Curtis for a friend. (Both knew him.) He played basketball and didn't have much of a home life. He never knew what the hell a homemade cookie or a pie was until he came over to our house. Funny how a little thing like a homemade cookie can change your life," I said with a smile. "This guy was as tough as Brother Albert and he really liked our folks." My sister beamed. "They gave him the love that he never had at home. Before he came along I had trouble with some of the white kids at school." I frowned. "I knew some Indian kids a couple grades ahead of me, they were ridiculed so much they had to go back down to the boarding school." With that we held a discussion of the various family offspring that played summers along Rapid Creek in Rapid City.

"Rapid's getting better," Rosemon acknowledged, "but when I was going to school the missionaries had an iron grip. When September came, the buses would load up the kids, little ones and big ones and down to the reservations they'd go." She ground her cigarette into an ashtray before she continued.

"I was in grade school with your sister Elsie when she got pneumonia. She was real bad off. Albert wrote back to your folks and told them how sick she was. You must've been pretty small yet 'cuz they were still living on the reservation then. Well, in those days they even censored the letters at the boarding school and your folks never knew about it until Elsie was almost dead. The Indian grapevine finally got word to them. When they did get there, she was too far gone. She died two days later. Goddamn, even an animal gets comfort from its parent when it's dying. What was wrong with that little girl having her parents with her when she was sick?"

"Albert was never told about it until after she was dead. He was sitting in class and heard it from his teacher. 'Albert, your sister died. They buried her this morning.' He didn't even get to go to the funeral. God, talk about mean. Those frustrated things were cruel." She shook her head. "It wasn't just the missionaries that were mean," Rosemon went on. "Back in my time, they had a big federal boarding school just outside of Rapid. Some fourth grade boys ran away. They were headin' for their homes back on the reservation but they got caught on the railroad track by Creston. They brought those little fourth graders back and chained them together just like a chain gang, like we always hear about in the South."

"Fourth graders chained?" I looked at her.

"That's right...fourth graders! I hate to even tell about the boarding school. People think you're nuts or a big liar."

"I believe you. Go ahead."

"They had solitary confinement in all those schools, too. I did two days on bread and water, locked in a place as big as a closet and pitch black, too. Well, those little boys were chained together and they had to march off all the miles down to Creston and back, around the flagpole on the drill field. It was about fifty miles. They stayed chained together until they finished the fifty miles. They ate together, slept together and went to the bathroom together.

"They had a long punishment table and they would march in step. If one fell down, they all fell down. When it was time to feed them, they'd all sit down and the dining hall girls would bring their food over to them on trays.

"How would you feel if that was your little brother sitting there?"

I stared out the darkened window. Rosemon took a drink from her cup and continued. "It took a long time to march off those fifty miles." She motioned with her head toward the door. "I wonder how that would go over if you did that to some fourth graders in this college town? Fourth graders, and then people wonder why the Indians got so many alcoholics!"

"You know Indians were always a clean people, but they really tried to make us clean. We had to scrub, scrub, scrub when we worked in those boarding schools. I scrubbed a lot of floors in my day. We even scrubbed porches in the wintertime. We worked either a morning shift and went to school in the afternoon or the other way around.

"The girls worked in the kitchen, laundry, dining hall, dormitories, sewing room or clean up details everywhere. The boys were in the dairy, machine shop, barns and in the kitchen too. Everyone worked half a day and went to school the other half. We always laugh about how we really got only half an education."

The older woman paused to push her cup toward the center of the table. "Government and mission schools, they all operated the same way. We got less education from the missionaries. At the mission we'd get up at 5:30 every morning, get dressed and celebrate a goddamn boring mass every damn morning. You got slapped or had to kneel on the floor the whole time if you fell asleep or whispered. We'd go to church in the evening, too, and sometimes during the day. Hell, we were always going to church. Boys were separated from the girls. If you looked at a boy, you'd have to tell about it in confession. You couldn't even talk to your own brother standing in a mess hall line. We didn't get much education from the boarding schools, but we got all the work and religion we could handle. When we tried to go to college and compete with the white kids that had gone a full academic day, we couldn't get the same grades. The sociology and psychology experts claimed we had lower intelligence."

"We never got to read any books telling anything good about our leaders. They wouldn't even let us make a dance costume on our own time, let alone go to a powwow dance. If you spoke Indian you got your mouth washed out with soap. If you weren't a Christian you were a pagan and would go to hell. God help you if you was related to the holy men. Those kids really received a brainwashing. That's why so many of us don't know much about our ways. We never heard anything good about the Indian ways…only the white ways. Yet most of the white people at those boarding schools were cold and mean, and every morning we'd look in a mirror and still see an Indian." She rose to turn the burner on the coffeepot. She turned it to high then adjusted the controls for low. "We used to drill every day. Right flank, left flank, to the rear march. I know all that stuff." She managed a stifled laugh.

"Discipline, everything was discipline," she said as she sat back down. "When our men and women went into the war, we did okay in boot camp. We all knew how to march." She studied the blue flames under the coffeepot. "I didn't tell you everything. I couldn't. Even you wouldn't believe me."

"I believe you," I answered.

She thought for a long while. She stared at the stove, then turned resolutely. "The last thing I'll mention about boarding school is hunger. You get so damn hungry that you'll do anything for just a little crust of bread. If you were smart or lucky, you'd be a waiter in the head nun's dining room or the head priest's table. Those people ate good. Hell, we'd be so damn hungry we'd eat off their plates, once we got them back into the kitchen. They ate a helluva lot better than the Indian kids ever did. The government schools were the same way. The employees stole them blind. When we unloaded the supply trucks, we saw butter and eggs but it never showed up on the tables for the Indian kids."

"You remember that old brother Herman down at Oglala?"

"Yeah, I remember him. You mean the one that limps. He used to hold kids down when Buchwald would put the belt to them. Course, now, I believe he was just following orders. I always think of him as being real scared, like God was always watching him. Kyle told me he had that scared look, the last time he held Albert down and that big fight broke out...they ran away."

"I heard it was Albert or Kyle that made him limp." Rosemon said.

Chick shrugged. "When you are little you can't remember much." Her response was matter of fact. "They told me they were going to leave. I remember being scared...and then the fight broke out. Cross Dog and Albert planned it that way. Everything happened so fast." She paused, trying to reconstruct what seemed so far back in the past. "Kyle told me about the two big fancy stones that Buchwald had on his desk. He picked one up and crashed it down on a brother's foot. It took him out of action, so he reached for the other rock. It was a polished rock and flat on a couple of sides and big, like the other one. He took another brother out of action and on the way to the railroad, Cross Dog and Albert were praising him. He said he felt like a Dog Soldier and warriors were singing kill songs over his exploit. He said he never was so proud in his life." A sad look shadowed her face. "I remember Cross Dog at the mission. Big and kind and sad, is how I remember him. That next summer, I heard he was dead and the war was going on. We were up at Rapid, the whole family. Dad had a job. It didn't take long for us to get out of the Indian camp. I was never separated from Mom and Dad again—not until I grew up. That's what I will always remember. No more boarding school."

"It almost seems like yesterday. I've seen that scared Jesuit brother a few times when I was watching you dance at the powwows. He seems okay."

"Yeah, he is, now maybe he is," Rosemon growled. "Back when he was young, your sister Elsie and I served him his meals. We'd get so goddamn starved, we'd let him feel our legs and he'd always leave a piece of meat and an extra piece of bread on his plate. We were just little girls though. I'd get so damn hungry that I'd let that horny son of a bitch feel my leg then damn near go nuts because I was afraid to tell about it in confession.

"It really bothered your sister and me. It got so damn bad that we decided to tell the head nun, especially when he'd come to feel us and he wanted to feel more than our legs. We got scared and we went to tell the head nun. We were both going to go in but I told Elsie to let me go first in case of a beating. 'No sense both of us getting beat up,' I told her.

"Well, I went in and told. I learned my lesson. I never was beaten so bad in all of my life. I can still see that nun. She called in two others to hold me down and she took off that big leather belt they always used to wear. That nun beat me and I can still hear her." Rosemon paused to look straight ahead at the refrigerator door. "Now you know brother would never do such a thing. You know he wouldn't. He's like a priest. He couldn't do such a thing. Tell us that you're lying. They beat me so damn bad that I said that I was lying."

"Not many people going to believe you, though. Not a helluva lot."

The older woman carried her coffee cup to the sink. "I'd better go. I said enough. You're right. Ain't nobody going to believe it." It happened. "Put that in your book," she said with angry tears in her eyes.

Sister Chick was the same. "Nobody will believe it," she added.

Well...Dear Reader, maybe you can now understand why I go after the gutless, collaborating, traitorous quisling Indians who seek a higher perching and preening spot in the White Man's lice-infested chicken roost. A sadder, more tragic story would unfold had I had a poor relative confined within the all Indian, federally built and staffed, lobbied for by missionaries, Hiawatha Canton Insane Asylum where our Medicine people were confined...and died. The South Dakota Humanities Director is right along with them—scheming cowards all. They don't want you to know what really happened. I'm the bad guy however, like Kennedy. I just don't like what I see!

As Black Elk declared. "To get to know me. You have to know my people." (And what happened to them).

17 BOOKS AND PLANETARY HEATING

Well, here I am on the short end of my journey. Do I hurry off to an old folks' home. Not on your life! Ahh, yes - Goals.

Goals

I have written over ten books that are published and surprisingly most are out on the market and still being read. There is a good chance that at least a few will go on for some time. I can't understand why so few Native North American writers have not taken up my subjects and issues. The academic Indians I can understand. Most never got what I say, never became involved with Indian-ness. They didn't dance, socially or spiritually. No, definitely not the arduous four-day, no food, no water Sun Dance. They never went off to a war and became a warrior, yet there were always plenty of wars provided by the U.S. War Department to fight in. They never came back from a war and joined forces with the Indian warriors such as AIM or other movements. In my time, I was the only Native academic-based warrior to fight in the Trenches of Change, the all-important and deeply symbolic fight for our religious freedom. Most importantly, for themselves, they went out to learn the White Man's culture to fit snugly into it, yet neglected to study the deep success for thousands of years of their own blood. Mostly agriculture and of course democracy from the Iroquois was indigenous man's greatest gift to ignorant fellow man.

Should I have entered politics?

That is the one occupation where you have less odds of becoming one than a kid dreaming to be a major leaguer. Regardless of how much common sense, honesty, proven track record, etc., you just do not have a snowball's chance in hell!

That said, what would I have done were I to be a politician? A biography usually is what you have done and not fantasy, but possibly the following may offer just a bit more insight despite being too old for such. Here are some bills I would be prone to introduce:

50% of the Senate would have to be Female! Why not? Best war preventive measure ever. Wars have so foolishly cost our nation. With the present environmental dilemma before us we cannot afford any more wars. How would that fit in with Nature? Look at Nature! Nature does not have wars!

Severely curtail the Military Industrial Complex. President Eisenhower warned of the danger of the MIC in his last address. His national project, the interstate highway system, created more commerce than the WPA (Works Progress Administration) of the Depression times.

Recognize planetary heating as the nation's greatest danger, actually the world's.

Recognize overpopulation as the root cause of climate change

Water Recovery for the Nation, beginning with the replenishment of the Oglala Aquifer utilizing Missouri River Spring run-off. Likewise for the Ohio River Valley and lesser aquifers across the nation as well. This ties in with a huge, practical, needed employment—a federal project akin to Eisenhower's highly successful interstate highway project.

Remove the impractical limit on ammunition procurement. Recently my son and his friend and a grandchild were going to go on my Rez' land and take out a few prairie dogs. They do eradicate thousands of acres- called over population. You can't eat them. Try getting through their restrictive gland system. If you eat beef, try raising cattle with them. We were limited to only a few rounds of under-powered .22 caliber ammunition. I was shocked. Such federal strategy to curtail the Nutso gun whackos isn't working.

Employment? The monies saved via MIC curtailment, higher taxes to the rich and super rich, and let's tax the churches as well; such could well pay for a nation-saving, water-for-agriculture dilemma. The largest, longest and most provisional, the Oglala, is a huge natural pipeline that supplies water all the way to Texas from my South Dakota reservation. A cavernous, wide, wide natural pipeline. Missouri River runoff is available every spring regardless of drought as it is fed by the Pacific evaporation. Other aquifers could also be replenished by their nearby rivers. As of this writing, the Kansas Bureau of Water has brought up the idea that I have promoted years ago— harness the Missouri. Feeding the Oglala from the Missouri, however, is the more practical answer for a national project. Such would feed four states: Nebraska, Kansas, Oklahoma and Texas. The excess could be piped off to the Southwest, namely Tucson and Phoenix. It will happen eventually since it is the only solution to save these states' agriculture. The longer it is postponed, the more farms and ranches are lost. You can't eat bombs and bullets.

Tax the Churches. Actually it is unconstitutional to let these institutions-for-profit remain tax exempt. They meddle in politics and as a result spawn one issue, narrow-brained-politicians. Palin, Bachmann, Rick Perry, Santorum, the two Ryans are obvious examples, and all presidential Vice or Presidential candidates. Palin is loaded with criticism but never offers a solution because she is incapable.

We all know who killed President Kennedy mainly because he was a man of Honor and sought to curtail government control operating under the guise of secrecy, terrorism and exaggerated national defense weakness.

I don't believe any of those presidential candidates could hold a candle to my track record. I volunteered for my combat tour and put my law school acceptance off for a year back when pilots and officers were bailing out of the military if they could work it or hiding in the National Guard. I volunteered for Korea, too. I have seen the tremendous waste of two major wars, the last one from the air, almost daily.

I support Warren Buffet: Congressional Reform Act of 2012

1. No Tenure/No Pension.
2. A Congressman/woman collects a salary while in office and no pay when they're out of office.
3. Congress (past, present & future) participates in Social Security.
4. All funds in the Congressional retirement fund move to the Social Security system immediately. All future funds flow into the Social Security system, and Congress participates with the American people. It may not be used for any other purpose.
5. Congress can purchase their own retirement plan, just as all Americans do.
6. Congress will no longer vote themselves a pay raise. Congressional pay will rise by the lower of CPI or 3%.
7. Congress loses their current health care system and participates in the same health care system as the American people.
8. Congress must equally abide by all laws they impose on the American people.
9. All contracts with past and present Congressmen/women are void effective 12/1/12. The American people did not make these contracts with Congressmen/women.

World Changes

Will there be significant world changes? I am no prophet, how should I know? Nature is my major prophet. Were there any genuine realistic prophets that accurately predicted the future? Name me one! None of the oft quoted Biblical prophets said a word about the greatest calamities approaching. I do suspect that planetary heating is the result of overpopulation. Heretically, (pun intended) I blame overpopulation on the influence and control of organized religion, specifically the Roman Catholic Church. I offer Mexico as an example and we (America) are their safety, spillover valve. Actually I should point out this applies to the rest of South America, too. All those unwanted South and Central American kids being dumped on America's door step need Tea Party-ites to line up and adopt them since all of them (Tea Party) got in political office via the Abortion-Banning ticket (It doesn't work!) Over-population is dooming the planet. Oddly, it is overpopulation that will severely alter/change America. Eventually Mexico will control our country. Unfortunately, they currently do not espouse our Spirituality nor the Democracy initiated by the Iroquois and passed on to the early Americans. Most foolishly deny they are Indios and are controlled by the overpopulating Roman Catholic Church and Spanish descendants.

Had there never been a science-halting development for five hundred years, (the Great Inquisition) technology would be so advanced now that possibly science would have answers and preparation for today's planetary heating. Organized religion does more than scare people and control them. It can and does screw up an entire planet. Why should such organizations be tax free?

How can that be? Simple. Who is responsible for the large amount of pollutants entering the atmosphere? It is entering by the tons daily, according to leading scientists. More people equals more pollutants. 2 and 2 makes 4. But some scientists are denying climate change. Yes, you are correct, and those are dependent on some coal company's payroll or other energy providers. Oil companies are not supporting climate change. If there were easier profits in climate change, you'd be surprised at how many naysayers of today would reverse their band wagons. Do commend the vast majority of honest scientists that readily recognize planetary danger.

What is a scientist? A Sioux name is, *Wahounspaeyea Wahshichu* - he seeks knowledge. At least those who are not under the employment of the denying corporations. A scientist is simply a person that probes and explores Nature down to the tiniest molecule, germ, virus or microbe. A true scientist constantly seeks for truth; actually, Creator's Truth.

Jesus

One of the greatest prophets of mankind, at least that is what I endlessly hear, was Jesus Christ. He is oddly mute about climate change or planetary heating for having so many followers. The Catholic population, I understand, is at 1.2 billion. Guess they outnumber my tribe, considerably. Hmmmm, wonder what their attitude and reaction will be when they start to starve? Jesus has such a large following, maybe we should all pack it in and join with organized religion's denial. 1.2 billion versus a paltry couple hundred thousand and probably only half of we Sioux are non-Jesus types, if that.

Wow! If that is so, then what do we do about drought? Well if the Bible or Koran doesn't mention it specifically for these times then, I guess we are going to just have to pretend it is not going to happen. Nature is unpredictable. Maybe it will hold off or diminish at least for a year or two. Hmmmm. But it is here already.

Oh that! It can't repeat itself. Not for long. I doubt if the Lord will let it.

Like How?

His Dad can do anything.

Like How?

Grrh. (Exasperation).

You don't have an answer do you?

You are beginning to irritate me with all your foolish, troublemaking questions. HE will lift up a magic wand. All will be taken care of.

All of us?

No, Stupid. Just us believers. Get on with you and don't listen to those heretics, deceivers—the unbelievers. Scientists are the worst. Go to China where you belong. They stupidly are controlling their population problem— at least making an effort. Other countries are not. It's all imagination. God will punish them. China, probably the most!

A magic wand? How does that overcome Nature's / Creator's laws of Physics and Math? Is that what they call the Resurrection and the Redemption?

Yah, kinda sounds like His Promises.

So we just have to sit back and wait for the magic wand waving?

Yup.

Can I ask you one more question?

Oh well. You have wasted my valuable time already. One more and that's all.

Well, if his Dad made the atmosphere, and this planetary heating is a reaction to too many chemicals pouring into the atmosphere, then "man-caused" has to be the reason why, and more and more humans creating more pollutants has to increase the temperature. Modern proliferation is causing planetary heating according to how the Ultimate Designer/Maker made the Laws of Physics and Laws of Chemical Reaction in accord with its Grand Design. Does the Man-God tell the Father-God that HE made a mistake in His creation or else, will He have to undo His Truth—the precise laws of Math/Physics/Chemical reaction?

Silence

Yah, I know you are pretty stymied. Seems to me you are 'Wishing' your way to a Hollywood type ending solution. You cannot admit to Creator structured scientific fact. My Dad made beautiful braided bridles, hackamores out of rawhide, bull whips, quirts and braided hat bands. Us Indians are always making things—sorta a cultural thing. The Trading Post owner was real good to Dad and paid him well. He was also an expert roper and Bud Duhamel, whose store was downtown, had Dad put on a roping event mainly for the summer tourists. He would put on quite a show. Tourist kids would run and he'd tell them which foot he would catch them on. Bud paid Dad fairly. Everyone enjoyed the show. Bud always sold me my jeans, boots and western shirts at half price when I was working my way through high school. I wish he'd have sold basketballs, baseball gloves and bats, and fly rods, too.

Well, I would never try and tell my Dad how he should rope and braid, nor tell my mother how to butcher a steer chased into a chute by Dad and killed by the back of her axe and then butcher it out after Dad's horse would pull it up on a pulley from a big cottonwood limb. No way would I try and tell Mom what to do. Even though they never bothered to learn how to drive a car, I have to add. Cars cause pollutants. Horses don't.

If I was Jesus, I'd be a bit hesitant trying to overrule the Great Spirit!

World Population estimate as of April 30, 2013—Seven billion. Every six seconds ten more are born. Could very well be eight or nine billion by now.

1. China 1,349,585,838
2. India 1,220,800,359
3. United States 316,668,567
4. Indonesia 251,160,124
5. Brazil 201,009,622
6. Pakistan 193,238,868
7. Nigeria 174,507,539
8. Bangladesh 163,654,860
9. Russia 142,500,482
10. Japan 127,253,075
    The United States—317,000,000 + by now

One birth every eight seconds
One death every twelve seconds
One international migrant (net) every forty-forty seconds.
Net gain of one person every fourteen seconds.

An unusual way to end a Biography? Well…a catastrophic ending potential for Planet Earth is a helluva lot more important facts and evidence warning than a mere man's events. Black Elk Speaks! You are now aware that this Blue Man exposure—environmental warning—initiated by Creator over a century ago could quite possibly be the same Higher Power that communicated with Moses on Mt. Sinai, many Millennia ago.

My Latest Adventure: Opening Brule's Show Singing in Lakota. "Wakan Tanka, Pilamiyah. Wi------choni ----Heyy!" (Oh Great Spirit, I thank you for my life).

ABOUT THE AUTHOR

Ed McGaa, also known as Eagle Man, is an enrolled Oglala Sioux tribal member, OST 15287. After serving in Korea he earned an undergraduate degree (St. Johns University, MN). He rejoined the Marine Corps to become a fighter pilot. Captain McGaa returned from 110 combat missions to dance in six annual Sioux Sun Dances. He is a Bush Award recipient wherein he studied under two Sioux holy men, Chief Eagle Feather and Chief Fools Crow, and Ben Black Elk, the interpreter for *Black Elk Speaks*. Eagle Man holds a law degree from the University of South Dakota.

OTHER WORKS BY ED MCGAA

Red Cloud: Biography of an Indian Chief
Mother Earth Spirituality—Healing Ourselves and our World
Rainbow Tribe—Ordinary People Journeying on the Red Road
Nature's Way: Native Wisdom for Living in Balance with the Earth
Eagle Vision—Return of the Hoop,
Native Wisdom: Perceptions of the Natural Way
Crazy Horse and Chief Red Cloud
Creator's Code—Planetary Survival & Beyond
Dakota Pheasant and Iowa too!
Calling to the White Tribe
Spirituality for America—Learning Earth Wisdom from the Indigenous
Black Elk Speaks IV

18102649R00176

Made in the USA
San Bernardino, CA
29 December 2014